The Washing Machine

Nick Kochan

THOMSON

Australia · Brazil · Canada · Mexico · Singapore · Spain · United Kingdom · United States

THOMSON

™

The Washing Machine
Nick Kochan

Library of Congress Cataloging-in-Publication Number is available. See page 327 for details.

For more information about our products, contact us at:

Thomson Learning
Academic Resource Center
1-800-423-0563

Thomson Higher Education
5191 Natorp Boulevard
Mason, Ohio 45040
USA

Contents

Dedication

The Washing Machine is dedicated to
Miriam Kochan, mater familias

Preface

THE WASHING MACHINE HAS ITS ORIGINS in the events of September 11 2001. That was the moment when the world at large was alerted to the importance of the money trail left by terrorists. The professionals had been making that case for some two decades that financial crime needed much greater resources, but their argument had fallen for the most part on deaf ears. An attack at the very heart and arteries of capitalism, symbolized by the Twin Towers of the World Trade Center, ironically put the spotlight on the financial methods used by those who would destroy capitalism.

Since then, money laundering has scarcely left the public gaze. Indeed, it is a term virtually indistinguishable in the public's mind from fraud and other financial misfeasance. I have sought to encompass some of this diverse range of money laundering activities in the following pages.

This is a book aimed at the general reader, and it should be accessible to someone who has a general knowledge of business and finance. I have sought to explain technicalities but if these are ever obscure, readers should skip them rather than get bogged down.

The task of covering the large numbers of topics, cases and countries which touch on the black and grey economies has required me to draw on the resources of a very large number of people with different skills, interests and abilities.

So, I would like to express my gratitude to Charles Piggott who contributed so enthusiastically to the chapter on Operation Casablanca, to Matthew Pym and David Evans who became experts on the Russian Mafia, to Lawrence Joffe, who helped with so much of my investigation into Islamic terrorism; to Nick Flavell who conducted wide research on internet crime, to David Porter of the Detica consultancy who shared with me his knowledge on fighting cyber and Internet crime, and to the Man Up the Hill who learnt more about diamonds and Russians than he could ever safely admit or be identified with.

I would also like to thank Judith Crosland for her help with the administration of this project, and Miriam Kochan for her proofreading and general guidance.

In addition to these friends and colleagues, numerous others contributed help and information but requested not to be named for understandable reasons. I would also like to express my gratitude to my wife, Laura, who tolerated with fortitude the long periods I spent researching and writing this book.

—NICK KOCHAN
March 2005

Introduction

Part One:
World at risk

OUR SECURITY DEPENDS ON IT. Our way of doing trade with trust is based on it. Global economic activity with nations relies on it. Money must be earned and spent fairly and openly. By the same token, money that is earned illegally or is unaccountable, must be excluded from the economic system. Its possessors must be apprehended. That is the money laundering mantra. Those who wage the war against economic crime are working harder than ever to stem the tide of black money as acquisitive crime threatens to get out of control.

The criminal who possesses black money and wants to pass it off as legitimate must fabricate an explanation to make the source look genuine. These tricksters make friends with corrupt elements in the financial system. They will hide their money so that it becomes untraceable to those who may want to hunt it. As more people or financial institutions handle money with dirty origins, those origins can be lost. And criminals are caught and convicted by the dirty money they possess.

So who are the elements in our society who close their eyes to criminal money? Most are those who committed the crime in the first place. There are four key groups. They are global corporations engaged in fraud; corrupt governments and their politicians who accept bribes; organized criminals who trade in drugs and other illegal goods; and terrorists. These are nebulous forces, and there will be those who say much talk of global money laundering is fuelled by paranoia and even hysteria. But the following pages will show that tyrants have triumphed by having their money laundered, drug gangs have ruined countries by passing their money through complicit banks, terrorists have waged wars on the financial system to fund their outrages and companies have made themselves available to organized criminals in a Faustian laundering pact. Laundering is as sinister as it is ubiquitous.

Global Corporations

Those who perpetrate bankruptcies, frauds, huge share scams and bogus schemes like Enron and WorldCom—not to mention executives at the Bank of New York, Citibank, and the Bank of Credit and Commerce International involved in laundering scandals—exploit the crevices within the financial systems of which they are themselves integral, even cartelistic parts. Launderers who work inside the gate undermine structures of governance and trust. Economic systems rely on the integrity of those who administer them and those who regulate them. When these key roles are shown to have been suborned by bankers in smart suits, as well as crooks and conmen, all participants in the economic system are weakened.

Global corporations are in many ways the most powerful, and certainly the wealthiest of the three groups listed above. Criminals need the services provided by global corporations especially banks and other financial institutions, to move and clean their money. Criminals and corrupt politicians in developing countries and the former Soviet Union look to Western banks for a huge array of devices that include offshore companies and tax structures, false names for their bank accounts, and lawyers and accountants for their complex financial structures. Some banks will provide them willingly, satisfying the authorities with the formalities of due diligence that have increased in volume in recent years in response to the perceived terrorist threat to the economic system.

Global corporations are driven by competitive pressures to spread into risky new markets and deal with unknown and possibly criminal counterparties. When doing business in many parts of the world contact with corruption and illegality is hard to avoid. Organized criminal groups grow and feed off the enforcement vacuum in many developing countries and these groups have reached positions of such political and economic power that they can determine the conditions under which Western companies do business within their markets. Trade with these criminal entities becomes a condition of entry into the market or country.

These criminal groups also extract a price for their collusion and the world's largest global banks and businesses move illegal wealth at the behest of launderers, creating a money laundering merry-go-round that sneaks black cash between the crevices of corporate and banks' anti-money laundering systems.

Huge financial ingenuity may be employed to create these deceptions but launderers understand the system at least as well as those who work in it legitimately, and often better. They use the language and instruments of the legitimate system to explain the provenance of their wealth. They are capable of sending stolen money along the same byways as legitimately gained wealth, harnessing technical developments such as the global electronic movement of money and complex financial derivatives. By diverting funds across borders or within financial or governmental institutions, they dodge police who challenge the validity or history of their illegal financial documents or instruments. Their corrupt money mingles with the hard-earned funds of genuine citizens who pay their taxes and trust their banks.

But however it comes about, when dirty wealth is moved, the bank participates in a theft, even if it has been duped by a criminal who is skilled at hiding the source of his funds. The maker of the corrupt or fraudulent money and the financial institution who helps moves it are equally complicit in a process, where both parties are conspirators, in both parts of the activity.

The processes that are apparently lawful are corrupted the more the corporation abuses the trust placed in its systems. The Western way of doing business and moving wealth becomes increasingly suspect as more criminal money is moved into the system. Turning the blind eye to the dubious transaction has become the norm for business in many parts of the world. Corporations benefit from money laundering by investing dirty money for fraudsters as well as hiding it in off-shore accounts. Either way, they will be beneficiaries when they gain a fee, paid from crooked funds. Chapter 2 on the Bank of New York, and Chapter 9, which is largely about Citibank, provide detailed investigations into banks' roles, knowing or unknowing, in money laundering.

Governments

The fruits of money laundering find most fertile ground where corruption is rife. Corruption not only puts dirty money into the hands of politicians through bribery, but corrupt politicians are exposed to extortion from mafiosi. Those hoodlums may be small-time hoodlums or they may be oligarchs (including most dramatically, but not exclusively, Russians) at the other. The two forms of black money-transfer link together in a vicious cycle of corruption.

Hoodlums that have obtained great wealth can make their position sustainable. The intelligent ones can acquire the trappings of honesty. They are in our midst and have achieved the status where they are considered 'upright citizens'. Money launderers operating on this global scale have great intellectual ability. They are also intriguing and complex personalities. Friends of Victor Bout (see Chapter 3) say he is charming, very talented and gregarious. He hobnobs well with powerful politicians, attracting admiration and trading favors with aplomb. Other Russian money launderers have demonstrated considerable intellectual ability in an academic context before turning their cerebral firepower towards breaking down the financial system's controls.

Western institutions have been content to treat with mafia, intelligence agencies and private individuals who have gained access to newly privatised state industries in countries experiencing economic and political change. The speed and efficiency with which the West has absorbed capital released from the bankrupt former Soviet Union over the last decade is a remarkable case study in how financial manipulation can be institutionalized. Established banks in the West collaborated with some dubious operators in Russia in a systematic process of pillaging that took place under the noses of politicians both in Russia and in the United States.

Both countries' political elites had reason to turn a blind eye to this criminal activity; Western politicians were still exercised by the Communist bogey and treated the launderers and conmen who came out from under the Russian dungheap when Communism expired, as legitimate entrepreneurs. Russian politicians were content to let the scams continue because they were corrupt and in the crooks' pockets. Those who were disturbed by what they saw had no means to reverse it because the country's administrative systems were in a shambles.

Intelligence agencies handling and distributing black money on behalf of their governments have the greatest opportunity to influence unstable regimes. Indeed, some argue that these shadowy groups are among the most active of all money launderers. The financial resources possessed by Oliver North, the architect of the Iran-Contra affair, puts him into the top echelon of money launderers, even though he was arguably guided by a political mission rather than personal enrichment.

Organized Gangs and 'Terrorists'

Organized criminal gangs have grown rich on the proceeds of the drugs trade or other contraband. This money has then been ploughed back into other criminal activity such as counterfeiting and the movement of people, the transportation of asylum seekers or economic migrants, and the trade in human body parts. The more established parts of organized criminal gangs seek to make investments in the 'legitimate' economy, by buying companies or real estate. The less established parts, the 'parvenus,' are likely to trade in illegal arms where commissions and profits are massive.

A key customer for arms and material are groups perpetrating political violence. These are easily defined as 'terrorists,' but definitions are difficult as the term can not be applied to groups seeking to overthrow illegitimate regimes. Definitions are equally problematic when describing terrorist money. This is because the money used by these groups may have legitimate origins—for instance from individual charitable donations or government funds. Whatever the case, in recent years we have seen growing political pressure on law enforcers to intercept this form of money as its significance on the stability of the social and political system is so much more direct and evident.

The 'war against terrorism' as it was dubbed after September 11, led to a new attack on the 'hidey holes' used by criminals involved in fraud and financial deception. But like so much of the Patriot Act, the authorities appear to have applied the machine gun—kill everything—approach rather than the rifle approach aimed to thwarting terrorism. The red flags of criminal money-making differ from those thrown up by terrorist money-making, because the first shows exploitation of the financial system for acquisitive ends. Most terrorist money, on the other hand, is spent in the black market buying arms, while small amounts are used to support terrorists while they prepare an illegal act. The first form of purchase is not applicable to conventional anti-money laundering solutions because such deals take place only in the black market. The second are unlikely to trigger suspicion because the amounts are very small and the transactions unlikely to be particularly complex. Today's anti-money laundering policies are convenient and cheap for governments as they place most of the burden on the legitimate banking and financial system. However, as this short analysis demonstrates, they are of questionable relevance to terrorist financing.

Intelligence agencies working in conjunction with police are likely to be more effective in stopping terrorist trade than banks as they can intercept the money flows between donors and terrorist groups. These take place in the underground economy, and intelligence agencies may be able to spot suspicious movements of cash or other valuable items like diamonds by using other participants in the black economy as sources. For example criminal gangs in the jewellery industry might be persuaded to work with intelligence agencies in breaking the link between the terrorist donor and the operating terrorists on the ground. Those money flows may issue suspicious signals if the donor creates complex trails to divert attention from his interest in the terrorist group. Chapters 3 and 6 indicate how Al Qaida raised money in Africa's diamond markets.

The Size of the Black Economy

The players in the money laundering merry-go-round are clear enough. But what sort of money do they handle, and where do they put it. The amounts are as vast as they are unquantifiable. Many inflated figures are proposed to scare governments, populations and bankers. But here are a few that may be more trustworthy. For example, The International Monetary Fund has estimated that drug use alone accounts for 5 percent of the global gross domestic product of some $33 trillion. That is some $1.65 trillion. Much of this acquired and laundered by organized criminal groups.

It is further estimated that $100 billion of illegal money moves annually from the 'undeveloped' world to the 'developed' world through illegal trade. This is pay into, or through global corporations.

These two numbers do not include the many unquantifiable figures like the value of trade in illegal arms, the payment of illegal commissions on those arms deals and the value of illegal trade in precious stones. They further do not include the amount spent by terrorists or the amount lost to the world's economy through fraud and counterfeiting. It would probably not under-estimate the scale of the problem to say that $2.5 trillion is now swilling around the black economy as well as white.

The Victims of Laundering

Those who secretly manipulate the sources and movement of money affect the security of nations and the wealth of people. We are all victims. Money laundering affects everybody who participates in the world's economy. It is a salutary thought that a large number of the currency notes that pass through our hands have been subject to laundering by crooks or their intermediaries, even though we may be using the money for quite legitimate purposes.

Dirty money is thus a tax on the global economy as well as a threat to the stability of the weaker parts of the global system. It is no exaggeration to say that the combined cost of money lost to governments through tax together with the cost to the economic system of imposing anti-money laundering controls amounts to 10 cents in every dollar of income.

When major financial or commercial institutions with a global reach handle criminal money, the wider economy is debased, and social and political structures devalued. Money laundering by criminal or terrorist groups also has far-reaching implications for the world's security.

However, perhaps the biggest losers are the ordinary inhabitants of developing countries. Skillful operators in the developing world apply the tools of finance to steal from their home countries. Wealth that has been criminally obtained, whether by bribery or fraud, needs to be hidden and moved if it is to be enjoyed or re-used. There are many reasons for this. Politicians in unstable countries fear that a government will be changed and their records and bank accounts examined; fraudsters are vulnerable to investigation by police or tax authorities.

Western financing schemes hollow out the wealth of poor countries, leaving behind economic deserts and volatile forces bent on political instability. This form of wealth transfer by deception benefits a few sharp or crooked entrepreneurs to the detriment of the larger economy. Ironically, it is most likely to occur in countries where there is least economic activity. If there were more economic activity in these countries, it might be argued there would be less scope or need for laundering as the financial system would be more dynamic and the regulators more powerful. So if the countries of Africa where diamonds are mined had their own viable diamonds markets, would sharp local operators (in league with politicians and Russian crooks—see Chapters 3 and 6) need to ship them off to Antwerp or Beirut under the cover of bogus companies, to launder them?

Short term theft has long-term implications for these poor countries. As we have seen, mafiosi and oligarchs use their illegally gained prosperity stored outside the country in secret offshore centers to rebuild their local reputations, and so wipe out the evidence of how the wealth was obtained. The shrewdest will take political office and run their criminal businesses under the cover of legitimate authority. The most ruthless will use criminal gangs to create a rule of fear and extortion in economic sectors.

These scenarios are particularly ominous as they destroy trust in political and civilian leadership. Governments that are 'up for sale' to the highest bidder must be prone to terrorist or mafia intervention, as we saw in Afghanistan where an alliance between drugs dealers and terrorists brought us the Taliban and then Al Qaida. These and other terrorist groups are examined in Chapters 4 and 5. Vulnerable countries are also in hoc to international banks, that supported the leaders on their way up, and now extract their pound or dollar of flesh when their man is in charge.

Attacking Laundering

Western governments and multilateral bodies have understood these dangers and sought to introduce some standards into banks' relationships with politicians and those close to them. These standards are embodied in the Wolfsberg Principles and all large banks subscribe to them. The implementation of such standards—however patchy—offers the best hope for poor countries eager to rebuild their economies without the depredations of mafia and their Western abetters.

Tax officials and police encounter these cheats and subject them to criminal trials. The penalties for money laundering, especially when drugs are involved, are very heavy. But in recent years, the financial police have turned their attention to another criminal use of the money-go-round. These are terrorists and others who perpetrate violence for political ends. Financial police—tax officials, police detectives, customs agents, bank money laundering reporting officers and the like—have been charged with examining suspicious money movements for terrorist links. This new dimension has dramatically raised the profile of economic crime and investigation from a discipline that was performed by a few specialized—and often under-funded boffins—to one that has come to pre-occupy every professional who handles money. Money laundering rules are their constant concern.

Today, the bank manager, the accountant, the lawyer, the estate agent, the seller of expensive yachts . . . you name it, is required to ask his customer about the source of his money. The money laundering mantra that prevails in this 'enforcement area' is the need to 'know your customer'. This process of acquiring 'knowledge' is performed by asking a series of questions about the bona fides of the money and the business activity which produced it. Clients interrogated in this way are often offended, whether or not they have anything to hide. It will also be argued that the time involved puts an additional cost on doing business and that is an economic burden on the economy. The inconvenience and bad feeling will be a small price to pay if this process of interrogation and due diligence succeeds in staunching the growing amounts of funds lost through acquisitive crime and fraud; allegedly two thirds of all reported crime is acquisitive. The 'know-your-customer' system, if it works effectively, not only puts the authorities on the tracks of those planning to behave dishonestly, but also deters would-be crooks from embarking on their schemes.

The need for the system to 'know its customers' has another, much more general context. The huge sums of money handled today by a machine or computer in a digital form has lowered levels of accountability and scrutiny and opened the way for abuse. When a criminal enters the system, computerization allows him to move greater amounts of money faster than was ever possible when money was in a intangible, note form. Interrogation of those participating in this 'immaterial' system introduces a personal element that has been lost as computers have taken over.

But will the imposition of today's money laundering regimes help to prevent orchestrated and elaborate abuse? Checks by banks may stop low-level fraud but, arguably, have much less impact on high-level and well-financed criminal activity.

Massive money laundering is likely to be performed by crooks and organized crime gangs operating through large companies and banks and it is highly unlikely the form-filling, 'tick-in-the-box' type controls involved in much anti-money laundering supervision will affect the well-financed and sophisticated crook.

Financial secrecy and manipulation are today viewed as the genie that escaped from the bottle during the free-wheeling 1980s and 1990s. Returning it to captivity is a vast task for law enforcement, let alone the governments that sponsor them.

Launderers menace a stable and fair society. The importance of keeping them outside the gate has never been greater. Likewise the need for a clearer and more focussed system of regulation is paramount. Laws passed round the globe since September 11 (not to mention those passed before and largely ignored), have given the authorities greater powers to tap phones, investigate individual and corporate bank accounts and seize illegally obtained wealth. Enforcement authorities also now encounter fewer obstacles now than before September 11 to cross-border collaboration. They face an unprecedented opportunity to attack money laundering and seize criminal and terrorist wealth.

But there is a cost to society and the individual entailed in this extension of power. The rights to privacy from state intrusion have been diminished as a result of anti-money laundering powers. This has been accepted by governments round the world in the arguable interest of security and the greater good of society. As a result, money laundering is much more likely to be cited as a pretext for 'fishing expeditions' where the police seek to obtain confidential documents referring to an individual's financial affairs without a specific cause. Worse still, police authorities, acting on a governmental agenda, may seek to use money laundering legislation to gain evidence from banks to pry into the affairs of political dissidents. The very nebulousness of the money laundering controls and legislation risks obstructing efforts by those pursued by the authorities to challenge the validity of this process.

The world watches and awaits a clampdown that is commensurate with the risks it now faces from money launderers, corrupt governments, criminal gangs and terrorists. It is paramount that the law enforcement authorities attack not merely the small fry but the ring leaders of crime and the dirty dictators. If these heinous operators are stripped of their wealth and liberty as a result of the new money laundering regimes, few would deny they had served a worthy purpose. If, on the other hand, those new laws add to the cost of doing legitimate business without the payback in terms of a growing number of convictions, leading to improved levels of honesty and integrity, anti-money laundering will be regarded as no-more than dead letters. Criminals will march on and society will have been shown to be powerless in touching their illegal wealth and systems. The opportunity to turn back the march of the vicious and greedy gangs will have been lost, and respect for proper ways of doing business will be diminished. To say the very future of the economic system is at risk, is no exaggeration.

Part Two:
The Early History of Money Laundering

The offshore system serves the interests of stateless and wealthy people who seek ways to dodge paying taxes to their home governments and pass beneath police radar screens, scanning the markets for criminality. Wealthy criminals have been quick to learn how to exploit this system and a few of course have become extremely rich on the back of it.

The most famous organized criminal to play the offshore game was Al Capone. In the 1920s and 1930s, Capone invested the Mob's money in pizza joints, café's and in casinos in Cuba. He ran his businesses and banks out of the Bahamas, keeping the local government on his side by allowing a few select and corruptible ministers to share in his gains. Switzerland and Liechtenstein later provided a safe haven for the wealth of Jewish refugees when it was under threat of confiscation from the Nazi regime. Switzerland's role won general approval and for quite some time after the War, the West chose to neglect small countries that offered wealthy people scope to hide their wealth.

Capone's friend, Meyer Lansky, who was dubbed 'the Mob's accountant,' took over where Capone left off in 1931, riding roughshod over flaky governments in Haiti and Bahamas during the 1940s and 1950s. Lansky also exploited Swiss liberality with an innovative scheme he called a 'loan-back'. Couriers carried cash from the US to Switzerland to escape the US tax net. The money was deposited in a numbered Swiss bank account (that is a form of account—now discouraged—which does not carry the name of the owner, only a unique number) from which Lansky 'borrowed' back his own money. The money returned to Lansky's accounts in the United States, without the US authorities realising that it was taxable. As part of their crackdown on the Mafia, US authorities stopped Lansky's schemes and put out a warrant for his arrest. He did a bunk for the Jewish homeland of Israel, but the US Internal Revenue Services sought and secured his extradition from Israel in 1975. He was subsequently convicted and imprisoned in the US.

By this stage, Lansky had been joined in the pantheon of abusers of tax havens by two notorious financiers. Bernie Cornfeld and Robert Vesco were early fraudsters who saw how secret havens could be used to rob the public. Cornfeld, for example, offered investments in his company Investors Overseas Services. He called this a 'mutual fund' to provide his investors—most of whom were themselves tax evaders—with reassurance. The money was secreted in tax havens where it was invested in pyramid schemes, that is schemes where each fraudulent transaction is dependent on the last, until a brick is knocked out of the construction and it collapses in a heap. IOS duly collapsed in a heap, leaving its corrupt clients out of pocket. Their funds had been hidden in offshore centres where information was scarce, and money scarcer. Cornfeld invested the money in another hidey hole out of reach of the original investors. For obvious reasons they did not seek to retrieve their money.

These schemes set the tone for much wider abuses during the last thirty years of the Twentieth century. This was an era when free-market economics reigned. It is no exaggeration to say that Western authorities— governmental as well as those in the financial markets—turned a blind eye to tax evasion. They would call it financial entrepreneurism or some such euphemism. R.T. Naylor wrote in 'Hot Money and the Politics of Debt,' of Cornfeld's schemes, 'The IOS "recycling" activities received virtual government endorsement when, from 1968 to 1971, U.S. officials suggested that countries politically and financially embarrassed by the flood of dollars put some of their excess dollars in the U.S. stock market.'

The U.S. government acquired a taste for financial manipulation of their own during this period. The Campaign for the Re-election of the President (CREEP) in 1972, made up of associates of former President Richard Nixon, arranged for money to bypass government checks on election funding by putting a $100,000 campaign contribution through a series of offshore centres, Nassau, Lebanon, Panama and Switzerland. This money was used to fund the bugging of Nixon's political opponents. The Nixon aides described their activity (apparently without so much as a blush) as 'money laundering,' and the term then entered the common currency.

Between 1970 and 2000, the number of offshore centres—and schemes to use them—grew like topsy. Hidey holes for the rich could be numbered on two hands in the Forties and Fifties, but by 1980s the number had grown ten fold, with obscure places like Nauru (in the South Pacific) and

Anguilla in the Caribbean coming into their own. The political free-marketers, who were content to see the expansion of the 'offshore' world, also allowed levels of regulation in the traditionally more conservative countries, including the UK and United States, to decline.

By the 1980s, the offshore ethos had moved onshore into the World's largest markets, such as London and Tokyo. Blue chip corporations applied tax avoidance schemes (often devised by London-based accountants) using the most obscure tax havens to satisfy shareholder demands for profits. For example, an international corporation could set up companies in Panama, Liberia and Caribbean centres to defer paying tax on dividends owing to the UK government. These were offshore or 'nameplate' companies without physical presence anywhere on the globe, but the scheme was accepted as legal by the UK's Inland Revenue.

Similar schemes were applied by accountants and financiers working on behalf of the Colombian cartels to hide the proceeds of drugs around the offshore world. The amount of money invested in these schemes grew to such a size that tax authorities and US law enforcement pushed for new and stronger powers to curtail them. In 1986, the first money laundering law was passed in the US. This tightened up the penalties for financial advisers who were found setting up devices for hiding drug money. Later legislation passed in Europe and the US widened the definition of black money to include the proceeds of tax evasion and terrorist finance.

The money that used the offshore world to dodge their own countries' authorities was as diverse as crime itself. So Panamanian drug money was joined by Russian flight capital and bribes destined for oil ministers in Middle Eastern countries in a glorious whirligig of tax evasion and legal obfuscation.

Dealers in goods like illegal arms and blood diamonds—those mined in conflict zones—were able to use paperwork provided by banks, trusts or other legal fictions to disguise trades that could not be legitimately disclosed. (See Chapter 3 on Victor Bout in Africa). The operators who made money from trading these commodities needed to find ways to take money out of the black economy to fund bribes to politicians, to buy investments or simply to fund an 'honest' lifestyle. The process of extracting the money, and of hiding its source by putting it through many different guises, is typically called 'laundering'. Laundering itself is perhaps an ironic term as money that has been treated in this deceitful way attracts the suspicions of financial investigators who can pick away the layers and reach the original criminal source. For this reason, if for no other, 'laundered' money is never quite as safe as those that handle it might like to claim.

Companies that have advised a list of blue chip clients how to play the offshore laundering game have been no less famous than many of their clients. Bank of New York (see Chapter 2) has played on the same money-go-round as Citibank (Chapter 9) to please a bunch of hoodlums who had made their money out of drugs, weapons, political extortion and the like.

As the Twentieth Century drew to a close, Western Governments began to register some of the consequences of low regulation and excessive offshore freedom. The most worrying concern was that global terrorist groups were using offshore structures to fund and organize their activities. Controls had been lost on the movement of funds through the black economy and governments suspected that money had leaked into some particularly unsavory hands. Low regulation of the financial markets coincided with under-funding of the intelligence community leading to some glaring mistakes. Moreover Russian criminality was beginning to spread Westwards. And this is where we will begin our journey to the heart of the laundering phenomenon.

Part Three:
The Structure of The Washing Machine

The following pages show corporations dealing with Russian mafia, diamond companies treating with organized terrorist groups, firms of accountants dealing with East European hoodlums and global banks dealing with dictators' gold. In each case, the corporate desire for untapped or illicit wealth coincides with the criminal gang's need for secret channels to funnel wealth away from the authorities.

Each of the chapters that follow deal with the four greatest threats posed by money laundering. Each threat is broadly encompassed within a section of the book.

The first section covers the specific threat to the safety of world markets posed by Russian criminals whose long arms and ruthless methods are practiced as far afield as Africa, Europe and the United States. The West searches out Russian money eagerly, but such is the country's instability that each new investment brings with it commercial instability and risk.

The second section deals with a quite different but related threat: terrorism. Their place in the global economy is far less tangible or evident than that of the Russians but its effect on the security of everyone is obvious. Western law enforcers are forced to follow the money trails, although many argue that the trails are less important than the places where the money is made.

The third threat is that posed by the injection of black money into the financial system. This section examines three ways in which that money can be generated, namely through the sale of diamonds, drugs and cigarettes. It also shows how dealers use these three commodities, as well as other illegal goods and activities such as arms and people-trading, interchangeably.

The fourth threat is that posed by corrupt banks. These are targeted by criminals with black money. When launderers succeed in using banks for laundering, crime is perpetuated. This section examines a number of banks and banking sectors to demonstrate how corporate policy, coupled with greedy or gullible bankers, undermine an effective and clean global economy.

The book's final section deals with those people who seek to understand and curb the threats just described. These are the law enforcers in Government service and money laundering officers in banks across the globe. Their remit is vast and their resources are invariably stretched. But the section shows how September 11 transformed the way law enforcers work, and the tools they work with. Whether these measures have worked to make the world a safer place is the question all of us with any role whatsoever in the world's economy, need to ask.

—NICK KOCHAN
London

Section I

Criminal Oligarchy

Chapter 1

The Russian Mafia

Illegal Russian wealth has been transferred out of the country since Communism gave way to capitalism, and Communist officials gave way to gangsters and oligarchs. The laundering of these funds has destabilized parts of the world's market system.

PERIODS OF SHARP POLITICAL CHANGE and unpredictability stimulate criminal activity. Those who possess wealth may feel insecure about devices to move it abroad away from the gaze of the authorities. Those who want to increase their wealth and lack scruple will exploit the insecurity experienced by government, police and regulatory officials to set up laundering and fraudulent schemes to service the wealthy and fleece the poor. Schemes set up by Russian mafia and their allies in conventional business to exploit political instability in Russia are described in the following three chapters.

In Chapter 1, criminal operations by Russian mafia spilled over into the international marketplace, causing havoc in Canadian and U.S. stock markets. In Chapter 2, a Wall Street bank teamed up with Russian bankers and mafia to undermine Russian tax and regulatory officials. This unholy liaison provided the laundering machinery for the washing of large amounts of the proceeds of crime outside Russia. In Chapter 3, Russian arms and diamonds trading operations in Africa were disguised using webs of offshore companies. In each episode, Russian criminality, with international connivance, undermined Western organizations and commercial trust and security.

Political Change and the Growth of a Mafia State

Criminal gangs had limited opportunities under Communism where the Party managed corruption for its own ends. But with the Communist Party ousted, the mafia gangs or "Thieves in Law" (*Vori v Zakonye*) were allowed to flourish. These descendants of seventeenth-century highwaymen and Cossack robbers had their own elaborate honor codes and intricate networks of social and family connections. These links enabled mafia to run extortion operations, smuggle contraband goods and currency into and out of the former Soviet Union, and run limited drug operations.

Political change, and the ensuing chaos, at the end of the 1980s and early 1990s enabled mafia, and their allies in the financial and newly-created business areas to lift their ambitions. People with the capacity to apply financial techniques linked up with the mafia and they helped gangs participate in the mass privatization schemes of 1992–1994, pressuring those holding privatization vouchers to surrender them for below-market prices. Mafia also set up international companies smuggling arms and even human body parts.

In one particularly audacious move, representatives of mafia linked up with apparently respectable bankers to penetrate the Central Bank of Russia and engineered the alleged theft of a $4.8 billion loan made by the International Monetary Fund to Russia. Insiders in the Central Bank of Russia diverted these funds through a web of offshore companies, including some in the British island dependency of Jersey. The money was then re-routed back to a group of wealthy Russian families in Moscow.

Financial chaos bred unlicensed greed. That in turn bred violence. Between mid-1991 and 1995, the Association of Russian Bankers reported that there were 83 armed attempts on the lives of high-ranking bank officials; in 1994, 50 bankers were murdered in Moscow alone. The head of one large bank retained a private security force of over 2,500 heavily armed men who had their own training school and firing range!

Enter Semion Mogilevitch

The Russian gang leader who has become an icon for Russian organized crime is Semion Mogilevitch. This senior member of the Moscow-based Solntsevo crime brigada or gang has subsequently been called "The world's most dangerous gangster." According to Frederico Varese, in his book, *The Russian Mafia*, the Solntsevo brigada is the largest and most powerful of the Moscow *brigady*. Named after the Moscow suburb from which it originated, the Solntsevo is an umbrella organization of mafia crews, probably twelve, active in different countries. Mogilevitch was the representative in Hungary. The proceeds of activities of each country are merged in a central pot, which is managed by several banks. In Moscow, the Solntsevo was involved in protection in sectors including drugs, prostitution, retail, and oil and gas. Mark Galeotti, an academic and the director of the Organized Russian and Eurasian Crime Research Unit at Keele University in the United Kingdom, says, "Mogilevitch is linked with the Solntsevo, which is the most international and most entrepreneurial of all the Russian criminal networks. Solntsevo represented his best client in business terms."

Mogilevitch has been involved in the Eastern European vice industry, liquor smuggling, arms manufacturing and trading and financial scams. At one time, some of Mogilevitch's money went through Benex and the Bank of New York. Benex was the secret company used by rogue traders within the Bank of New York to transmit money out of Russia. (See Chapter 2 for connections between Benex and the Bank of New York.) When the Federal Bureau of Investigation raided Benex's London offices, they found paperwork for at least nine transactions undertaken by Mogilevitch's Canadian company, YBM-Magnex. The FBI subsequently put Mogilevitch on its most wanted list, accusing him of racketeering, securities fraud, wire fraud, mail fraud and money laundering.

The short and brutal story of Mogilevitch's YBM-Magnex company is told later in this chapter. There were also allegations that Mogilevitch gave Natasha Kagalovsky, a Bank of New York official, wire transfer instructions to move funds from the Bank of New York through Brazilian banks to offshore companies for the Cali drugs cartel. Kagalovsky has never been charged with any wrongdoing.

Semion Mogilevitch was born to a Jewish family in Kiev in the Ukraine in June 1946. His mother was a podiatrist and his father was the manager of a large state-owned printing company. He studied economics at Lvov University, gaining a qualification that would later earn him the nickname of the "Brainy Don." Detail is thin on his early years, but he is said to have acquired early experience of business manning a fruit stand on the streets of Moscow.

Russian authorities first encountered Mogilevitch while investigating counterfeiting in the 1970s. He was convicted of illegal currency speculation in the Ukraine and spent eighteen months in prison. A few years later, he was again arrested for dealing currency on the black market and received a four-year prison term. Black money was already his medium.

Mogilevitch made much of his early "seed capital" by conning Jews who were fleeing Russian anti-Semitism in the 1980s into selling him at bargain prices their Russian currency, antiques, and art. He led them to believe that he would re-sell the items on the open market, get a full price, and send on the proceeds to the original owners in Israel or the United States in hard currency. But Mogilevitch simply kept the proceeds and so became a wealthy man.

Gangland wars in Russia in 1990—rather than anti-Semitism—were Mogilevitch's prompt to take up his inalienable right, determined by his religion, to Israeli citizenship. According to an Israeli intelligence report published in the late 1990s, Mogilevitch regarded Israel as a place to which he could move without restriction. The report said that he succeeded in building a bridgehead in Israel and took advantage of the fact that his new citizenship allowed him to travel freely in and out of the country. He was also said to have developed significant and influential business and political ties there. He made contacts with Russian and Israeli criminals and maintained control of several businesses.

Mogilevitch became a player in Israel's poorly regulated financial system. The intelligence report mentioned above claims that his bank accounts in the country date back to 1991. An Israeli bank with branches in Moscow, Cyprus, and Tel Aviv was allegedly owned by Mogilevitch, who was reported to be laundering money for Columbian and Russian organized crime groups.

The roaming Mafioso married a Hungarian in 1991 and moved on to Hungary. Hungary was a congenial environment for Russian émigrés, with its thriving black market, relatively advanced entrepreneurial economy (for an Eastern European country at that time), and little financial or even criminal authority. Mogilevitch moved to Budapest, and in an interview with the Russian newspaper *Moskovsky Komsomolets* at the end of August 1999, explained an early project, which showed some semblance of business enterprise. He said, "There was a factory in Hungary then which manufactured some sweet soft drink which ended in the magic word, 'Cola.' I bought a truckload at 30 cents a liter and sent it to Russia. In

Moscow, it was sold at $1.65 a liter. A single truckload brought $12,000 profit. I sent many trucks to Moscow."

Other commodities were also available cheaply in Hungary that Mogilevitch could exploit for profit. One of those was women. He bought the Black and White chain of strip clubs in Prague, Budapest, Riga, and Kiev. German and Russian women worked in these areas, using illegal passports provided by Mogilevitch. It is widely reported that other Moscow crime groups joined with Mogilevitch and his Russian partner, Monya Elson, in the prostitution business. One of these was the brigada founded by Vyacheslav Ivankov, who was known as Yaponchik, or the "Little Japanese," because of his prominent Asian features.

Nightclubs and strip joints offered Mogilevitch more than a supply of women, however. Catering operations, in general, can be used to serve the money launderers' ends in a number of ways. First, dirty cash can be used to pay wholesalers for the commodities consumed at the clubs. Secondly, they provide useful covers to explain false invoices or large cash consignments as tax, and police authorities find it very hard to measure the amount of alcohol, food, or cash that comes in and goes out of these places.

The Black and White club in Budapest (since closed) is said to have become the hub of Mogilevitch's worldwide operations. Using cash flow from the strip chain, he acquired a casino in Moscow and more nightclubs in Eastern Europe. Mogilevitch had quickly become a major tycoon in Eastern Europe's sex industry.

Rising prestige and power made Mogilevitch a figure of notoriety, attracting attention from other organized crime groups such as the Japanese Yakuza and the Italian Camorra, one of the leading Mafia families. Mogilevitch provided the Camorra with synthetic narcotics along with expert money laundering services to wash profits. Camorra members came to the Czech Republic and Camorra's leader Salvatore DeFalco teamed up with Mogilevitch in trading weapons.

Narcotics profits fuelled Mogilevitch's ambition and he acquired a bankrupt airline in the former Soviet Union Republic of Georgia, allegedly to ship heroin out of the Golden Triangle—a vast area bordering Thailand, Burma, and Laos where poppies are cultivated for opium production—into Europe. An Israeli intelligence report says some of the drugs were to be smuggled into the United Kingdom by sea. Cocaine and heroin were also smuggled into Russia from the United States and Canada. The profits are believed to have been introduced into British banks before being transferred abroad.

His business grew rapidly in the early 1990s. The many-headed hydra of the Mogilevitch corporate empire was run by his company, Arigon, domiciled in the secretive Channel Islands, and whose seven investors each held approximately 14 percent of the stock. The next company down the line from Arigon was Arbat International, a petroleum import/export company of which Mogilevitch owned 50 percent. Arbat was domiciled in Aldeney, one of the smallest of the Channel Islands. His friend Vyacheslav Ivankov held a 25 percent stake in the company. Ivankov is known to have set up several international companies and bought others. The other partners in Arbat were Solntsevo partners Sergei Mikhailov and Viktor Averin.

The narcotics income that flowed round the corporate empire needed to find a home. So in 1993 Mogilevitch underwrote a massive art fraud, reaching an agreement with the leaders of the Solntsevo crime family to invest huge sums in a joint venture aimed at acquiring a jewelry business in Moscow and Budapest. One company would serve as a front for acquiring jewelry, antiques, and art stolen by members of the Solntsevo organized gang from churches and museums in Russia, including the Hermitage in St. Petersburg. They also set up a large jewelry factory for fabricating Fabergé eggs, some of which were sold at auction as the genuine article.

The black money was invested in commodities, including alcohol, which were smuggled around Eastern Europe. The only information about the operation comes from the authorities who seized a consignment of 643,000 gallons of vodka out of Hungary. Mogilevitch also invested in arms trading. In the mid-1990s, he made a string of acquisitions in this sector. This diversification reflected both his growing power-base in Hungary's political establishment and the recognition that the global arms market was growing rapidly and was largely unregulated.

A giant magnet manufacturer in Budapest, co-owned with Sergei Mikhailov, was the first acquisition. Then his company Arigon bought 95 percent of Army Co-op, which owned a mortar and anti-aircraft gun factory. A license permitting him to trade in weapons through Army Co-op and with other arms companies was granted to Mogilevitch in 1994 and a

Mogilevitch company participated in at least one legitimate arms exhibition in the United States, where mortars modified by Israel were exhibited.

Mogilevitch built up sufficient credibility to persuade Banque Francaise de l'Orient to extend him a loan of $3.8 million against Balchug, a company he controlled, which manufactured and sold office furniture. This money was used to buy Digep General Machine Works, an artillery, shell and mortar, and fire equipment producer.

The Mogilevitch criminal empire had largely thrived in the domestic Hungarian and Eastern European markets he knew so well. But his challenge in 1993 was to break out of Europe and go for the big time in North America. If he could break in to the United States, that black European empire would quickly be dwarfed by much larger American ventures.

The route into the United States took two tracks. The first involved the establishment of a company in Pennsylvania, where Mogilevitch could invest his black money. The second led to the creation of a public company in which Mogilevitch could invest his money on behalf of some straw shareholders. This collapsed in a heap, leaving a host of shareholders out of pocket and regulators in Canada, the United States, and the United Kingdom deeply embarrassed. It also shook the international accountancy firm Deloitte & Touche, whose credibility would be called into question as a result.

In the course of a series of interviews in late 1999, Yosif Aronovizh Roizis, a member of the Russian mafia who cooperated with American and other Western authorities, gave some revealing insights into Mogilevitch. Roizis told the authorities in November 1999 that Mogilevitch was described to him as one of the kingpins of the Russian mafia. Roizis helped Mogilevitch buy a large quantity of Italian furniture for use in his chain of bar rooms and nightclubs in Czechoslovakia. Roizis met many Russian criminals working for Mogilevitch and says that at Mogilevitch's 46th birthday party on July 30, 1992, "I was introduced to many Russian criminals visiting him. 70 percent of them are by now dead, the remaining 30 percent are the present leaders of Russian organized crime around the world."

Many meetings took place in Budapest, attended by several Russian criminals who were operating in various European countries, over the two weeks immediately before and after the birthday party, to organize laundering the proceeds of crimes, which had been carried out in Germany, Poland, Hungary, Russia, and other European countries. Roizis recalled, "They decided, among other things, to buy an arms manufacturing company in Hungary and they actually did so."

Mogilevitch laundered proceeds from crimes he had committed by purchasing large numbers of buildings, bars, and restaurants in many Eastern European countries, says Roizis. He refers specifically to property purchases in Bulgaria's thermal resort of Carlovyvari and in Prague. Property was also purchased in Austria, Germany, Hungary and Great Britain.

Roizis referred to a business relationship Mogilevitch had with a mysterious woman called Alla, who "had control of the money at the Central Bank in Moscow." He said that this allowed him to borrow millions of dollars to use for fictitious business transactions. Roizis said he met the woman at Mogilevitch's house in Budapest, where she was accompanied by her husband, a former general of the KGB (the intelligence and internal security agency of the former Soviet Union).

Roizis gave another interview to the authorities the following month where he described the money laundering scheme set up by Mogilevitch. He said, "Mogilevitch set up offshore money laundering schemes wherever he could." Roizis said he (Mogilevitch) would have money transmitted to the Channel Islands to purchase goods and legitimize the monies. Roizis recalled, "Everything goes through the Channel Islands, where one can benefit from particular financial facilities and conditions."

Roizis recalled attending a meeting with many members of the Russian Mafia where they decided how they would divide illicit monies. "Mogilevitch would receive travel bags full of money every day, forwarded by air, railways, or carried by trucks. Seven accountants were participating in that meeting and counted the money. I saw heaps of banknotes with my own eyes. There was a separate room inside the office and this money would then be funneled into various channels. All this was achieved through the Central Bank of Russia because Mogilevitch had a person he trusted, a woman, in this bank to whom he would give some of the money. She was one of the senior officers at the Central Bank of Russia." Roizis said, "The scheme would operate following precise procedures, and it is still the same even today, this system is still operating in this way and the person I'm talking about is still at the Central Bank." Roizis is, of course, referring to the time of the interview, in 1999.

Roizis also told the authorities about money laundering schemes operated by some Mafia groups through Benex, the company used to launder funds through the Bank of New York—see Chapter 2. He said, "The procedure followed by Benex is the one devised by Mogilevitch in the course of the 1992 meeting. He had some financial advisors he had brought with him from Moscow and they would suggest to him what to do. Mogilevitch started to operate with England. The people working for Benex came from England and now they are fleeing back there. I heard that a friend of Mogilevitch's second wife is a finance expert working for the Bank of New York and for Mogilevitch." It must be assumed that Roizis is referring here to Lucy Edwards, the Bank of New York employee who set up Benex with her husband Peter Berlin (see Chapter 2).

Roizis also described another laundering operation involving Russian organized criminals Cyril Kouznetsov and Boris Rizner. He said that Kouznetsov and Rizner were high-powered academics who lost their jobs after the fall of the Soviet Union. Kouznetsov was a professor and computer expert while Rizner was, according to Roizis, the third most important nuclear physicist in the Soviet Union. They began their business careers by obtaining loans legally to finance trade. Their initial business involved buying pantyhose in Bologna, Italy and selling it through stalls or kiosks dotted round Russian towns.

Kouznetsov and Rizner later teamed up with the mafia and they spent several million dollars of dirty money buying consignments of pantyhose. Roizis, in his interview with the authorities, showed how it worked. He said, "Two truckloads of pantyhose cost approximately $2 million. A truckload generally consists of about 1,450 boxes, each containing two packages of pantyhose. There are 60 to 120 pairs of pantyhose in each box. The average cost of each item is 5,000 liras, sometimes slightly more or a little less, it varies according to color . . . The money used was money that had to be laundered. I don't know how these funds would get to Italy, certainly through some banks (sic) like Benex. I witnessed the whole pantyhose operation carried out to launder money and in nine months their turnover in Italy rose to $18–$19 million."

Roizis says the two men acquired twelve stalls selling pantyhose and were "offered Mafia protection to run the kiosks business" but had to pay the Koptovo Mafia organization $1,500 a month for their protection. Every month at a fixed date, if Rizner and Kouznetsov did not pay the protection money, a "meter would be started," that is, the money owed would increase by 100 percent per day. For this reason everybody was ready to pay at the pre-fixed deadline. They scared Kouznetsov to death. He was beaten up, together with Rizner. The pantyhose operation fell apart as its academic instigators were forced to pull out.

The Israeli Bridge

The Russian mafia, not to mention the Russian business community more generally, has a high proportion of Jewish members. This may be explained by that religious group's marginal place in Russian society. During the period of the Tsars, the Jews experienced much anti-Semitism, ill treatment, and discrimination. To survive, many had to develop forms of marginal existence, struggling to make a living while evading discriminatory laws. Some were forced to exploit the system and became tough operators. Others resorted to mysticism and their religious faith that provided another gentler world. Many lived on the margins of society.

The dawning of capitalism in the late 1980s under Mikhail Gorbachev presented an opportunity for Russian Jewish businessmen to come in from the margins and to make money in the newly legitimized Russian capitalist economy. The oligarchs, who themselves are exclusively Jewish, grasped the opportunity of making a great amount of money in the privatization and other parts of the newly liberalized economy.

Jews brought up under a cruel mix of Communism and anti-Semitism could have little respect for Soviet law (though this was not, of course, limited to Jews), and that disdain endured through the Boris Yeltsin and Vladimir Putin eras. There were even Jews who emerged as leaders in the Moscow brigady or criminal gangs. Russian politicians later sought to win political advantage by tapping into historic Russian anti-semitism and referring to the religious origins of newly-enriched oligarchs and mafia members.

The creation of the Jewish state of Israel in 1948 presented Russian Jewish businessmen and Mafiosi with a second country in which they were entitled to live, purely by virtue of their religion. Israel welcomed the Russians both because they were Jews (one of the country's missions is to be a home for Jews) and because they brought cash. Israel had sought to develop an economy that matched that of the West, rather than its poorer Arab neighbors, so Russian wealth was accepted without care for its provenance. Israel's political insecurity and its lack of international friends outside the United States have exacerbated its dependence on dubious sources of funds. Black money similarly was sought by South Africa and Rhodesia (now Zimbabwe) when they were subjected to international boycotts.

Israel's desperation for foreign exchange means Russian Mafiosi have been allowed to integrate themselves into the country's political and financial system. It also means Russian Mafiosi have been given shelter and a great deal of security, which they would not have experienced either in Russia or in Western Europe. Meyer Lansky, the Jewish American Mafioso, for example, fled there to escape American tax and criminal authorities. Lansky is the exception to the general rule as he was extradited to the United States. But many Russians with criminal records have used their wealth to promote themselves into the top echelons of Israel's political parties.

One consequence of the country's receptivity to Russian money is a reputation for a relaxed stance on money laundering. Israel has not fully implemented stringent anti–money laundering rules and the Financial Action Task Force (FATF) has blacklisted the country.

The amount of black money swilling around the Israeli economy is estimated to range between $4 and $20 billion according to Israeli police officials who say Russian mobsters have bought factories, insurance companies, and a bank. They have attempted to buy a newspaper and even a kosher wine company. The risk that unsavory elements could secure control of a part of the military complex remains a concern of law enforcement officials.

As much as 10 percent of the newly emigrated Russian population of Israel is allegedly criminal, and Israeli prostitution and some elements in its powerful diamond industry are now in the hands of Russian operators. Jonathan Winer, a Washington lawyer and the former deputy assistant secretary of state for international law enforcement under President Clinton, has claimed, "There is not a major Russian organized crime figure that we are tracking who does not carry an Israeli passport." The problem has become so great that Israel's former chief of police intelligence, Hezi Leder, prepared a report on Russian organized crime in the country for the Israeli government that concluded that Russian organized groups had become a strategic threat. An intra-agency intelligence committee was set up by the Israelis as a result of the report, but it appeared powerless to act.

The financial system's weak money laundering controls explain some highly unusual cash payments allegedly made into Israeli banks. Thus no less an authority than the former Israeli minister of National Security, Moshe Shahal, told a gathering of intelligence heads in 1996 that a corrupt deputy ex-prime minister of the Ukraine smuggled $300 million of illicit cash into Israel in several suitcases and deposited it in an Israeli bank. Robert Friedman, writing in his book, *The Red Mafiya*, quotes an American underworld crime figure saying, "I've watched Russian mobsters exchange suitcases full of cash out in the open at the Dan Hotel's swimming pool in Tel Aviv."

The infiltration of the financial system was demonstrated at the trial of Gregory Lerner, a Russian mobster living in Israel who travels the globe in part to do business and in part to escape his victims and those pursuing him. Lerner, using the Israeli name of Zvi Ben-Ari, was arrested at Tel Aviv airport in May 1997 as he was about to board a flight to the United States. He was charged with attempted bribery, defrauding four Russian banks of $106 million using a pyramid scheme, and attempting to set up a bank in Israel to launder money for the Russian mafia. Lerner pleaded guilty to bank fraud, forgery, and bribing government officials and was sentenced to eight years in jail. He served five years before his release in February 2003.

Lerner's involvement with the Russian mafia dates back to the 1980s, when he was convicted in Russia for major fraud. He later came under suspicion during the investigation of a $20 million larceny case. In 1994, the manager of one of the Russian banks in which Lerner was involved was killed in a mysterious explosion while he was riding to Moscow airport on his way to Israel, where he was due to inform Israeli police of Ben-Ari's activities.

Ben-Ari was later arrested during a business trip to Switzerland and deported to Russia, where he managed to jump bail and return home to Israel.

There can be no more colorful mobster than Joseph Kobzon, who made his name in Russia as an immensely popular singer of patriotic ballads. Indeed, he was said to have brought Leonid Breznev to tears at public functions with his soulful renditions. But, according to the CIA, Kobzon supplemented his performing income with the proceeds of crime. The Americans described Kobzon as a spiritual leader of the Russian mafia in Moscow. It has been alleged that Kobzon brokered the sale of surface-to-air missiles to Iran, according to a U.S. federal wiretap affidavit.

When the U.S. State Department revoked Kobzon's American visa in June 1995, citing his links to the Russian mafia, Kobzon's need for an Israeli home was reinforced. Israel has come close to excluding him, but Kobzon managed to exert enough "protexia" (influence with powerful friends) to ensure his safe admission on every occasion.

Many Russian Jewish businessmen regard Israel as their bolthole when they find the heat uncomfortably strong in their native land. Equally, they regard North America as having streets paved with gold. Semion Mogilevitch had great plans for the launch of a company to raise money in Canada to fund his Eastern European business interests. The outcome would be rather less glittering than the initial golden promise.

The YBM-Magnex Bubble

Mogilevitch needed critical mass to break into North America and, in 1993, merged his two main operating companies with Magnex 2000, the Hungarian company that sold industrial magnets and military hardware, to achieve it. He refinanced the new venture by arranging for his Jersey-based company, Arigon, to send $30 million to his American company, YBM. The money was "smurfed" in the form of numerous wire transfers of funds, in chunks ranging between $10,000 and $1 million plus. This form of laundering, first encountered by New York police officers investigating a banking scam, involves breaking up large sums of money into amounts that are small enough to be deposited into the American banking system without arousing suspicion. Smurfing takes its name from a popular children's cartoon series about the adventures of a horde of tiny people known as smurfs. They take their orders from a benevolent father figure called Papa Smurf. Benevolence is far from the minds of the players in this particular activity.

Igor Fisherman, Mogilevitch's trusted childhood friend and adviser, was given the job of pulling the two companies together and making them a presence on the North American scene. Fisherman, now YBM-Magnex's chief operating officer, was a trained mathematician with a respectable pedigree, having once served as a consultant to Chase Manhattan Bank in New York City.

The two men plotted the financial path that would enable them to expand the company while enriching themselves and their own enterprise. They set their sights on a stock market listing and targeted the lightly regulated (at that time) financial markets of Canada, which were already notorious for scams perpetrated by bogus gold, precious metals, and oil prospecting companies.

The duo of Mogilevitch and Fisherman would be joined by a third scholar and financial whiz kid, Jacob Bogatin, a professor of physical metallurgy and Mogilevitch's long-time colleague from Saratov, near Kazakhstan. Bogatin had served on the boards of Mogilevitch's Arbat and Magnex companies in Budapest but had yet to cut his teeth in the West.

In 1995, Bogatin traveled to Northern Canada with the mission to turn Mogilevitch's financial interests into something that could be marketed to the investing public. He did extensive research into Canadian stock markets, before deciding on one of the country's less regulated exchanges, Alberta. The stocks listed there were mostly agricultural and the investors were rich but financially unsophisticated farmers. Alberta's regulators would not trouble to delve into the background to a new listing.

Bogatin obtained a listed company called Pratecs Technologies Inc. as a shell with nothing more than a name. The YBM shareholders register read like a role call of Mogilevitch's extended family. Mogilevitch, his ex-wife Tatiana, their daughter Mila, and Mogilevitch's former mistress, Galina Grigorieva, were among the major shareholders. Another shareholder was Mogilevitch's associate, Alexei Viktorovitch Alexandrov.

Alexandrov, a director of Arigon, was nicknamed "the plumber" for his deft handling of leaks and planting disinformation on behalf of Mogilevitch's organization. He was also Mogilevitch's contact with the Hungarian police and responsible for procuring Russian women for Mogilevitch's sex industry operations, which stretched across the width of Eastern Europe. Alexandrov was another smart operator, holding degrees in economics and engineering.

Shortly after the company was listed, the directors announced plans to issue ten million shares at twenty cents per share to enable Pratecs to acquire a string of off-shore companies owned by Mogilevitch. This was almost defeated when the British security services, which had been investigating Mogilevitch's empire for some three years, told the Alberta Stock Exchange, in advance of the listing, that YBM and Pratecs were not only controlled by Mogilevitch but that the probable intention of obtaining a Pratecs listing was to have a vehicle to launder dirty money, manipulate shares, and deceive legitimate investors. A British intelligence report describes the money as largely the proceeds of Russian organized crime in Eastern Europe from the Mogilevitch and Solntsevo organizations.

The Canadian authorities were shown some of the work undertaken by British police in an operation they called "Sword." Documents seized from the London offices of Arigon and Arigon's lawyer, who was arrested and interrogated, purported to show that the lawyer had used his client's accounts to launder more than $50 million in criminal proceeds on behalf of Mogilevitch. The funds, allegedly laundered through the Royal Bank of Scotland, were said to have originated from a variety of dubious sources in the former Soviet Union. The Alberta authorities suspended the listing of Pratecs but waited to be convinced by the outcome of the lawyer's trial in London to see if the sources of Mogilevitch's money were as "black" as the UK authorities claimed.

But the trial did not deliver the goods the British had hoped. The Russian government had refused to cooperate in providing evidence against the solicitor and the trial was abandoned. The Canadians gave the go-ahead to the Pratecs share issue, saying that without a criminal conviction, they could not accept the veracity of the police evidence.

In fact, the damage had already been done to the Mogilevitch empire, whose UK companies were closed down and whose Channel Islands–based assets, primarily Arigon itself, were frozen. Mogilevitch was banned from entering the United Kingdom and the Royal Bank of Scotland was subjected to a high-level internal enquiry by the UK Special Investigation

Unit. The solicitor involved was disbarred although he has long denied any involvement in laundering Mogilevitch's money. Mogilevitch's own fortune was decreased by these events. Mogilevitch's associates were boiling in anger at a $3.5 million debt Mogilevitch owed them and plotted to have him killed at a party to be held at Mogilevitch's restaurant in Prague, U Holubu. Mogilevitch was warned and survived.

In July 1995, Bogatin arranged for Pratecs to acquire the Mogilevitch assets and it began trading on the Alberta stock exchange. The first stage of Mogilevitch's plan to acquire and build a financial asset in the West was completed. The authorities had not been a problem.

Pratecs was now on the move. A year later, in 1996, Mogilevitch was sufficiently confident to move Pratecs to the much larger Toronto stock exchange. Its name was changed to YBM-Magnex International. Reflecting its size and its founders' claim to respectability, they appointed the international auditing firm of Deloitte & Touche as its accountants. The firm was happy to take the Russian money, but it is not known how much due diligence they used to look into its sources. But there is one thing to be sure of—the responsible partner rues the day he first met up with Igor Fisherman, YBM's finance director.

The shareholders appeared to have taken the message that YBM was respectable and ignored concerns held by the British police, published in the form of obscure court reports in the United Kingdom, about the sources of the company's money. Instead, they saw a diverse industrial conglomerate with assets as far afield as Philadelphia and Budapest, and they were enthusiastic. The Exchange made it their favorite stock with a market capitalization approaching a billion Canadian dollars. This ensured its admission to the prestigious Toronto Stock Exchange 300 index. In another bid for respectability, Mogilevitch appointed David Peterson, the former premier of Ontario, to its board.

The British Metropolitan Police continued nagging away at Mogilevitch and his booming stock market company. They produced a report, written by detective John Wanless, which said that Mogilevitch was using the stock exchange listing primarily to legitimize the criminal organization by floating on the stock exchange a corporation that consists of UK and U.S. companies whose existing assets and stocks had been artificially inflated by the introduction of the proceeds of crime. Mogilevitch was said to be using

YBM to transfer funds between Britain, Hungary, the United States and Canada.

When doubts began to be expressed in 1997 about the company's financial practices, its auditors Deloitte & Touche came to its aid, saying that the company was sound. Investors' fears were temporarily allayed.

But law enforcement authorities on both sides of the Atlantic now started to act on their earlier warnings. Undercover surveillance of YBM's factory in Pennsylvania showed that it occupied no more than a small section of a former schoolroom and was not capable of supporting either the 165 employees or the $20 million in sales claimed in its glossy published report. The U.S. Attorney's Office in Philadelphia followed up the FBI investigation with its own and came to a similar conclusion. Similar surveillance of the firm's activities in Budapest revealed questionable activities. One auditor who visited the factory reported that armed guards were posted at the gates and cars with Russian license plates were stationed in the car park. There was a strong suspicion, he commented, that YBM-Magnex appeared to be in the business of making magnets for the defense industry.

The employees of Deloitte & Touche now tried desperately to reverse their earlier commendation of the company. In 1997 they reported that one or more illegal acts might have occurred which may have a material impact on YBM's 1997 financial statements. This referred to the inclusion of $15.7 million worth from the sale of magnets to the Middle East and North America, which later analysis had shown to be invented. The firm issued YBM-Magnex an ultimatum—hire an outside auditor to conduct a sweeping re-evaluation of the business or we resign. YBM refused and the auditors resigned. The firm's audit partner is reported to have been understandably extremely distressed following the affair.

YBM-Magnex did not have much longer to run. The firm's offices in Pennsylvania were raided in May 1998 by no less than five American law enforcement agencies, including the Federal Bureau of Investigation and the Drug Enforcement Administration. The authorities took no chances, salvaging virtually every piece of paper they could find in their bid to prove that YBM-Magnex was a money laundering machine. The stock was suspended as soon as word of the raid was passed to the Toronto Stock Exchange. It never resurfaced.

Information released by the investigators showed the company was little more than a hoax. Its advanced process to desulphurize oil, which accounted for 20 percent of its 1997 revenues, did not exist and, in September 1998, court documents filed in Alberta showed that $20 million in revenues was missing. After Mogilevitch's men quit, money was found to have passed through front companies and banks in Moscow, the Cayman Islands, Lithuania, Hungary, and a branch of Chemical Bank in Buffalo, New York, in the United States. Among a massive number of funds transfers in and out of YBM-Magnex, the FBI discovered that YBM had received $270,000 from Benex, the laundering scheme discussed in the following chapter.

The charges against the company—of mail fraud and of securities fraud—were anti-climatic, given the events that preceded them. In 1999, YBM-Magnex pleaded guilty and was fined $3 million, a laughably small sum in the light of the tens of millions of dollars that had been laundered through YBM-Magnex.

Deloitte would not be allowed to forget their involvement. In 1999, two of the YBM-Magnex shareholders sued them, amongst others. The suit alleged, "Deloitte breached its duty of care to the plaintiffs and the other class members, made negligent misrepresentations in connection with the issuance of its audit opinion in respect of YBM's financial statements for the year ended December 31, 1996 . . . Deloitte was negligent . . . in failing to identify and warn [about] irregularities relating to related party and other suspicious transactions in Eastern Europe."

Russian payments to YBM-Magnex made using the Benex system alerted police to Mogilevitch's sources of money, and these sources continue to be investigated. The Brainy Don's empire has yet to yield all its secrets. Benex sheltered inside the prestigious American bank, the Bank of New York. As the following chapter reveals, Semion Mogilevitch was far from alone in using that system to move his crooked money around the globe.

Chapter 2

BoNYGate

The tentacles of the Russian mafia spread globally. Their money went into laundering schemes in Italy, London, Lithuania, France, and many places we don't yet know. But the schemes started in New York, in one of America's most prestigious banks, the Bank of New York.

WE EXPECT OUR BLUE CHIP BANKS to deliver honest and reliable service. We expect them to handle our money with care, and to be scrupulous with their customers and their staff. So it comes as quite a shock to discover that money launderers exerted great influence over the Bank of New York (BoNY), one of America's leading banks, for the best part of the 1990s. BoNY's lack of oversight enabled Russian money to escape the net of revenue officials and local police, while the bank's managers allegedly made a turn on the process of capital flight. Worse than that, some of Russia's most heinous mob members were customers of a secret bank-within-a-bank nestling inside BoNY.

That is the conclusion of a number of legal documents that have been filed since two Russian bankers were charged with money laundering at the bank, and other offenses.

The following account reviews the allegations in three sets of court documents in particular. The first and largest was a civil complaint filed in the U.S. District Court, Southern District of New York by shareholders of The Bank of New York Company Inc. The second case was brought by a group of depositors of the Russian bank, Inkombank, against The Bank of New York Company Inc. Finally, there is a series of documents detailing the indictments produced by the government in the criminal case brought on October 5, 1999, against Lucy Edwards, Peter Berlin, Alexei Volkov, and Svetlana Kudryavtsev. Kudryavtsev worked in the Bank of New York's Eastern European division.

If the allegations in these documents prove to be true, BoNYGate is among the biggest single money laundering exercises in history. Despite the allegations, no action has been taken against the bank's chairman and former chief executive officer at the time the laundering was committed, Thomas Renyi, and the bank itself, flourishes. Renyi has admitted that there was a "lapse" of internal controls on the part of BoNY. Renyi made this admission when he gave evidence before the House Committee on Banking and Financial Services of the U.S. Congress investigating the BoNY case on September 22, 1999. Renyi has denied all allegations in both the BoNY shareholders and the Inkombank depositors complaint referred to above, and he has never been charged by authorities with any wrongdoing.

Lawyers acting for shareholders of the Bank of New York claim that BoNY's top management is culpable. They say BoNY received a percentage of the dirty money that was deposited with them by Russian tax evaders, on the assumption that tax evaders with something to hide would never complain to law enforcement authorities.

They allege that Renyi, "knew and assisted in the Bank's participation, with private banking leaders, in the implementation of these illegal tax evasion, money laundering, and capital flight schemes." It is stated elsewhere in the complaint that "Renyi actively conspired, directly participated in, and personally benefited from schemes to illegally divert and steal Russian assets." These allegations have never been tested in court but if true they would be extremely damaging as Renyi remains chairman of the company. Another defendant named in the civil complaint filed by Bank of New York shareholders was John Malone, the prominent chairman of Liberty Media and a member of the bank's board since 1986. He, too, has denied all allegations of wrong-doing.

The Bank of New York

The Bank of New York was probably the least likely place to expect such illegality. Its Number One Wall Street headquarters indicated blue blood and establishment. Its founder was Andrew Hamilton, a father of the U.S. Constitution. BoNY was the sixteenth largest bank in the world in the late 1980s and well respected for its integrity.

But the bank had hit hard times when the Russian bonanza beckoned. The value of its investments in real estate had collapsed and it needed new revenues. Enter here Bruce Rappaport. He was BoNY's largest shareholder and saw Russia's potential. Rappaport was a self-made American lawyer, who was in addition a linguist. He had also taken advantage of the land of opportunity. Born in Israel of Russian and Jewish parents, he had made a massive fortune financing oil and energy-related projects. He had been involved in a financially dubious Indonesian oil company and had worked with the Gulf Group, owned by the Gokal brothers. Abbas Gokal, one of the brothers, would later be entangled in the Bank of Credit and Commerce International (BCCI) laundering scandal and in due course received a fourteen-year prison sentence in the UK. Two banks in Antigua and Barbuda, purportedly controlled by Rappaport, were the subject of a suit filed in the Boston federal court by regulators seeking to retrieve $7 billion worth of drug money. The judge, citing lack of jurisdiction, dismissed the case and Rappaport denied wrongdoing.

Finally, Rappaport, through his friend William Casey, a former head of the Criminal Intelligence Agency (CIA), has had a long history of involvement with U.S. intelligence operations. Rappaport's bank, Inter-Maritime Bank (IMB), based in Geneva, directed the Bank of New York's expansion plans in Russia. Rappaport worked closely with BoNY's chairman at the time, J. Carter Bacot, to expand contacts in Russia and bring in Russian money. In fact, the two banks set up a joint entity, called IMB-BoNY, to forge links with Russia. Rappaport said in a statement following the Bank of New York exposé, "I know none of the individuals involved in this matter, and I certainly have no knowledge of whatever their business was about."

The architects of the scandal that enveloped Bank of New York worked much further down the bank's food chain. They were a Russian husband and wife team, Lucy Edwards and Peter Berlin, who created a secret bank-within-a-bank in BoNY to facilitate the movement of the flight capital and illegal earnings of Russian politicians and leading Mafiosi. Their money and clients would later be traced to numerous crimes. Benex International, the company they created to make the criminal transfers, would become synonymous with Russian illegality.

Benex: Lucy Edwards and Peter Berlin

Lucy Edwards' name suggests little of her origins. She was born Ludmilla Pritzker in Leningrad, in the then Soviet Union. Today it is St. Petersburg, a major city on the River Volga. The "Edwards" part of her name comes from her unlikely marriage to a nineteen-year-old American merchant seaman Brad Edwards in 1977, a man she met casually at a club in her hometown. Shortly afterwards, the couple moved to Illinois where their daughter Amy was born. They then moved to Colorado where she worked as a bank teller and waitress. After the marriage fell apart in 1988, Lucy got a low-level job handling commercial accounts at BoNY.

Four years later, Edwards met a fellow Russian, Peter Berlin, and they married within a few months of their first meeting. Berlin was a scientist who had graduated from the Moscow Institute of Physics and Technology in 1978, with a degree in molecular chemical physics. But he had not pursued science, instead he had set up small import-export firms. He had left Russia in 1989 and started exporting electrical goods to Russia from the United States, but business was poor and by 1992 he was down on his luck.

Edwards' career, on the other hand, was thriving. Her energy had brought her to the attention of her boss at BoNY, Natasha Kagalovsky, with whom she traveled to Russia on several occasions. In 1994, she was promoted to loan officer. A year later, Edwards and Berlin hatched a scheme to make themselves rich. The scheme was designed to shift around the world Russian money.

Natasha Kagalovsky was married to Konstantin Kagalovsky, one of Russia's most influential financiers. This archetypal "New Russian" had started as an academic economist, and been recruited into the government as an adviser to Yegor Gaidar. Gaidar was an economist, who from November 1991 to January 1994 had played a leading role in the transformation of the Russian economy. Kagalovsky had also advised Boris Yeltsin, and used his public influence to win major positions in the banking and oil companies controlled by the oligarch, Mikhail Khodorkovsky. He held senior positions at Bank Menatep and Yukos.

Natasha Kagalovsky and Lucy Edwards visited Russia frequently, showing off BoNY's Micro/Ca$h system. This was a money transfer system, which allowed a customer to transfer money across BoNY's entire banking network. BoNY did not enquire who used Micro/Ca$h or where the money came from, but users were treated as customers of the bank. When they wanted to put the money into another bank, the BoNY name ensured it got sanctuary. Micro/Ca$h undoubtedly could be used properly. But there were those who saw its criminal possibilities.

Micro/Ca$h gave Edwards and Berlin the technology and the banking networks for launching a secret money transfer business. They gave this business the name Benex International. Now they needed a client and sources of funds. These came through Depositano Klearingovi Bank (DKB), a bank recruited by Edwards on one of her visits to Russia. DKB had many Russian clients with large quantities of funds to whom this secrecy appealed. In late 1995, Edwards suggested to Kagalovsky that her husband wanted to set up a finance company on behalf of DKB with an account at BoNY. Kagalovsky raised no objection although it was probably against BoNY's rules for a bank manager to have access to an account on behalf of a relative.

There was no shortage of clients for Benex, and they came from the highest and lowest echelons of Russian society. Tatyana Dyachenko, the daughter of former Russian President Boris Yeltsin, the former finance minister Alexander Livshits, oligarch Vladimir Potanin, and prominent Russian politician Anatoly Chubais were among them.

But so too was Semion Mogilevitch, the notorious Ukrainian gangster whose YBM-Magnex company was involved in market rigging in Canada. He made nine transactions through Benex accounts, as was revealed in Chapter 1. The Colombian Cali drugs cartel (see Chapter 7) also channeled money through Benex.

In February 1996, Peter Berlin set up an account at One Wall Street, BoNY's New York headquarters on behalf of Benex International; another, opened six months later, was on behalf of a related company, BECS. They had their offices on Queens Boulevard in Forest Hills, New York, and Edwards set up the Micro/Ca$h computer system there. Berlin appointed his Russian friend, Alexei Volkov, a director of Benex International, alongside himself. DKB now had access to one of the world's most advanced money transfer systems.

DKB expanded by taking over Bank Flamingo, a Russian commercial bank, and Berlin gave Flamingo a set of the Micro/Ca$h equipment. This time the equipment was put into Bank Flamingo's Moscow offices and

Berlin created a company called Lowland, based in New Jersey, to handle Flamingo's affairs. It is unclear to what extent BoNY's board was aware of the scale of funds movement and their sources and destinations.

Lucy Edwards was promoted to vice president in BoNY's Eastern European division in 1996, reporting to Kagalovsky. Edwards and Berlin moved to BoNY's London office with their two children but they made frequent visits to New York and Russia to build up the Benex client base. Benex boomed. The U.S. Government indictment in the criminal case against Berlin and the others alleges that between February 1996 and August 1999, more than $7 billion of funds originating primarily from Russia was deposited in, and transmitted through, the Benex, BECS, and Lowland accounts. It also alleges that approximately $4.9 billion was deposited in or transmitted through the Benex account at the Bank of New York. It further alleges that between December 1996 and August 1999, approximately $2 billion was deposited in or transmitted through the BECS account at the Bank of New York. Some $358 million went through Lowland.

The money they sent ranged from advance payments made by companies that vanished shortly after their registration to payments for exported goods, where the due amounts were wire-transferred directly to third-party beneficiaries in foreign countries, instead of being transferred back to Russia. The full gamut of fraudulently acquired and criminal money flowed down this pipeline.

No less than 87,000 separate transfers passed through Benex, BECS, and Lowland either on their way to or on their way back from Russia. Reports of transactions are said to fill entire rooms at the Federal Bureau of Investigation's building. Police authorities say that not all Benex dealings were criminal, although the majority were designed to assist the owner of the funds, at the very least, to avoid tax.

BoNY's tentacles spread much further than Benex. In fact, they percolated throughout the Russian banking system. The American bank, for example, forged links with a Moscow-based commercial bank called Inkombank, which had many rich Russian clients with money to hide in offshore hideaways, out of sight of Russian tax authorities. Natasha Kagalovsky and Vladimir Doudkin, Inkombank's vice chairman, joined in a common cause to allegedly provide what we would call today tax shelters.

The class action suits contend that they acted with the knowledge of high management. The clever schemes they created were dubbed *prokrutki*, or "spinning," on the basis that the schemes involved whirling millions of dollars of Russian money around the world's financial system so fast that nobody could catch it.

Prokrutki worked in the following way according to the allegations in the suit filed by BoNY shareholders and referred to above. "After a major 'investment' was placed by a Russian customer with Inkombank or one of its satellite offshore companies, BoNY would execute a series of electronic funds transfers (EFTs) from the Inkombank dollar account to specific offshore front companies and bank accounts. Usually several layers of these transfers were executed in succession, hence the name *prokrutki*. The ultimate goal of this spinning around was to obscure and disguise the true origin of the funds being moved through the BoNY accounts . . ." Offshore shell companies, sham loans, fake stock transactions, and contrived bankruptcies were allegedly used by Inkombank to disguise the fact that vast sums of black money were being spun through a sophisticated international washing cycle.

The lawsuit filed by the depositors of Inkombank against the Bank of New York Company Inc. describes the trail of money in detail. For example, Inkombank allegedly used a Cyprus-registered shell company under its control, Aspirations Holdings, to purchase 1,200 common registered shares in Inkombank with a face value of 1,200,000 rubles. At that time, the existing rate of exchange was 200 rubles to one dollar, but Aspirations paid four times the face value, namely $24,000. Inkombank then bought back its shares for $2,400,000, one hundred times the amount paid by Aspirations. The 1996 audit of Inkombank by the Central Bank of Russia showed that the "agreement" had no requisites such as the address or other personal details for Aspirations, and the signature of the purported "foreign shareholder" (Aspirations) was illegible. This transaction had thus purportedly allowed Inkombank to embezzle $2,376,000 of bank assets, which were then funneled through the Bank of New York's accounts with the Bank of New York's advance knowledge that the transaction was bogus.

Sham loans were alleged to be another effective way of muddying the money trail. The civil complaints allege that Inkombank principals employed this technique to move assets out of Russia and into their personal control. The basic format of these sham loan transactions is alleged to be as follows:

Step One: Inkombank made a bogus United States dollar "loan" to Company A, which was secretly controlled by bank principals.

Step Two: Company A in turn "lent" or "invested" the proceeds in Company B, also secretly controlled by bank principals.

Step Three: When the original loan from the bank to Company A fell due, Company A defaulted.

Step Four: Rather than take a bad debt charge on its books for the original loan to Company A, Inkombank assigned the defaulted loan to Company C, also controlled by bank principals, in exchange for promissory notes of Company C. In this way, the loan was carried forward on the bank's records; in effect, it was "extended" rather than defaulted on.

Step Five: Company A dissolved. Ultimately, Company C also dissolved, when its promissory notes fell due. Proceeds of the "loan" remained in Company B, or were transferred through additional shell companies controlled by the bank's principals.

One of the complaints recounts a set of transactions dated December 15, 1995, as an example of this technique. Inkombank allegedly lent $35 million to three companies called Neftegaz, First Moscow, and Tokur. The three companies defaulted but not before they passed on the loans to two shell companies controlled by Inkombank's shareholders. They were called Overseas and Mathur, and they issued the bank uncollateralized promissory notes. The shells in turn went bust, but not before the original borrowers, Neftegaz, First Moscow, and Tokur, had sent the original $35 million to offshore entities controlled by Inkombank principals and officers of the Bank of New York using international wire transfers and Bank of New York accounts. The upshot of the alleged scheme was to provide a false trail for any auditor or regulator who wanted to try to follow or understand the illegal payments.

But the cover would not last and in 1996 the Bank of New York's relationship with its Russian correspondent banks, in particular Inkombank, attracted the attention of officials who were particularly concerned about its Russian customers. On June 6, 1996, the Central Bank of Russia issued a report of its audit of Inkombank, detailing evidence of widespread misconduct by Inkombank and its senior officers. The report said that the misconduct pervaded all aspects of the bank's operations, including "improper funding of the Inkombank capital account, illegal inside deals between Inkombank and its senior executives and shareholders, and the making of unsecured, interest-free loans to Inkombank insiders and companies they controlled."

BoNY's correspondent banking facilities are used in all the alleged schemes that have been listed so far, but to what extent did the bank and Natasha Kagalovsky realize what was happening? Kagalovsky has vehemently protested her innocence and claims to have no knowledge of the scams being perpetrated in the Inkombank case. However, she is frequently referred to in the complaints. Some allegations relate that Natasha Kagalovsky and others at Inkombank created "sham contracts and back-dated contracts . . . to falsely verify transactions that, in fact, had never occurred in order to validate illegal money transfers. As part of these schemes, Kagalovsky provided Inkombank with confirmations of fictitious wire transfers. For example, on one occasion in 1996, Inkombank, at Kagalovsky's request, created false documents, backdated to 1993, concerning a supposed transaction involving a Russian company, Transneft. Kagalovsky was among those who used the term *konformashka* (translated as 'confirmation') to refer to such phoney documentation."

Multitudes of offshore companies were allegedly created in the *prokrutki* process. One of these was Tetra Finance Establishment, based in Liechtenstein. Testimony to New York banking regulators shows that Tetra was controlled by principals of Inkombank "to divert the bank's money through offshore accounts." It was reported in November 1999 that earlier in the decade Natasha Gurfinkel, who became Natasha Kagalovsky, had been given power of attorney over the company.

The complaint filed by shareholders of the Bank of New York suggests that certain of BoNY's bankers and their Russian colleagues divided the money that they had allegedly skimmed from Russian clients in the course of the *prokrutki* just described. The alleged skimmng was performed using a computer program which investigators later analyzed. In other words, people from BoNY and Inkombank allegedly deceived the Russians who were evading taxes, presumably because people who handle or steal black money are unlikely to incriminate themselves by "snitching" to the authorities.

The complaints say that, "in April 1994, Vladimir Doudkin, Inkombank's vice chairman, sent the computer specialist who wrote the program a chart showing the movement of funds through a web of offshore companies and accounts. The chart aroused the specialist's suspicion because the scheme depicted involved a pre-planned default on a loan by the entity to which the loan was to be made. The chart also made explicit references to 'fake promissory notes.' The specialist refused to proceed with the project, telling Doudkin that the global custody system appeared to be an illegal money laundering scheme. Doudkin replied, 'what do you care? You'll be handsomely paid.'"

One of the complaints further alleges that BoNY's leading bankers involved in the scam gave themselves code names to disguise the ownership of their share in the "Retirement Fund." Code names are part of the banker's armory of disguises to blot out from their printed records the names of sensitive or high-profile clients. (See Chapter 9 for Citibank's code names for its politically sensitive private clients.) Natasha Kagalovsky, BoNY's head of the Eastern European department, was called "Gurova," Doudkin became "Illyinsky," and his colleague at Inkombank, Vladimir Winogradov, was named "Winoff."

It was a cast list that might have come out of *War and Peace*. Indeed the plan might have been just as fictional, but if these complaints are to be believed, the system was created to allow bankers to apportion their share of the proceeds as anonymously as possible. Secrecy prevailed as the bankers allegedly slipped in and out of America to organize their affairs. Winogradov was admitted under his code name, Winoff, to Pascack Valley Hospital in Westwood, New Jersey, for treatment of a kidney condition. The complaints allege that, while he was at the hospital recovering from quite an uncomfortable biopsy procedure, he had a visit from Renyi. They purportedly chatted about schemes to move money out of Russia through the Bank of New York. Winogradov used the back of a hospital menu to illustrate the flow of money through various entities, resulting in a $10 million fall-out payment for an offshore account.

The shareholders' allegations in the complaint go on to say that the men talked about the details of offshore accounts that might receive the black money. Renyi is alleged to have said that he wanted to use FirstTen S.A., a Panamanian company, because it was an older, less suspicious company. The two men also purportedly discussed a loan from the American Export-Import Bank (Eximbank) that was on its way to Inkombank. Eximbank was a federal agency of the U.S. government. The two men saw opportunities to make money, and they allegedly later met in New York at the Waldorf Astoria hotel to talk about their percentages.

In much the same way as the bankers allegedly fabricated names and accounts to keep safe their own shares of the laundered money, so they allegedly fabricated paperwork and false auditing trails for their punters to explain unusual transfers and losses. The complaints later indicated how the alleged scheme worked. One alleged: "the conspirators established 'independent' offshore companies to which they caused their banks to make unsecured loans, never intending the loans to be repaid. The conspirators also caused offshore companies to engage in fictitious business transactions using bogus sales contracts, letters of confirmation for electronic funds transfers, and other documents . . . It was precisely these types of transactions, in high risk locations such as Russia and offshore havens that FinCEN (the U.S. Financial Crimes Enforcement Network), the agency responsible for administering the Bank Secrecy Act, had specifically identified as being potential money laundering schemes."

Bust

The Bank of New York was first investigated by British police in 1997, following the affairs of a tipster named Stuart Creggy. Creggy was prosecuted in 2001 in New York for forgery and falsifying business records. In November 2002, Creggy was convicted of seventeen counts involving conspiracy and falsifying business records. An appeal hearing is expected to take place in 2005. The UK's National Crime Squad passed the information on to Neil Giles, a British police liaison officer and quasi-intelligence officer working at the British embassy in Washington, D.C. Giles in turn passed on the information to the FBI's Russian Organized Crime Unit.

Russian police authorities, who had seen kidnapping and ransom payments pass through Benex, noted the name at the same time and asked the Federal Bureau of Investigation for help. Finally, in August 1998,

Republic National Bank reported to the FBI a suspicious movement of $10 million from Russia through Benex.

In fact, Republic National Bank was claimed to have had some links of its own with Russian mafia. In December 1999, one year after it went to the authorities to explain this unusual movement of money through Benex, Republic's billionaire owner Edmund Safra died in a fire in his Monaco apartment. Monaco has a wealthy ex-patriot Russian population. The circumstances of the fire were highly suspicious and there was an uncorroborated rumor of Russian mafia involvement.

The Benex trail took British investigators to the house in London of Berlin and Edwards. They put the address in London's chic West End under constant surveillance. The British National Crime Squad worked in conjunction with the FBI to set up some elaborate traps for them, although it seems that none was particularly successful. For example, it has been reported that Federal investigators set up an undercover agent posing as a diplomat to approach Berlin to discuss a deal to convert a Russian defense factory for civilian use. British investigators were later said to have taped Berlin boasting of his ties to the diplomat, but nothing more came of it.

Benex International provided the U.S. and UK intelligence community with a window into Russian and East European organized crime. It seems obvious that they would have good reason to keep it open as long as possible. But the investigation was brought to a sudden end by the publication of a revealing account in *The New York Times*. This is widely believed by UK police insiders to have come from a source inside BoNY itself, which had collaborated with the investigating authorities. Certainly, police sources could barely disguise their anger at the leak.

In August 1999, the investigating authorities were phoned by the reporters from *The New York Times*, Raymond Bonner and Timothy O'Brien, telling them that they were about to reveal news of the investigation and they had a few hours to comment. It hit the investigators hard.

One police officer serving with the UK's National Crime Squad said, "The FBI went to BoNY in order to discuss the problem surrounding the accounts and of course if you do that you are telling a bank you may have a serious problem. Well, the bank's got to look after its own interest. So it would make sense for the bank to say, well if you say we've got a potentially big problem here but we can't do anything about it because you're investigating it, where does that leave us? So it would make sense to leak it so you could bring it to an end from the bank's point of view. Once it's made public they shut the accounts down so you then reduce the risks to the bank. I don't know if that's the case but I'd be surprised if it wasn't. I can understand them doing it. If I were a senior manager at BoNY I'd have done exactly the same, if I'd have suddenly been told I was in the center of what could be biggest money laundering case the world's seen and it was."

The same source in the National Crime Squad said that the police had to act as soon as they received the newspaper report on August 18, 1999. He said, "It didn't help because we were in the middle of the investigation and we were getting fantastic intelligence on what Berlin was up to because he was involved in all sorts of things. It just meant that we had to take immediate action in order to preserve evidence, we had to go and execute a search warrant."

Another National Crime Squad source commented, "We were looking very hard at Berlin and Edwards in London, when we were forced into a situation where we searched the London home of Berlin and Edwards. The decision was to search 62 Montague Mansions, Baker Street. Computers were seized; Berlin and Edwards were not arrested or interviewed. A load of stuff was taken, Edwards's office at BoNY in Canary Wharf was searched and a load of stuff . . . we had a long negotiation with BoNY over legal privilege matters, arguments about documents. The FBI came over to the UK."

On the following day, August 19, 1999, a detailed account of the Benex operation was published in *The New York Times*. The front page story, entitled "Activity at Bank Raises Suspicions of Russian Mob Tie," said, "billions of dollars have been channeled through the Bank of New York in the last year in what is believed [by law enforcement officials] to be a major money laundering operation by Russian organized crime . . . Investigators say the transactions seem to add up to one of the largest money laundering operations ever uncovered in the United States, with vast sums of money moving in and out of the bank in a day."

It was an effective demonstration of the power of the press, as U.S. police then had to close their investigation and prepare something for the lawyers. On October 6, 1999, an indictment was unsealed in the Southern District of New York charging Lucy Edwards and Peter Berlin with "conspiracy to violate United States and New York State banking laws. The United States

Attorney for the Southern District of New York has announced that the investigation of money laundering and other possible crimes involving Bank of the New York is wide-ranging and continuing in nature."

On February 16, 2000, Lucy Edwards, her husband Peter Berlin, and three of the shell companies they controlled—Benex, BECS, and Lowland—pleaded guilty to a number of federal crimes, including, first, "conspiracy to launder money through international funds transfers in violation of Russian law, defrauding the Russian Government of customs duties and tax revenues;" second, "to making corrupt payments to members of Bank of New York's Eastern European Division for their participation and facilitation of, and to earn and launder commissions from, the unlawful banking schemes;" and third, "to conducting unauthorized and unregulated banking activities through accounts at Bank of New York."

Edwards and Berlin were named in two counts that each carry a possible maximum five-year prison sentence. They both agreed to forfeit to the United States more than $1 million in proceeds from their criminal conduct, including their London residence and the contents of two Swiss bank accounts. In their testimony, Berlin and Edwards admitted that between late 1995 and September 1999 they were part of the money laundering conspiracy that allowed Russians to defraud their government by wiring money out of the country to avoid customs duties and taxes. The money-transmitting scheme was also used for other criminal activity, including the payment of $300,000 in ransom to the kidnappers of a Russian businessman. Some four years later, none of the guilty parties has been sentenced. Alexel Volkov, who was indicted alongside Edwards and Berlin, has not entered into any plea agreement with the Federal authorities, said his lawyer.

Officials working for the Bologna Public Prosecutor's Office, Anti-Mafia District Division, subsequently observed how the weakness of U.S. banking regulations facilitated the Russian scheme. They said, "The Russian banks Flamingo and Depositano Klearingovi, through the accounts at the BoNY opened in the name of three named companies (Benex, Lowland, and Sinex), could operate without being duly authorized by the Federal Reserve, as if they had licensed branches in the United States." The Italian authorities said the scheme accounted for the disappearance of some $8 billion from the former Soviet Union.

Italian investigators had taken a particular interest in the Benex scheme because a company based in Rimini (an elegant seaside resort on Italy's east coast) called Prima had engaged in numerous transactions with Benex. Their research found that Prima was controlled by two Russian hoodlums, Oleg and Igor Berezowski, whom Italian police have since charged. Italian police believe that Prima was a front for the repatriation of money to Russia that had been secretly spirited out of the country during the late 1980s.

The investigation of Prima—a massive exercise called Operation Spiderweb—led to the discovery of a series of other companies based in Paris which were controlled by a reputedly brilliant Russian called Andrei Marisov. These Paris-based companies have been the subject of French prosecution and have been closed down. Marisov has been arrested and charged with fraud.

However, these companies were allegedly linked through an export company called Kama Trade AG to another company called Nordex which greatly intrigued the authorities. Nordex had been founded in 1989 by Dr. Grigori Loutchanski, a Russian businessman who has been the subject of much investigation for alleged financial irregularity. Western authorities have never charged or convicted Loutchanski of an offence. He was however convicted for embezzlement by Latvian authorities in 1983 and served a prison term. Loutchanski has since said those charges were motivated for political rather than judicial ends.

Loutchanski successfully sued *The Times* newspaper in 2000 over an allegation that he was linked to the Russian mafia. He said in a witness statement made to the UK High Court in November 2000, that, "I am aware of the suspicion that the Nordex group of companies has been used to launder money for criminal entrepreneurs in Russia. This is completely untrue. All the monies paid into off-shore companies are covered by invoices bona fide raised by the trading transactions of the Nordex Group. The payments from these accounts have been made by way of commissions and . . . . Incidental benefit to our partners in Russia, with whom the Nordex group have made contracts." Loutchanski has also denied in the same document having any involvement with the Bank of New York, or Benex.

Concern over the Bank of New York case gave rise to a report by the U.S. Senate Sub-committee on Correspondent Banking. This was published in

2001 and explained the role of United States Correspondent Banking in International Money Laundering. Following the publication of this massive and shocking investigation, pressure was placed on banks to investigate their correspondent relationships more thoroughly and make them more transparent.

The international links of the largest banks enable Russian criminals to export illegal capital and corrupt schemes to the most far-flung corners of the globe. But laundering can also be facilitated using commodities. Africa's most precious natural asset is its diamonds and its most eagerly sought product, in some quarters, is tragically weapons. Victor Bout sought out people who controlled the diamond fields who wanted weapons, and he found people who owned weapons who were prepared to accept or do deals with diamonds. Bout's networks spanned the globe, as we shall discover next.

Chapter 3

'Merchant of Death'

Victor Bout has been described by a British cabinet minister as "Africa's merchant of death." Bout deals in the wealth of illegal and unstable African regimes and guerilla groups. They provide him with diamonds, cash, and other commodities; in return he supplies arms. It is a laundering whirligig that makes the blood run cold.

VICTOR BOUT IS A MASTER OF FINANCIAL ENGINEERING, money laundering, and deceit. The complex structures of his transportation companies have baffled law enforcement and intelligence agencies across Africa, the United States, and Europe. The scale of his operations is such that Bout is reputed to have made many millions. Whether his wealth is invested in diamonds, oil, dollars or the currencies of Africa, or indeed all of them, must be a matter for conjecture. While numerous allegations have been made against Bout, as we shall see now, it should be realized that no charge or conviction has been sustained against him.

Bout came out of the former Soviet Union, and some may judge him to be a shady oligarch, with political roots going deep into Boris Yeltsin's government. Unlike some of his fellow oligarchs, he has become one of Vladimir Putin's friends. But Bout's biggest political triumphs have been in Africa, where he has fed the hunger for arms of military and political leaders, legitimate or illegitimate, without scruple. He treats Africa's democratically elected politicians and terrorist leaders on the same basis, namely their ability to pay for his deadly merchandise. Bout also provides the machine to launder black or gray money or precious stones with an efficiency no other launderer in Africa has ever achieved. The basis for his friendships with the continent's wealthy and powerful is easily understandable.

Bout has been the subject of two international arrest warrants, one issued by the Belgian authorities and Interpol, the other issued by the

Central African Republic. The latter was later withdrawn under suspicious circumstances. Most recently, the French government has sought international help in freezing Bout's assets and having him placed on a United Nations (UN) sanctions list. But these attempts appear to have been blocked by the United States and the United Kingdom acting in consort. United Nations officials believe the United States has taken this stance because the U.S. military used Bout's fleet of planes for operations in its war on Iraq in 2003, although this has not been confirmed. It seems that Bout's political connections have allowed him to slip through the net once again. Today he lives freely in Moscow.

Bout's Beginning

Victor Anatoliyevich Bout was born on January 13, 1967, in Dushanbe, then in the Union of Soviet Socialist Republics, now the capital of independent Tajikistan. His father is reported to have been high up in the KGB, the intelligence and internal security agency of the former Soviet Union. Bout joined the Russian air force in the mid-1980s, and was based in Vitebsk, working as a navigator before beginning to train as an air force commando. Bout is a brilliant linguist, fluent in at least seven languages: Farsi—the native tongue of Tajikistan, English, French, Portuguese, Spanish, Xhosa, and Zulu. He entered Moscow's Military Institute of Foreign Languages, graduating in 1991. At this point the story becomes obscure. In some versions he also joined the KGB and was sent to Angola. Whether or not this is true, his army career ended shortly afterwards as the Soviet Union crumbled and his regiment was disbanded, leaving the 24-year-old Bout to make his way in the free market. He didn't hang around.

The former air force officer decided there was money to be made in transportation. He claims to have started by purchasing three Antonov cargo planes in 1992 for $120,000 but he will not say from where the money came to buy them. He moved to Dubai, one of the United Arab Emirates (UAE), in 1993, and began to import gladioli from South Africa. By his account, the cargo business steadily grew from these beginnings, with the next big breakthrough in 1997 when he launched an enterprise to fly frozen chickens from South Africa to Nigeria. This history may even be true, if incomplete, for it is generally thought that many of Bout's business ventures—one source close to him says the great majority—have been legitimate. Bout was prepared to fly anything that would pay.

In 1993 Bout founded the Transavia Export Cargo Company, which flew Belgian peacekeepers to Somalia as part of Operation Restore Hope, the U.S. military-led famine relief effort. Meanwhile, he was cutting his teeth on a very successful scheme begun the previous year which was building up his business. He could never have foreseen what a profound effect it would have on his fortunes ten years down the line. Bout was running arms to Afghanistan.

In the first half of the 1990s, Afghanistan was sunk in a bitter multi-party civil war that lasted until the Pakistan-sponsored Taliban rolled into Kabul in September 1996, bringing peace and fanatical repression to much of the country. By the spring of 1992, the former Soviet-sponsored government had fallen and the Mujaheddin, the Islamic force created by America during the Cold War, split into several factions that fought amongst themselves. A faction led by Burhanuddin Rabbani had the upper hand and formed the de facto government in Kabul, but the lines of battle and territorial control frequently changed. To supply armies under these conditions, and in the mountainous terrain of Afghanistan, was risky and required brilliant and flexible logistics. Shipments had to be flown in at short notice; avoid enemy fire, usually by flying in at night; and land on makeshift airstrips, which often were hidden from the air until the time the plane was due, when they would then be lit by beacons.

The arms came from a vast market in surplus Russian weaponry, which grew up in Eastern Europe after the fall of the Soviet Union and still exists today. While some of the weaponry was stolen, or at least illegally sold by officials in charge of the armaments factories and warehouses, much was legally acquired from newly independent countries such as Slovakia and Moldova, which had been left with enormous armament industries and stocks. Desperate to keep some of the industry going and vying for any of the limited trade available, they added large quantities of cheap weapons to a saturated market. Slovakia, a major exit point for arms flown to the Third World by Bout, had 40,000 people employed in armaments in 1989. Between 1992 and 1998, the value of its arms exports dropped from $1.83 billion to $213 million. During that period, Hermes, the state arms export company, sold weapons to Pakistan, Indonesia, Rwanda, Sierra Leone, and

Sudan, among other friendly regimes. Their most notorious sale was of 58 T-72 tanks to Syria, in 1993.

Bout, with his contacts in the military and the government, evidently had no trouble obtaining the weapons. He paid his pilots $10,000 per trip from Eastern Europe to Afghanistan, and an extra $1,000 for every landing they had to make. He is even alleged to have provided a Boeing 707, registered in Zaire with a Swiss crew, to a group of Afghan generals. Bout has a reputation for supplying both sides in a conflict and is reported as having armed Rabbani's forces, the Taliban, and other groups. Supplying the Taliban or any of the other groups in Afghanistan was not actually illegal under international law. The UN only put an embargo on arming the Taliban on December 19, 2000. However, Bout, who struck up a friendship with Ahmed Shah Massoud, the renowned commander of what became the Northern Alliance (the resistance movement against the Taliban) and who was assassinated by Al Qaida on September 9, 2001, vehemently denies helping the Taliban. He insists he only armed Massoud and Rabbani, an ethnic Tajik, like Bout, and proudly claims "my aircraft was the last one out of Bagram air base, outside Kabul, Afghanistan, before the Taliban came."

Bout undeniably came into contact with the Taliban, though not in a way he desired. On August 25, 1995, an Ilyushin-76, owned by a company called Aerostan, based in Tatarstan but leased by Bout's company, Transavia, and registered in the United Arab Emirates, was intercepted and forced to land in Kandahar by a Taliban Mig-21 fighter jet. The plane was en route from Albania to Kabul, carrying 30 tons of AK-47 ammunition to Rabbani's forces. The capture made international news. Bout and Russian diplomats met with the Taliban to try and secure the release of the crew, but without success. However, one source claims that Bout managed to turn even this defeat into a business opportunity and used the contact with the Taliban to arrange his first deals to arm them. The crew and the plane eventually got out a year later, but how they did so is shrouded in mystery. The widely reported version has them overpowering the Taliban guards and escaping in the Ilyushin to Sharjah, another emirate of the United Arab Emirates.

While fueling the war in Afghanistan, Bout had a finger in many other pies. He is said to have been involved with the supply of arms to the Hutu extremists who carried out the massacre of 800,000 people in Rwanda in

1994. He claims, on the contrary, that he flew French peacekeepers to Rwanda to stop the massacre. Both could be true. In 1995 Bout started a company called Eastbound BVBA with a Belgian pilot, Ronald de Smet, which lasted until 1996 and supposedly exported new and used cars from Western to Eastern Europe. In March 1995, Bout and his business partner Michel-Victor Thomas founded the Trans Aviation Network Group (TAN). It was run by de Smet. Later that year TAN is alleged to have sold an aircraft to a billionaire Islamic fanatic hardly known in the West at the time, Osama Bin Ladin. The plane is reported to have been in use almost constantly for the following six years, shuttling across Iranian airspace between Afghanistan and Saudi Arabia.

TAN was based at Ostend airport, a major arms trafficking center because of the lax oversight of the Belgian authorities. Ostend would remain Bout's primary base for the next two years. TAN also had an office at Sharjah airport in the United Arab Emirates. Vast quantities of cargo transit the free trade zones of the UAE every year, much of which is not even recorded by the authorities. Airports like Ostend and Sharjah have been dubbed "airports of convenience," vital ports for the illegal traffickers. They are hubs where dubious cargos can disappear, commingled in the vast quantity of legitimate goods. Just as importantly, they are places where goods can appear. Regular flights on a lonely flight path from, say, Moldova to Liberia might arouse the suspicion of anyone looking out for arms smuggling. But if the flights came from the United Arab Emirates, the cargo could be anything: televisions, radios, rice, or building equipment. Concealed by the general traffic, it wouldn't attract the attention of observers—not that there were many people watching.

In 1996, a company called Starco Investment & Trade, claiming to be registered in Israel, presented the Romanian authorities with an end-user certificate (EUC) from the Togolese government. An EUC is a warrant given to its broker by a government that wants to purchase arms. The certificate guarantees that the arms will not be resold; it's a system to control arms circulation. Arms deals without an EUC are illegal. The EUC specified the purchase of 2,000 assault rifles, worth $156,000. The guns were duly bought from ROMtechnica, a Romanian arms company, and shipped by AVIA Services, registered in Bulgaria. However, they never reached the Togolese government. Starco Investment & Trade and AVIA

Services were both sanctions-busting companies and it is likely the arms got to UNITA, the National Union for the Total Independence of Angola, probably via Kinshasa, capital of Zaire and the domain of President Mobutu Sese Seko, a staunch ally of the Angolan rebel group. At the time, UNITA was voicing commitment to a peace process while it clandestinely rearmed and prepared an offensive. Starco was registered in Israel as Starcon—slightly altering the names of companies was a standard technique used by sanctions busters to confuse investigators. It closed down shortly after the deal. The EUC was forged (although Togo illegally provided UNITA with an EUC in 1977). This is the earliest discovery of an arms deal involving UNITA to be uncovered. It laid the ground for much bigger deals that followed, as Bout became Africa's number one gunrunner.

That year, 1996, Bout registered an airline, Air Cess, in Charles Taylor's Liberia. Taylor, once applauded by everyone from President Jimmy Carter to Reverend Jesse Jackson as Africa's great hope, was, by the 1990s, running a modern-day pirate state where he seemed to be in business with every type of international criminal syndicate on the planet. Bout started arming Hutu forces plundering the Congo. With increasing business in Africa, Bout wanted to use South Africa as another hub for his network. The country had a vast number of small airstrips, poorly supervised by the government, and was a thriving center for smuggling, a significant portion of which was in arms and diamonds. Bout had recently moved to a heavily-guarded villa in Johannesburg worth $3 million, but it was difficult for him to get an air operator's license immediately, which was needed to operate an airline in South Africa. Thus in June Bout went into partnership with Norse Air Charter, the small African agency of Air Foyle, owned by Christopher Foyle, nephew of the founder of the London bookshop, Foyle's. Norse Air Charter already had the requisite operator's license; Air Cess brought a huge capacity to the partnership. They formed Pietersburg Aviation Services Systems (Pty) Ltd., trading as Air Pass, which operated from the hitherto virtually abandoned Pietersburg airstrip. Bout held 90 percent of the shares and Deirdre Ward, manager of Norse Aira South African Cargo Company, held 10 percent. The business thrived, and under this arrangement Air Cess became one of the biggest air cargo operations in South Africa. Most of its trade was legitimate—crayfish and vegetables were flown to Europe, mining equipment was flown around Africa. It also provided essential cover for the secret arms flights. Bout regularly arrived at the Air Pass offices carrying $250,000 in cash in supermarket bags, which he then put in a safe there. Ward and Foyle deny they had any knowledge of Bout's illegal activities. Bout's air armada grew to between 50 and 60 Russian planes, including the largest fleet of Antonov aircraft in the world. Air Pass received an unrestricted license from the government in June 1997, which Bout celebrated by throwing a glamorous launch party in September in Johannesburg. The great and the good of the South African aviation community were in attendance. It seemed that Bout's star would just keep on rising.

Meanwhile, Bout didn't neglect his Afghanistan business. Once the Taliban captured Kabul, Bout allegedly made a deal with the United Arab Emirates, one of the only countries in the world to grant the Taliban diplomatic recognition, whereby Air Cess got the contract to supply and service the Soviet-built fleet of the national airline of Afghanistan, Ariana Airways, and the Afghan Air Force. It was also arranged that Bout would supply weapons to the Taliban in partnership with an air cargo company called Flying Dolphin. This was owned by Sheik Abdullah bin Zayed al Saqr al Nayhan, a member of the ruling family of the United Arab Emirates. Flying Dolphin had an office in Dubai but it was registered in Liberia.

There was one minor fly in the ointment. Human rights groups who were trying to monitor illegal activities at Ostend airport had mentioned Bout in connection with the arms supplied to the Hutu for the perpetration of the Rwandan genocide. Local press in Belgium picked up the story and the Belgian authorities launched an investigation. Bout decided it was time to leave Belgium, and in June 1997 he moved most of the Ostend operations to his base at Sharjah. He retained an office of Air Cess at Ostend, on premises formerly occupied by TAN.

The previous month, Bout had another triumph. He extracted President Mobutu from Zaire when rebels seized control of the country. The rebels' gunfire strafed the aircraft as it took off and Mobutu's son later remarked, "We were lucky it was a Russian plane. If it had been a Boeing, it would have exploded." The fact it was an Air Cess plane may have added to the security. The hulls of many of Bout's planes were sheathed in lead, as hails of bullets are an occupational hazard for gunrunners.

The unceremonious departure of Mobutu from Zaire, subsequently renamed the Democratic Republic of Congo (DRC), necessitated a rearrangement of Bout's supply lines to UNITA. Lomé, Togo, and Ougadougou, the capital of Burkina Faso, replaced Kinshasa as arms procurement centers for UNITA outside Angola. The Côte d'Ivoire was also used. The new arrangements proved less secure. In summer 1997, the Togolese authorities, acting on intelligence from the UN, seized a cache of missiles and launching equipment destined for UNITA. Investigations revealed they had been flown there on three separate Air Cess flights in July and August. The first flight had started in Sharjah. The destination was falsely logged as Berbera, Somalia, and other flight details were recorded incorrectly in Sharjah, including its registration as a passenger flight. The plane actually diverted to Beirut. From Beirut it flew to Khartoum, in Sudan, and then on to Niamtougou, Togo. The source of the weapons before they got to Sharjah was never established, if indeed they were on board at Sharjah and weren't loaded at one of the intermediate stops. Another of the three flights to Niamtougou came from Nairobi, and traveled there from Gomo in the Democratic Republic of Congo. The final flight recorded an arrival from Johannesburg with the Niamtougou airport authorities, which is probably not true. The investigators haven't uncovered where it actually came from because of poor and non-existent record keeping by national aviation authorities, coupled with the deliberate confusion and document falsification created by Bout and his associates.

In August, Bout rearranged the documentation of part of his fleet, creating Air Cess Swaziland (Pty.), registered in Swaziland. Some of the planes that had been registered in Liberia were reregistered on the Swaziland aviation register, with the tails repainted accordingly. In reality Air Cess Swaziland operated from Pietersburg, South Africa. The purpose of this paper reorganization appears to have been simply to construct another layer of confusion for any law enforcement agencies looking into Bout's affairs. International criminal networks like Bout's seek to make things so complicated and impenetrable that investigators either give up or take so long that by the time they have got to the bottom of it the criminals have had full use of the setup and have discarded it like a lizard shedding its skin.

One of the schemes discovered by UN investigators began in July 1997 and was completed the following year. Again, it involved ferrying arms to

UNITA, but in a much greater volume than the scheme of two years earlier. Bout supplied UNITA with $14 million worth of arms through a company he established in Gibraltar, called KAS Engineering. The arms included 100 anti-aircraft missiles, over 6,000 anti-tank rockets, 20,000 mortar bombs, as well as cannons, assault rifles, and a mind-boggling amount of ammunition, enough to keep a huge army going for several years, which is exactly what it did. All this weaponry came from Bulgaria. KAS Engineering Gibraltar (represented in Bulgaria by another company, KAS Engineering Sofia) obtained the arms on the basis of eighteen EUCs for the various shipments from the Togolese government. These turned out to be forgeries, but were based on a genuine EUC given to UNITA in July 1997 by the army chief and later Minister of Defense of Togo in return for a cut of the deal. Some of the EUCs were brought to Bulgaria by the captain of an Air Cess flight from Togo; others were sent by Bout by express mail from Dubai. The weapons were loaded onto Air Cess planes at Burgas airport in Bulgaria by EMM Arab Systems, a company based in Dubai and owned by an associate of Bout called Oleg Orlov. They were flown from Burgas on 36 flights between July 1997 and the following January and two further flights in October 1998. The planes flew to various destinations, but mostly to Mwanza in Tanzania and Kindu in the DRC, transiting Khartoum and Nairobi airports. It's not known whether the arms reached those destinations, or whether they were unloaded at Khartoum or Nairobi or at another stop not scheduled on the official flight plans.

Investigators found that KAS Engineering was administered by a company called Skysec Secretarial Limited, in Cyprus. But Skysec claimed to be a nominee secretary and to know nothing of the activities of KAS. The directorate of KAS Engineering was held by another company, Armart International LT, registered in the Isle of Man. This in turn was owned by yet another company, Intercon Nominees Ltd., also in the Isle of Man, beyond which point the trail ran cold. The financial trail was equally convoluted. Payment to the Bulgarian arms dealers was traced back to an account at the Sharjah branch of Standard Chartered Bank, held by one Hjalmar Stefan Dijkstra, a Netherlands passport holder and General Manager of KAS Engineering Sharjah, another branch of the ubiquitous company. Dijkstra also had another account at the bank in Sharjah, over which Ivanov Pentchev Gueogui, a Bulgarian, had power of attorney.

Millions of dollars were passed through both these accounts into a third account at the same branch, the account of KAS Engineering Sharjah. The money came from an account at the New York branch of Standard Chartered Bank. To complete the circle, the money in the Sharjah account of KAS Engineering was sent to a different account back at the New York branch. All the accounts in Sharjah had been created at the end of 1996 and were closed at the end of April 1998. Shortly afterwards, Bout allowed the license of KAS Engineering Sharjah to expire quietly.

As the flights from Burgas were wrapping up, Bout was conducting another deal in neighboring Moldova. In partnership with Joy Slovakia Bratislava, a company run by three arms dealers, Peter Jusko, Alexander Islamov, and Andre Izdebski, Bout flew at least two shipments of arms to Africa via Air Cess in January and March 1998. A forged Guinean EUC was used to justify the sale. Sanjivan Ruprah, a former associate of Bout, claims Jusko was a major provider of fake EUCs to Bout's network, and could always come up with one in 24 hours at a cost of $50,000.

At around this time, Bout ran into several difficulties in South Africa. Motorcycle gunmen and hired thugs began to terrorize him, his family, and his employees. In March they broke into his mansion and knocked his mother-in-law unconscious after she smashed one of the intruders over the head with a watermelon. The harassment was probably part of a dispute with a rival criminal syndicate. Meanwhile, the South African authorities were trying to crack down on smuggling and sanctions-busting and turned the spotlight on Bout's operations. Officials began to appear at the hitherto undisturbed Pietersburg airstrip and at other airstrips used by Bout, and examined the cargos and documents with a fine-tooth comb. The investigators didn't uncover any arms shipments but managed to charge Air Pass with 146 breaches of aviation law. In May, Air Pass was dissolved and the Johannesburg mansion sold. It was time for Bout to leave South Africa.

The South African aviation authorities alerted their counterparts in Swaziland, who responded by de-registering many Air Cess planes. Bout had to rearrange his logistics once more. He registered several new air cargo companies including Centrafrican Airlines which came into being in the Central African Republic. The planes which had been de-registered in Swaziland were re-registered in the name of the new company. It operated almost exclusively from Sharjah and Ras-al-Khaimah in the United Arab

Emirates, where it was officially represented by another new company called the Transavia Travel Agency. This shared a company address with Transavia Travel Cargo—which again has a slightly different name from Bout's previous Transavia companies—and Air Cess. Under the laws of the Central African Republic, Bout should not have been able to set up an airline operating like this, but he allegedly paid off the Director of Civil Aviation. Bout also created Cessavia in Equatorial Guinea, where it was later re-registered as Air Cess. It too operated from Sharjah. Another company, Air Cess Inc., was registered in Miami. Joy Slovakia Bratislava was renamed Morse. Meanwhile, de Smet and Michael Harridine, another associate of Bout, bought the Liberian civil aviation register from Charles Taylor, giving their company, Aircraft Registration Bureau, based in Kent, the right to register airlines and aircraft in Liberia. Later, the company reached a similar arrangement with Equatorial Guinea. Several more Air Cess planes were registered in Liberia. So was another airline, Santa Cruz Imperial, a subsidiary of Flying Dolphin, Bout's alleged partner in arming the Taliban. Like the others, it operated from Sharjah.

Now that Bout had come to the attention of law enforcement, albeit on a minor level, for no one knew the scale of his network, he concentrated his arms-dealing network in Sharjah. With its secretive banking rules and lack of regulation, and Bout's cozy business relationship with a member of the ruling elite, his activities were virtually impenetrable to outside investigators. He avoided direct arms flights from Eastern Europe to Africa, and routed the majority of the flights through Sharjah. At Sharjah the arms were typically reloaded onto flights combined with legitimate cargo and flown to major airports in Africa. When they landed at those airports, the plane's arms shipment would no longer be there, offloaded via an illegal landing at a hidden rebel airstrip during the flight. The sources for the arms flown into Sharjah have not been pinpointed. Some suspicion has fallen on Irbis, a company established by Bout in Kazakhstan. It had no planes and exclusively chartered Air Cess. Under this arrangement 91 flights were made between Kazakhstan and Sharjah or Ras-al-Khaimah in 1998. The Kazakh authorities have denied, however, that anything illegal left Kazakhstan on these trips.

The following year was another profitable one for Bout. UNITA remained a good customer, even though it was losing airstrips, so weaponry often had to be flown to neighboring countries, notably the Democratic Republic of Congo, and was transported across the border by truck or on foot. Other shipments were delivered by airdrops. To supply UNITA and other rebel groups, Bout reactivated KAS Engineering, the European branches of which still existed on paper. One hundred anti-tank grenade launchers, 4,000 AK-47 sub-machine guns, and large quantities of ammunition were bought in Bulgaria using EUCs ostensibly issued by the Rwandan government. They may have been genuine, as Bout had a good relationship with the Rwandan authorities. His aircraft were used for transporting coltan and cassiterite, two locally-mined minerals with industrial value, illegally plundered in the DRC by the Rwandan army, to Rwanda. He also flew military and mining equipment around the Democratic Republic of Congo for them. Bout had a mansion in Kigali, guarded by the Rwandan police and referred to locally as "the Kremlin" because so many Russian pilots lived there. He allegedly held discussions with Rwandan government officials about setting up a diamond-cutting factory in Rwanda, and in 1996 even traveled with a Rwandan diplomatic delegation to Europe although the Rwandans have denied he was an official member.

Bout himself visited Bulgaria in February to see the KAS engineering deal through. He then went to Romania, where a deal to ship arms to Togo through a company called the East European Shipping Corporation was brokered (see Chapter 6 Diamonds and Arms). Another batch of arms were then bought in Romania, under the guise of yet another company, Armitech, which claimed to be registered in Cyprus. The arms were purchased from Arsenalul Armatei Ltd. using a genuine EUC that Bout obtained from the government of President Blaise Compaore in Burkina Faso (although the Burkina Faso authorities deny this). The shipment was flown from Romania, probably to Sharjah, by a company called Acvila Air. Investigations into this case found that Armitech went by the name of Arminpex Hightech Ltd. in Cyprus, and the director was a Russian named Ivan Tsourkan. Arsenalul Armatei had been paid for the arms from an account at the Banca Turco-Romana held by another Cypriot company, Loratel Trading, whose directors were Yugoslavian. In the meantime, Bout kept up the socially conscious work of his early days, picking up the contract to fly platoons of Pakistani UN peacekeepers to East Timor in September 1999.

Just when everything was going well for Bout, his network was dealt two serious and unexpected blows. The first was a stroke of appallingly bad luck. In January 2000, President Ange-Félix Patassé of the Central African Republic traveled to a summit of African heads of state in Libreville, Gabon, to discuss poverty. Toward the end of the conference, fellow delegates making conversation complimented the President on the gleaming Ilyushin-62, painted in the colors of the Central African Republic and emblazoned with the logo of Centrafrican Airlines, that they had seen parked on the runway at Libreville and had assumed was the new presidential plane. But Patassé had never heard of Centrafrican Airlines, and it transpired that a diplomatic delegation from Gambia had arrived in the plane. When he returned to Bangui, capital of the Central African Republic, Patassé launched an investigation which uncovered massive fraud by the Director of Civil Aviation. Centrafrican only had a license to operate three small aircraft on domestic flights, but the Director of Civil Aviation had improperly registered dozens of planes and provided the company with international flight documents. It emerged that Centrafrican was owned by three companies registered in Gibraltar: Southbound, ATC, and Westbound. The first two were owned by Victor Bout, while Westbound was owned by Ronald de Smet. The Central African Republic authorities closed Centrafrican, de-registered its planes, and charged Bout and the Director of Civil Aviation with fraud and aviation law offenses. The corrupt bureaucrat was jailed for a year and Bout was sentenced to two years in absentia. The authorities also tried to seize the plane at Libreville, but documents showed it had been bought from Centrafrican a few weeks earlier by an airline no one had ever heard of called Gambia New Millenium Air. It emerged that this company was run by Baba Jobe, the Gambian politician who allegedly provided EUCs in a diamonds-for-arms and money-laundering scheme involving Charles Taylor, the Revolutionary United Front (RUF) rebels in Sierra Leone, and Al Qaida. Jobe was close to Ibrahim Bah (see Chapter 5 on Terrorist Finance and Al Qaida), the middleman in those dealings; the two men were old comrades from their student days in Libya in the early 1980s.

The Central African Republic's international arrest warrant for Bout was universally ignored. Nevertheless, it was a landmark in the fight against arms smuggling, the first criminal charges to be brought against Bout anywhere in the world. Bout wasn't going to brook this from an upstart African country. The cogs of his powerful network started to turn behind the scenes and, three months later, a special court in Bangui was convened which mysteriously nullified the sentence on Bout and withdrew all charges. As another of Taylor's clique of business partners explained, "We are the government."

The second blow to Bout's organization was far more serious. For several months, a UN panel of investigators into UNITA-related sanctions busting had been following his trail. In March 2000, their report was released, which exposed his network in public for the first time. Bout achieved overnight infamy among law enforcement officials and human rights activists around the world. Newspapers recounted the story, which sounded like something out of a Hollywood film, and concerned politicians, like Peter Hain, the Rhodesian-born British Foreign Office minister, discussed it in national parliaments. Bout didn't cut and run, though. Instead, the unwelcome publicity occasioned the most fundamental shake-up of his business yet. The network was restructured in a far-more fragmented pattern, using many more partners and subcontractors from whom Bout leased aircraft, disguising his involvement. According to a UN report, these partners included John Bredenkamp, the British-based arms dealer who provided Mugabe with parts for Hawk jets in early 2002, in breach of sanctions against Zimbabwe. In the place of Air Cess, many flights were flown by companies called Air Zory (Cyprus), Pilot Air (South Africa), and Volga Air (Russia). The latter is run by Yuri Sidorov, who is allegedly involved with organized crime in Russia. Volga Air armed the Rwandan-sponsored Rally for Congolese Democracy (RCD) terrorist army in the DRC and flew daily supply flights to UNITA. Bout's legitimate business ventures were harmed as business associates distanced themselves from him, but the arms trafficking remained in action. However, the smoke screens became much more complicated.

During 2000, Bout's network organized a massive rearmament of Charles Taylor's forces in Liberia. For years, Taylor had been secretly acquiring weapons in violation of a UN arms embargo. Through Taylor these weapons reached various rebel groups he was associated with in other countries, particularly the RUF in Sierra Leone. Guns provided by Bout were used against British peacekeepers in Sierra Leone in early 2000. In May, Bout obtained two Mi-24 combat helicopters, rotor blades, and spare parts from the Kyrgyzstan Ministry of Defense.

The broker who approached the Kyrgyzstan Ministry of Defense on Bout's behalf was Alexander Islamov, the representative of a Guinean company called Pecos. The helicopters needed some repairs, so Islamov arranged for them to be flown to a military repair plant in Slovakia. With the help of a corrupt Kyrgyzstan military attaché, he produced questionable documentation to make the Slovakian authorities believe their contract to repair the helicopters was with the Kyrgyzstan Ministry of Defense. The first helicopter was transported to Slovakia in June on an Ilyushin-76 run by another company set up by Bout called MoldTransavia, registered in Moldova but operating from Sharjah. The plane was officially owned by the Transavia Travel Agency and had previously been owned by Air Cess. It was one of those that had been improperly registered in the Central African Republic, and was still recorded in this manner on documents. The helicopter was repaired and the same Ilyushin-76 picked it up, ostensibly to fly it to Kazakhstan. In reality it was conveyed to Taylor in Liberia. This routine was due to be repeated with the second helicopter in October, but the smugglers were thwarted, as will be seen.

Meanwhile, the rotor blades and spare parts were flown to Liberia in July. The plane on which this consignment was flown was an Ilyushin-18 leased from a Moldovan airline company called Renan. It had a Moldovan registration ER-ICJ; the first two letters are the code of the country in which it is registered and the registration is displayed on the plane's tail. The arms smugglers painted over the registration with a fake registration number EL-ALY. EL was the national code for Liberia. However, the plane was never legally registered on the Liberian air registry. The company that leased it from Renan was West Africa Air Services, a company set up by Bout in Monrovia, the capital of Liberia, but not on the books of the International Civil Aviation Organization, a legal requirement for airlines. One advantage of the name was it might easily be confused with West African Air Services, a legitimate airline based in Mali.

On July 17, 2000, the consignment of helicopter parts was flown from Bishkek, Kyrgyzstan, to Monrovia via Cairo. The Ilyushin communicated with air traffic authorities using the call sign WAS, which it had no right to use as that code belonged to a small airline in Ontario. On paper, what arrived in Monrovia was recorded as a consignment of Mi-2 rotor blades. The Mi-2 is not a combat helicopter so such parts would not have been proscribed under the sanctions. The contracts said they had been bought by West Africa Air Services from a company called San Air General Trading, directed by Sergei Denissenko, a close associate of Bout. San Air had the same address as all Bout's other companies at Sharjah airport. Denissenko later claimed San Air bought the "Mi-2" parts from Islamov.

West Africa Air Services was officially represented in the deal with the Liberian government by Sanjivan Ruprah. Ruprah is a Kenyan diamond-dealer and owned diamond mines in Kenya and Liberia. He was married to the sister of the leader of the RCD, and close to Taylor, who allegedly provided Ruprah with several Liberian diplomatic passports. Taylor had also obligingly made Ruprah the Deputy Commissioner of the Liberian Bureau of Maritime Affairs, a key government department in Liberia because a high proportion of Liberia's revenue comes from its shipping register, a flag of convenience that constitutes the second largest maritime fleet in the world (after Panama). The management of the register is contracted to an agent called LISCR, audited by the now-defunct accountancy firm Arthur Andersen. In June and July LISCR, on the instructions of Ruprah, made two payments of approximately $500,000 each to the account of San Air General Trading at the Standard Chartered Bank in Sharjah.

Once the plane with the fake tail registration had delivered the helicopter parts, it had another job. It flew to Abidjan, in Côte d'Ivoire, and picked up a payload of 7.62 mm caliber cartridges, with which it returned to Monrovia. Over the next two weeks, the Ilyushin-18 shuttled back and forth between Abidjan and Monrovia, delivering a total of 113 tons of ammunition to Charles Taylor. This ammunition had been flown to Abidjan from Ukraine via Libya on July 15 in an Antonov-124, a far larger plane than an Ilyushin-18. Again, the plane had been chartered from another company, Antonov Design Bureau, by a broker company calling itself Aviatrend. The ammunition was bought on the basis of an EUC signed by General Robert Guei, then head of state of Côte d'Ivoire. In this case it wasn't a forgery, Guei was an old ally of Charles Taylor, and provided the document to get a cut of the arms himself. Aviatrend was run by Valerie Cherny and Leonid Minin, associates of Bout.

Minin, an Israeli of Ukrainian origin, had been involved in Liberia for a while. The previous year he had used a similar setup and shuttled 68 tons of ammunition from Ougadougou to Monrovia in his private jet. Minin was paid by Taylor in timber concessions and tax relief of millions of dollars for his company Exotic Tropical and Timber Enterprises, with which he decimated hundreds of thousands of acres of Liberia's remaining forests. Minin in turn paid the money via offshore companies into Aviatrend accounts at Chase Manhattan Bank in New York. Aviatrend still had $750,000 worth of arms stockpiled in the Ukraine waiting to go to Côte d'Ivoire when, on August 5, Minin was arrested in Italy with several prostitutes for possession of cocaine. The arrest was by chance but the Italian police soon found they had stumbled onto a mafia figure notorious in international intelligence circles. The Italians found on Minin several original and forged end-user certificates issued by General Guei, and letters from the son of Charles Taylor, Charles Taylor Jr., who acted as a middleman between Taylor and Minin and got a cut, a role that was usually his father's specialty in criminal deals. They also found bags of polished diamonds and price lists for missiles and missile launchers from Erkki Tammivuori, a Finn. Tammivuori gave prices with or without an EUC. According to Ruprah, these missiles were delivered to Taylor in May 2000. Minin had directed the Aviatrend pipeline, and with his arrest the operation was thrown into disarray. The Ilyushin-18, which would have delivered the remaining arms, lay idle in Monrovia for the rest of August. It made a final flight to Abidjan in early September, carrying soldiers of Taylor's ironically named Anti-Terrorist Unit to rescue General Guei from a riot, then flew back to Moldova, where its tail was repainted with the original registration number and returned to Renan.

In October, an opportunity materialized for Bout to make up for some of the arms that should have been supplied by Aviatrend, but which were languishing in the Ukraine. An Egyptian arms dealer, Sharif Al-Masri, who ran a company called Culworth Investments Corporation that was based in Monrovia, had a contract to supply 2,250 assault rifles to the Ugandan army. When they arrived, the Ugandans found the consignment didn't conform to the specifications of the order, and told Al-Masri to return them to the manufacturer in Slovakia, where they came from. Bout got to hear about the rejected rifles—it's not known whether initially he approached Al-Masri or vice versa. Bout arranged that Pecos, the Guinean company, would buy the rifles, and provided Al-Masri with a forged Guinean EUC. Centrafrican Airlines—which still kept an office in Sharjah and operated dozens of planes illegally, having been struck off the International Civil Aviation

Register—chartered an Ilyushin-18 from Vichi, a private agent of the Moldovan Ministry of Defense, to fly the rifles from Entebbe, in Uganda, to Monrovia. The plane was chartered in an extremely roundabout way, which shows the pains Bout was taking to cover his tracks following the UN report in March. The Vichi plane was lured from Moldova to Ras-al-Khaimah by Pavel Popov, owner of MoldTransavia airline and former agent of Air Cess. It had ostensibly been chartered to fly a passenger flight of MoldTransavia from UAE to Moldova, as a replacement for a MoldTransavia plane with technical problems, which consequently was all that was recorded on the documentation in Moldova. However, when the Vichi plane arrived in the UAE on November 4, the crew was informed that the MoldTransavia plane had been repaired. They were then approached by Serguei Denissenko, who claimed to be a representative of Centrafrican Airlines, and offered an alternative job. They signed a contract with Centrafrican to fly to Entebbe, pick up sealed crates labeled "technical equipment," and fly the crates to Monrovia. On November 22 they arrived and collected 1,000 rifles, half of the weaponry Al-Masri had sold Bout. The crew was accompanied by Carlos "Beto" Alberta La Plaine, a diamond dealer and colleague of Ruprah. His presence raises the strong possibility that Taylor was paying in diamonds for this part of the rearmament program. The loading documents at Entebbe were signed by a Ugandan military officer, a representative of Culworth Investments, and Popov, on behalf of Peter Jusko, the dealer previously involved in Joy Slovakia Bratislava and now, according to these documents, a representative of Pecos. Three days later the Vichi plane went back to Entebbe for the remaining rifles. But by this time, the Ugandan authorities had got wind of the fact they had been sold instead of returned to Slovakia, and suspicious of the affairs of Pecos, they blocked the consignment from leaving. Vichi was paid not by Centrafrican Airlines but by San Air General Trading, and the Ilyushin-18 returned to Moldova.

It would have been unlikely for the Ugandan authorities to impound the rifles prior to the publication of the UN report in March, and this reflected a heightened vigilance by many export authorities. Improvements were by no means universal and procedures widely remained inadequate, but the lives of the arms dealers were made much harder.

The fiasco of the rifles was followed by another setback for Bout. By the end of January 2001, the second helicopter from Kyrgyzstan had been in the repair factory in Slovakia for four months and was now ready to be picked up. Bout wanted to send the Ilyushin-76 operated by MoldTransavia that had been used before to ferry the helicopters, and Popov applied for the requisite permits from the Slovakian civil aviation authority. The aviation officials were suspicious that a Moldovan company with a billing address in Sharjah wanted to pick up military hardware using an aircraft registered in the Central African Republic, and they contacted their counterparts in Moldova to check up on MoldTransavia. They learned that the company only had a license to operate a small passenger plane, not an Ilyushin-76. Popov protested, but the authorities were implacable. In mid-February, the arms dealers sent a second application to the aviation authority asking to pick up the helicopter, this time in the name of Centrafrican Airways. The same Ilyushin-76 would be used. The aviation authorities again requested to see documents, including insurance certificates for the plane. Bout insured all his planes with Willis, the United Kingdom insurance broker. The certificate for the Ilyushin-76 showed it was insured for operation by MoldTransavia, Centrafrican, and San Air. In the words of a UN report, these company names were "randomly interchangeable" on Bout's paperwork. Despite the illegality of Centrafrican, successfully concealed by the arms dealers, permission was granted to pick up the helicopter and the Ilyushin-76 arrived on February 22. Just as the helicopter was about to be loaded onto the plane, it was seized by customs officials, who had also become suspicious. An outraged Jusko, representing Pecos, turned up with documents showing his company—and not the Kyrgyzstan military, as had previously been claimed—owned the helicopter, and demanded its release using forged Guinean EUCs. This last-ditch attempt failed. Bout would have to try to get a helicopter for Taylor elsewhere. Jusko has denied involvement in any wrongdoing in the transaction.

Bout turned his sights to Moldova, where the cash-strapped Ministry of Defense had many helicopters. A complicated deal was arranged between the Ministry of Defense, Renan, the Moldovan airline that had provided the plane which then had a fake registration painted on the tail, and Pecos. The latter claimed, as usual, to be working for the Guinean government. In the deal, damaged Mi-8 helicopters of the Moldovan Air Force would be transported to Guinea, repaired there, and leased on a long-term basis to the Guinean and Namibian governments. On March 10, the Ilyushin-76 taxied down the runway at Marculesti military airbase, Moldova. This time the aviation authorities had been told it was operated by Centrafrican on behalf of

MoldTransavia. Just as they were about to load the helicopter, the Moldovan security services intervened. Inquiries had ascertained that the Guinean government had no knowledge of the deal, and there were no helicopter repair facilities in Guinea. MoldTransavia was struck off the Moldovan aircraft register. The quest for helicopters was in tatters. So was Bout's reputation as the arms dealer who always delivered.

Nevertheless, other ventures proceeded well. There were still many Air Cess flights recorded in South Africa in 2000 and 2001, and in March 2001, two Belgian journalists stumbled upon Bout at a tiny airstrip in DRC. Bout, a self-proclaimed ecologist (who, according to former colleagues, tried to persuade rebel leaders in the Congo to set up nature reserves) and admirer of the simple lifestyle in harmony with nature led by Pygmy tribes, was photographed by the Belgians filming the surrounds and the local Pygmies on his camcorder.

Bout's oldest business, running arms to Afghanistan, allegedly had had a recent boost. In October 2000, with UN sanctions imminent, the Taliban wanted to stockpile weapons. Flying Dolphin initiated an intensive flurry of suspected weapons flights between the United Arab Emirates and Kabul. A Belgian intelligence document and other sources claim Bout made another $50 million arming the Taliban in this period. After the December sanctions, the company successfully applied for a UN exemption to run passenger-only flights on the route. Flights continued until January 21 when the UN, suspicious that they were being used to carry arms, withdrew Flying Dolphin's dispensation.

More troubles beset Bout's operation. The UN, concerned about the misuse of the Liberian air registry, asked Charles Taylor to provide a full list of aircraft on it. He sent them a list of only 11 planes, although UN investigators had identified at least 117 flying with Liberian registrations. The UN Security Council responded by issuing an order through the International Civil Aviation Organization grounding all Liberian-registered planes at airports anywhere in the world. The Liberian air register was only allowed to start operating again after re-registering all planes with a new mark, A8, replacing EL, which was abandoned. The new registration process occurred under international supervision, so it was of no use to Bout. Instead, he re-registered the Liberian-registered planes, together with many that had been registered in the CAR, on the aircraft registry of Equatorial Guinea. His base in Sharjah was also under threat. Following the March and subsequent UN reports, countries were under pressure to tighten their regulation of airlines. In January 2001, the United Arab Emirates passed a law, to come into effect the following January, to prevent criminals from using the Emirates' airports as so-called "airports of convenience." Airlines and their planes would have to be licensed by the United Arab Emirates aviation authorities to be allowed to use it as their base. Bout had registered a new company, in Ajman, another emirate. CET Aviation Enterprise apparently absorbed Centrafrican Airlines and San Air General Trading. However, it continued to fly planes registered in Equatorial Guinea, which are currently barred under the new regulations. Meanwhile, law enforcement agencies were closing in on Bout.

The U.S. intelligence service had lost interest in international arms dealing after the Cold War, and shut down the last program still monitoring the illicit trade in Africa in 1995. But after the Al Qaida embassy bombings in Africa in 1998, and mounting rumors of links between Islamic terrorists and global criminal networks, they realized they had made a mistake. In the summer of 1999, the U.S. National Security Council (NSC) started eavesdropping on Africa once again. In all the government offices they bugged, and on the rebel phone lines they tapped, the same name kept coming up: Victor Bout.

The intelligence agents realized they had stumbled across something big. As they uncovered more, they were increasingly amazed at the extent of his network. Gayle Smith, the woman who ran the National Security Counsel Africa program, said "Bout was brilliant. Had he been dealing in legal commodities, he would have been considered one of the world's greatest businessmen."

The arms dealers knew the intelligence agencies had woken up. After the UN report of March, Ruprah, apparently hoping to strike a deal with the authorities, contacted the Federal Bureau of Investigation, which was working separately from the National Security Counsel, and offered to provide them with information about Bout's activities. Over the next year, he had several meetings with the FBI. This may have been the moment when Ruprah volunteered Bout's assistance with American military operations in Afghanistan and later Iraq.

The arguably less incompetent NSC was working with its counterparts in other countries, trying to close the net. In February 2001, the NSC requested the co-operation of Belgian intelligence to gather vital information. The latter mysteriously refused and enraged NSC staff found that Bout had been told all about their unsuccessful meeting with the Belgians. Soon afterwards, the NSC put into place a plan to apprehend Bout in Sharjah. The UAE authorities co-operated with the Americans and a Special Weapons and Tactics (SWAT) team was put on standby to grab Bout. At the last minute, the plan was abandoned. A call came through from high up in the American administration; it had been decided to keep Bout in circulation to see if he would lead them to someone else. The Americans believed that Bout was receiving orders from above.

Later that spring, the new presidency of George W. Bush scaled down the program monitoring Bout, part of a shift across the board away from attempts to tackle or monitor international crime. President Bush and his advisors had again decided that gun trafficking in Africa was not their problem. The argument that it was a national security issue fell on deaf ears. Instead, the U.S. government poured its energies into attempts to deregulate global trade of every kind. In July, the United States, together with China and Russia, successfully derailed the attempts of an international conference to impose modest controls on the trade in small arms. United States diplomats also worked to water down the Kimberley Process, the diamond certification launched in 2001 in Botswana (see Chapter 6). The intelligence policy was short lived and catastrophic. It culminated in the greatest failure of any national security service in history: the attacks of September 11.

After 9/11, Bout and the other arms dealers were in peril. The world's law enforcement agencies had belatedly been galvanized into action. Air Cess Miami was dissolved, Jusko was arrested in Slovakia but released soon afterwards. Bout, a photo-fit for the role of the individual aiding terrorism, loomed large on their radars. Linked to the Taliban and living openly in Sharjah and Moscow, American intelligence knew it could arrange to have him arrested. But surprisingly, after the attacks, Condoleezza Rice, then National Security Adviser in the Bush administration, ordered the National Security Counsel to terminate any operations to go after, or even to monitor, Bout. The U.S. government wanted Russia on its side in the War on Terror. To win this co-operation, they apparently felt the need to assure Russia that it wouldn't be pressured about Bout. There may have been another factor in their reluctance. Ruprah conveyed an offer from Bout to his FBI handlers to run guns to the Northern Alliance in Afghanistan for

America (with, claimed Ruprah, the pledged co-operation of Tajikstan and Uzbekistan). Whether Bout really made such an offer, or whether it was invented by Ruprah to try and safeguard his position, is unknown. It appears that Bout didn't become involved in such an operation, but it's plausible that the Americans gave serious consideration to the offer.

Bout's security was flimsy, though. There were high-profile media reports in January 2002 which claimed, based on leaked intelligence, that Bout had supplied the Taliban with arms in the 1990s. Ironically, these allegations are surrounded by more uncertainty than any others about Bout. Also, gunrunning for the Taliban, unlike many allegations relating to his activities in Africa, was not illegal then. Nevertheless, this public exposure intensified the pressure on law enforcement agencies to act. The authorities in the United Arab Emirates closed down Transavia, Air Cess, and the other Bout companies. On February 8, the Belgian police raided eighteen houses and arrested Ruprah. On February 25, they issued an international arrest warrant for Bout on charges of money laundering and criminal conspiracy. Bout fled from Ajman, where he narrowly avoided arrest, to Moscow.

On February 28, the head of the Russian bureau of Interpol, the International Criminal Police Commission, gave a press conference at the Kremlin where he announced, "Today we can say with certainty that Victor Bout is not in Russian territory." Public confidence in this assertion was somewhat undermined by a live interview Bout gave at the studio of a radio station a few hundred yards from the Kremlin, while the press conference was going on. Seeming remarkably relaxed, he protested his innocence, and asked, "What should I be afraid of?" Under the circumstances, he evidently had a point. A few days later, the Russian authorities changed their line. Yes, Bout is in Moscow, but "there is no reason to believe that this Russian citizen has committed any illegal actions." He continues to live openly in Moscow, and apparently elements of his operation are in gear again. He has been seen back in the Congo. More ominously for the West, in the summer of 2002, intelligence sources believed that Taliban gold which had been conveyed by boat from Pakistan to either Iran or the United Arab Emirates was flown on to Khartoum by a new airline linked to Bout called Air Bas. Khartoum is a major hub for traffic related to Al Qaida, and intelligence officials are terrified of a lethal partnership between Bout and the Islamic terror group.

Jonathan Winer, the former deputy assistant secretary of state for international law enforcement under President Bill Clinton says, "Victor Bout is a creature of the Yeltsin era, of disorganized crime, who adapted to live in the era of Putin and more organized crime."

Most observers believe the Russian government and Bout's network are interconnected in multiple ways. As Grigory Omelchenko, former head of Ukrainian counterintelligence puts it, "There's total state control." It's no surprise that they are so cynical.

Bout's own account of his activities and proximity to the Russian government can be surmised from an extraordinary interview he gave the *New York Times* in August 2003. He started the interview denying any involvement with weapons, then changed tack and admitted flying arms around, but argued that he flew any cargo he was paid to fly and it wasn't his business what was in the crates. Finally he abandoned that line, apparently admitting arms dealing, but implied that he was small fry, and received his orders from powerful governments. Bout tells the story of an aircrew getting away from the Taliban in 1996 differently. He dismisses the tale of a bold escape against the odds, and darkly suggests they were extracted by a secret Russian government operation about which it is too dangerous for him to speak. The *New York Times* interview abounds with melodramatic lines from Bout in this vein which trail off in ellipses—due, we are led to assume, to the danger of telling more.

Prominent on lists of favorite public enemies, there are good tactical reasons for Bout to try and portray himself as a mere cog in a much larger organization. Bout is certainly very close to Vladimir Marchenko, Director of Russia's Ministry of Internal Affairs and, allegedly, head of a crime syndicate. He is also said to be deeply connected to Ernst Werner Glatt, the apolitical Cold War gunrunner courted by both the CIA and the KGB. Richard Chichakli, a Syrian-born naturalized American who is a member of Syria's ruling family, a former U.S. intelligence officer, and Bout's accountant, said, "Victor is the most politically connected person you have ever seen." While he remains at liberty in Moscow, in the face of one of the most concerted efforts by international law enforcement bodies ever, many people find that statement rings true.

"Bout is good because he takes the chances," said one former associate. This is only half the story, though. Lee Wolosky, of the National Security

Counsel, said: "Bout's procurement and logistics network is fully integrated . . . Weaponry is harder to both get a hold of and to transport than women and drugs. There is really no one in the world who has put it all together the way he has." Employing around 300 people, Bout and his partners repeatedly escaped the arm of the law by keeping everything in motion—the air fleet, arms, people, money, and companies. Bank accounts and companies were closed after being used for an operation. By the time an investigation creaked into action, the arms dealers were beyond its reach.

The UN reports say Bout offered his customers a ready-made sanctions-busting formula, including provision of forged documents, contracts with arms suppliers, and handling of circuitous financial operations aimed at obstructing investigations. No hard evidence of payment for arms shipments by Bout using diamonds has ever been uncovered. However, the involvement of many diamond dealers like Ruprah in Bout's network, and the bags of diamonds found on Minin, contribute to the strong suspicions of the international intelligence community. According to the UN, "diamond circuits are used to launder the arms deals." Between 1998 and 2001, the value of diamond exports from Dubai, the United Arab Emirates, leapt from $4.2 million to $149.5 million. Could this partly be accounted for by Bout's dealings? As long as financial channels can be used to launder the profits of gunrunning, the most abhorrent of criminal activities will persist, and there will be no peace for vast parts of the world.

SECTION II

Terrorist Finance

Chapter 4

Al Qaida:
A Recipe for Sustainable Terrorism?

Money laundering and terrorist financing are invariably linked in the minds of politicians, police, and bankers. But the two are, in fact, very different. Terrorism, unlike hiding the sources of illegal wealth, is a cheap activity. The well-coordinated events of September 11, are said to have cost no more than $500,000. That puts a modest hole in Osama Bin Laden's reserves. So, what can investigators learn about the use of classic money laundering techniques in the wake of that outrage? And what approaches need to be adopted if terrorist money is to lead us to the terrorist masterminds or—at the very least—enable us to keep cash out of their hands? The answers to these questions are of critical importance to the future security of the West.

ANTI-MONEY LAUNDERING STRATEGIES rely on two sources of information. The first is the source of the dirty money. The second, is the money's destination. Investigation of terrorist funding largely precludes the latter source as terrorists spend the bulk of their money in the black market, buying arms for example, where anti-money laundering procedures do not apply.

This means that investigators must concentrate on the source of terrorist funding. Here, the key is to understand the role and financial activities of the financiers of terrorism. These financiers tend to be outside the organization as terrorist groups are primarily engaged in the business of ideological struggle rather than that of making money. Here of course these groups differ dramatically from the money launderer whose primary purpose is making, or at least protecting, his criminal funds.

Terrorist financiers may not identify themselves as such. Indeed, many will put Chinese walls between their money and the terror groups. This is because the discovery would expose them to prosecution and their organization to investigation. As we shall see later, Osama Bin Laden and Al Qaida are exceptional. Political groups are equally reticent about advertising their funding links with terror groups whose cause they espouse as they invariably claim to be democratic and political voices who eschew violence. The terrorists want to keep their sources secret as the money trail will disclose not just the origin of the funds but also their destination, namely the terrorist group itself.

The financial supporters will send their money to terrorists via a circuitous route to divert attention. But this route may give investigators a clue if it involves many changes of jurisdiction and transfers through off-shore and secretive jurisdiction. To avoid alerting authorities in this way, terrorists eschew the standard financial system and are more likely to use physical instruments, like cash, anonymous valuable financial documents such as bearer bonds and precious commodities like diamonds.

The trail between a terrorist and his backer may be cracked by the surprise discovery of a courier at a national border carrying cash or other precious objects. Equally, investigation of a company involved in commer-cial illegality, such as tax evasion or paying off extortionists, may reveal links to terrorists. When organized crime groups involved in the Colombian drugs trade or Irish groups active in counterfeiting have been investigated, links to terrorist groups have been unearthed.

The discovery of a financier of terrorism may reveal both the source of funds and their destination, namely the terrorist group, and in particu-lar those handling the money. This will provide an important source of financial evidence about the terrorist group's modus operandi and networks.

This information is fed through to criminal investigators tracking the movements of individual terrorists. Financial evidence will be critical not merely to stopping an outrage but also to a subsequent prosecution.

The closeness of the organizational and financial links between Osama Bin Laden and Al Qaida poses an exceptional challenge to investigators. His companies, political networks and wealth appear to have been placed at the disposal of the terror group. The Chinese wall that separates funders and terrorists does not exist. Indeed, for investigative purposes, Bin Laden and Al Qaida are identical. Money transfers which usually take a circuitous, and therefore suspicious, route between the two parties can, in this case, take place without surfacing into the legal economy. In short, there is closed loop between the financier and his group.

One route to intercepting this loop is to penetrate Al Qaida's financing operation with an intelligence source. This would enable the authorities to track sources of wealth and the money's destination. However such penetration presents an enormous challenge. The more realistic route to staunching the flow of Al Qaida's funds is to investigate the sources of Bin Laden's own wealth. Some work has been done in this area, as we see in the discussion of Al Qaida's banking arrangements that follow.

An understanding of the sources would lead to a discovery of Bin Laden's banking, commercial and even political alliances. They in turn could reveal the identity of the organization's charitable and political supporters. The process can work in reverse, and an analysis of charitable funds may give clues to Bin Laden's own financing sources. But this is far from fool proof as charitable and political entities linked to Al Qaida, especially those based in Saudi Arabia, may be as umbilically linked to Bin Laden as is Al Qaida itself.

Bin Laden's capacity to invest his money is now largely restricted to cash purchases in the black economy. However, the discovery that FARC (the Revolutionary Armed Forces of Columbia) terrorists bought the services of Irish operatives raises the ominous possibility that terrorist groups are now prepared to join forces to create a global terrorist black market. Market forces will enable the economically more powerful groups like Al Qaida to live longer, and even take over other weaker groups.

The fight against terrorism requires Al Qaida to be detached from its financial source as no organization runs for long without money. The concern for society's long-term security is that Bin Laden started a wealthy man and his Al Qaida organization has a lot of money to run through before it has to go to the bank. At that point, anti-money laundering systems ranged against terrorists, may at last kick in.

Al Qaida:
A Case Study in Terrorist Money Laundering

There could be no better example of the terrorist group sponsored by a single wealthy individual than Al Qaida. The origins of its funds lie in the wealth and influence of its founder and its inspiration, Osama Bin Laden. Family networks, business contacts, political blackmail, and his own personal wealth enable Bin Laden to channel reputedly $1.6 million a day from Saudi Arabia to Islamic causes. Some of that has gone to genuine charities, but some has gone to charities that are fronts for terrorist groups. The two are mostly indistinguishable, presenting major obstacles in the path of law enforcers and bankers.

The Al Qaida group has used its resources to create a global laundering infrastructure second to none. Bin Laden occupies the unique position of being both the subject of the myth and the launderer-in-chief. He employs skilled financiers and institutions to handle his organization's money laundering.

Al Qaida's businesslike structure owes its origins to Osama Bin Laden's own upbringing. He is the seventeenth of 52 children born to construction magnate Muhammad Bin Laden. The unschooled Yemeni-born Muhammad built up the Saudi Bin Laden Group (SBG) to become the largest construction firm in the Middle East. He assiduously nurtured royal connections, met the needs of the booming oil industry, and applied sheer hard work—values he passed on to his offspring. SBG won the prestigious multi-billion dollar contract to rebuild the mosque complexes at Mecca and Medina. Business acumen and political astuteness ran side by side with piety in Osama Bin Laden's early life. In 1979 he graduated from King Abdul Aziz University in Jiddah, Saudi Arabia, with a degree in civil engineering. He also took courses in business management. Bin Laden used his engineering skills to build roads in Afghanistan and later in Sudan.

The name "Al Qaida" is something of a misnomer. It literally means "the base," and refers to offices Bin Laden ran in Peshawar, Pakistan, near the Afghan border, during the war against the Soviet Union that lasted from 1979 to 1989. Al Qaida grew out of the Maktab al-Khidamat, or Welfare Office, which a younger Bin Laden founded as a rallying point for foreign mujaheddin, together with the late Palestinian ideologue and sheikh, Abdullah Azzam.

Before he became known as a terrorist mastermind in his own right, Bin Laden was spoken of as more like a terrorist fund-manager. The Saudi Bin Laden Group was valued at $1 billion or more; at one stage, Osama Bin Laden's personal fortune was estimated at $300 million. The Saudi businessman confirmed his role as the world's leading financier and practitioner of terrorism during his first period of exile from Saudi Arabia, between 1991 and 1996. Bin Laden had expressed powerful opposition to the Saudi King Fahd; he had funded opposition activities and was facing arrest.

The World Islamic Front, as Al Qaida is now correctly called, grew through mergers and acquisitions. Those who signed Bin Laden's famous August 23, 1996, fatwa, entitled the "Declaration of War against the Americans Occupying the Land of the Two Holy Places" included numerous allied groups. His February 1998 fatwa against "Crusaders and Jews," demanded "killing Americans everywhere," and was co-signed by the Egyptian Islamic Jihad and officers of Egypt's Islamic Group (Gama'a), the Jihad Movement in Bangladesh, and the Jamaat ul Ulema e Pakistan.

Before September 11, 2001, many of those who came across Al Qaida would not have known that its rationale was purely terror. It brought together charity, religion, and illegality to perplex its pursuers. The Bank of Credit and Commerce International (BCCI), another Muslim institution, performed a similar juggling act, preaching great religious ideas, charitable giving, and the principles of genuine Islamic banking. Foremost among these is the prohibition on charging or receiving "riba," or interest. One might speculate that Al Qaida would have been a key client of the Bank of Credit and Commerce International, had the bank not been peremptorily closed down in July 1991. Abu Nidal, a terrorist born in Palestine who ran his own army, was a client of the bank, and the bank helped fund the building of Pakistan's nuclear weapons development program.

Ideology and politics merged in the two organizations, Al Qaida and BCCI. Both claimed to detest globalization and Western capitalism while secretly practicing it. Indeed, it has been argued that Al Qaida is the quintessential global conglomerate. It has or had offices and cells throughout Europe, the Middle East, Africa, Asia, and even South America. It draws expertise from personnel with myriad skills. Its structure mimics the horizontal cellular hierarchy so typical of progressive multinationals. This devolution of power from the center to outlying cadres has increased since the United States launched its full-scale war against the movement in 2001.

The central command may have largely broken down, leaving behind a number of small and fragmented groups, says Ahmed Lutfi, an expert on terrorist affairs at the International Institute of Strategic Studies in London. He told the BBC on May 21, 2003, that Al Qaida had changed markedly since 2001. He said that half the senior leaders have either been captured or killed. So the group has devolved from a rigid hierarchy to a more loosely based and diffuse cell structure. Smaller subgroups now exercise more initiative. The media has played a large role in conjuring up an image of a monolithic organization, which is no longer true. However, this publicity has raised the status of Al Qaida, which has attracted new recruits. Thus the group remains a huge threat, and its warnings should be taken seriously.

Joseph M. DeThomas, U.S. Ambassador to Estonia, amplified the paradox of Al Qaida as a business-like entity in a speech he gave to the business daily *Äripäev* in June 2002. He said, "The global society has helped engender global villains. Groups hostile to democratic values have also gone global. Al Qaida is the equivalent of a terrorist multinational corporation with branches in more than 30 countries. Sitting in Afghanistan, Osama Bin Laden had operatives in Germany designing an attack on the United States using operatives who were hosted and trained in the U.S. itself."

Sudan's Role

Exile for Osama Bin Laden meant finding a home where his ambitions to build a terrorist group could be realized. He chose Sudan, a Muslim country with little law enforcement, a highly corrupt leadership, and a population where there was much sympathy for fundamentalist Islamic views. Sudan became both a military base and an important financial center for the group. Bin Laden knew well that money and munitions were umbilically linked.

Al Qaida established its early potency by setting up its own bank to launder its funds. Political support and benign neglect from local financiers were easily acquired when the Al Shamal Islamic Bank was founded in Sudan as a purist Shariah enterprise in 1990. According to a 1996 U.S. State Department report, Al Shamal Islamic Bank in Khartoum, Sudan, was capitalized by Bin Laden and wealthy members of Sudan's National Islamic Front. Bin Laden allegedly invested $50 million in the bank. Mohammed al-Faisal is an investor and board member at Al Shamal. Al Shamal has denied that Osama Bin Laden contributed to the bank's capital.

Some 50 wealthy Saudi and Sudanese participated in Shamal's share capital with the bank's biggest initial investor the Dar Al-Maal Al-Islamic

Trust (DMI), headed by a Saudi Prince, which owns nearly a fifth of Al Shamal. DMI is a Geneva-based bank with connections to Bin Laden. Its board includes Haydar Mohamed Bin Laden, Osama's half brother, and Khaled Bin Mahfouz. Bin Mahfouz once owned Saudi Arabia's largest private bank, the National Commercial Bank of Saudi Arabia until he was allegedly linked to the Bank of Credit and Commerce International (BCCI) scandal and, though charges against him were dismissed, reputedly fell out of favor with the King of Saudi Arabia.

Another powerful player in Al Shamal was Adel Batterjee, who was said to know Bin Laden well. Batterjee had founded the Pakistan branch of Lajnat al-Birr al-Islamiya (LBI) to provide assistance to Afghan civilians involved in the anti-Soviet jihad. Batterjee was later involved in forming the Benevolence International Foundation (BIF), an effective Islamic fundraising organization in the United States and elsewhere.

The bank allegedly served a key role in the financing of the bombings of the U.S. embassies in Kenya and Tanzania in 1998. A number of Al Qaida operatives testified at their trial in New York before the U.S. District Court in July 2001 to having accounts there. The four defendants were convicted and sentenced to life imprisonment. Bin Laden, who had at least three accounts at the bank, is believed to have used Al Shamal to move money round the world via its global correspondent banking relationships. Al Shamal had close relationships with at least three major American banks and three London banks. The London-based *Sunday Times* newspaper of September 30, 2001, reported that the London branch of American Express Bank, the British Arab Commercial Bank, and Banque Francaise de l'Orient were United Kingdom–based correspondent banks of Al Shamal. Banque Francaise de L'Orient is substantially owned by the former Prime Minister of Lebanon, Rafiq Hariri.

The bank's alleged role in funding the early activities of Al Qaida included wiring $230,000 to a bank in Texas to acquire a jet trainer fighter plane in Arizona, sending $100,000 to Islamists in Jordan, sending $100,000 to an Eritrean Islamist group, and sending further sums to Baku to help smuggle Islamic fighters into Chechnya.

The Al Qaida member who organized the acquisition of the fighter plane was Essam al-Ridi, a long-time Bin Laden associate and professional pilot. His assignment was to find a plane that could be used both to carry arms and Al Qaida personnel. It is believed he was intending to carry a consignment of Stinger missiles from Peshawar to Khartoum to attack a U.S. civilian airline when the plane flew out of control at a Khartoum airport and crashed into a sandbank. Al-Ridi did not attract the interest of the Federal Bureau of Investigation until he was questioned about the East African bombings in 1998.

Sudanese leaders initially welcomed the wealthy Saudi who was enthusiastic about investing in their fledgling Islamic republic, and by January 1994, Bin Laden was financing at least three terrorist training camps in North Sudan for rebels from six nations.

Al Qaida used official patronage in Sudan to run a weapons shipping network from the Hilat Koko military facility. This was designed to test a container of uranium from South Africa, purchased for $1.5 million in 1994. At the Hilat Koko center tests were allegedly carried out to assess the viability of chemical artillery shells apparently made with anti-riot paralyzing agents.

But by the middle of 1996, the Sudanese authorities were facing pressure from the United States to curtail Bin Laden's activities, and they eventually expelled him from Khartoum. He went to the mountains of Taliban-controlled Afghanistan. The Taliban regime guaranteed his security, and was receptive to his offers of investment to further their mutual cause.

Al Qaida and Diamonds

While Al Qaida had its headquarters in Africa, a number of its members got involved in the diamonds trade. The use of diamonds as a laundering tool is also discussed in Chapters 3 and 6. The activity in Africa goes back to 1993 when two senior members set up an operation in Tanzania. Abu Ubadiah al-Banshiri, also known as Ali al-Rashidi, a co-founder of Al Qaida and its first military commander, and Wadih El Hage, Osama Bin Laden's former secretary, wanted to make the local Al Qaida cell economically self-sufficient, and thus harder for intelligence agencies to detect, with no paper trail, electronic trail, or signal intelligence to link it to the rest of the organization. To do this they established companies in Tanzania to trade precious stones.

One Tanzanian company, Taheer, was set up in 1993 and was used to trade diamonds. The other, Tanzanite King Mining Co., was set up in 1994 and traded tanzanite. A third company for mining diamonds never got off the ground. Tanzanite smuggling is a massive business, worth an estimated $300 million in 1998, and Al Qaida was a participant. But its main activity was in trading diamonds, and its East African diamond business prospered, selling $1 million worth of diamonds a year. El Hage's notebooks, seized in a raid on his house by the FBI in 1998, give an insight into his diamond business. They show him to be an intermediary between sellers of diamonds mined in Africa and willing buyers in Europe and the United States. The notebooks also contain an ominous, but unexplained, reference to the cost of hiring a large plane from East African Airways for 120 hours.

El Hage's business worked like this. His partner, Abu Ubadiah al-Banshiri, would bring diamonds from Tanzania to Kenya where El Hage was based. El Hage then visited buyers and other middlemen in dozens of countries, including Belgium, the United Kingdom, and the United States, sometimes sending them diamonds in parcels by DHL, the courier company, once they had made a deal. El Hage traded through major centers for illicit diamond smuggling, such as Gomo in Zaire (now called the Democratic Republic of Congo) and Kampala, the capital of Uganda.

El Hage's business established Al Qaida as a player in African diamond trading and the profits went to funding Al Qaida's bombings of the American embassies in Kenya and Tanzania. In 1998, El Hage was arrested and charged with involvement in the bombings. He was convicted and imprisoned in the United States. The diamond expertise developed in the East African Al Qaida cell was later applied by three of El Hage's fellow terrorists, Abdullah Ahmed Abdullah, Ahmed Khalfan Ghailani, and Fazul Abdullah. They received an instruction from Al Qaida's top command, although it is not known whether Bin Laden himself was involved, to move their center of diamond operations from East Africa to West Africa, and in particular to Sierra Leone. Al Qaida was attracted to Sierra Leone because it was a politically unstable country where the rule of law was non-existent and the group could operate without hindrance. There were untold riches in diamonds for anyone prepared to flout a United Nations (UN) embargo against dealings with the Revolutionary United Front (RUF), the rebel group bringing Sierra Leone to its knees. Al Qaida jumped at the opportunity.

In September 1998, Abdullah Ahmed Abdullah made his first contact with the RUF. It took place in neighboring Liberia when he met Foday Sankoh, the organization's notorious leader. Abdullah flew to the meeting with Sankoh, which had been brokered by Charles Taylor, the Liberian president. Sankoh made clear that he wanted arms for the RUF in exchange for giving Al Qaida access to Sierra Leone's rich diamond resources in the parts of the country they controlled.

The RUF's fee for the introduction to Sankoh was $100,000; Taylor's own cut is not known. Another key intermediary in Al Qaida's entry into the West African diamond smuggling business was Ibrahim Bah, a Somalian advisor to the RUF and a devout Muslim. In the early 1980s he had trained with Taylor and Sankoh in Benghazi in Libya, under the patronage of Colonel Ghadafi. Bah was close to Al Qaida's leadership. He had fought alongside Hezbollah, the Syrian-backed terrorist organization based in Lebanon in the early 1980s and was later part of the mujaheddin forces in Afghanistan combating the Russians. Bah would be a critical element in Al Qaida's dealings with the RUF.

The following March, Ahmed Khalfan Ghailani and Fazul Abdullah came to Monrovia, Liberia's capital, to finalize arrangements. They had official approval and were able to bypass all immigration procedures at the airport. Nevertheless, they could not come up with the arms that would satisfy Sankoh, and this first foray into West African diamonds failed. Al Qaida tried again eighteen months later, when the RUF was in disarray following the arrest of Foday Sankoh. Bah again brokered meetings between Al Qaida and RUF, but this time he involved Aziz Nassour, a well-established Lebanese diamond dealer based in Antwerp with alleged links to Hezbollah, and runs the Lebanese mafia in Antwerp, West Africa, and elsewhere.

Nassour has admitted he worked for AMAL, the Lebanese terrorist organization representing the country's Shi'a community, but has denied having any links with Al Qaida.

Nassour was brought in to provide the laundering and operational expertise in the diamond world as well as networks throughout the illegal arms trading world. Al Qaida operatives took a backseat as financial partners. As part of his service, Nassour supplied satellite phones and code names to all participants.

In late 2000, Nassour started looking for arms to furnish Al Qaida's part in the arms for diamonds exchange and contacted a number of Israeli arms dealers. These included Shimon Yelenik, the former head of security for Mobutu Sese Seko, the President of Zaire, and Uri Zoller, the owner of a Guatemalan arms dealership and representative of Israeli Military Industries. He was allegedly a former Israeli spy. Once Zoller produced the arms, the RUF gave the Al Qaida/Nassour partnership a monopoly in diamonds from RUF-controlled territory. Nassour provided his Antwerp-based company, ASA Diam, as the vehicle for the diamond laundering. Al Qaida paid RUF $200,000 a month for the license to the monopoly. Half of the money went to the RUF and half to the Rwandan government, which was supporting them.

The deal between Al Qaida and RUF lasted less than a year. In the middle of 2001, money started to disappear from the enterprise and Al Qaida's headquarters dispatched a financial executive from Pakistan to Liberia to conduct an audit. Following a flurry of long phone calls between Nassour's company, ASA Diam, in Antwerp and Afghanistan, Nassour went to Liberia to investigate. When Nassour arrived in Monrovia, he found that $500,000 had been stolen. Among the losers from the theft was Charles Taylor, who demanded a $250,000 political donation from Nassour in recompense.

At Nassour's instigation, the RUF doubled its production of diamonds to fill the gap left by the theft, and in August, mining in RUF-controlled areas took place at an unprecedented rate, using much forced labor of men and children. But cash flow problems persisted to the point where Nassour and his Al Qaida partners had to resort to desperate measures, such as selling a generator for $4,500 to meet the cost of renting their Monrovia house. Mistrust over money was so bad by November that RUF even took one of the Al Qaida men hostage until more money was brought. By the end of 2001, the RUF had revoked Nassour's license to the monopoly because he was not buying enough diamonds.

The Nassour/Al Qaida partnership's diamond trade had been profitable to all parties. For example, Nassour and his terrorist partners had bought about $500,000 worth of diamonds every ten days, contributing no less than $2 million in tax to the RUF, over the period of his license. The trade did not stop with the withdrawal of the license. In May and July 2002,

Nassour brought two shipments of arms to Liberia from Bulgaria via Nice, using a French arms trader. The May consignment consisted of 30 tons of arms, including 20 Glock submachine guns; the June consignment was 15 tons of ammunition.

The UN estimates that between $25 and $75 million of RUF diamonds were mined in 2000, and production did not slow in 2001. In the first half of 2001 Nassour withdrew $20 million and passed it through various banks to Beirut. Nassour's accounts displayed the classic signs of money laundering, with over $1 billion routed through the account of ASA Diam in 2001, although some of it may have been from other Nassour family businesses. The large amounts involved suggest Al Qaida must have put millions of dollars into the operation. Al Qaida's dividend from the operation may have been a share of laundered money in a bank account in the West, as was Nassour's. Al Qaida's share of the profits may equally have been paid in diamonds, which never made their way to Antwerp but were diverted from Liberia to a terrorist diamond hoard.

Experts and intelligence agencies disagree on the extent of Al Qaida's involvement in the diamond trade. Some believe this case is the tip of an iceberg, while others doubt whether Al Qaida has the capacity to trade in these rough diamonds. There is a small and close-knit network of dealers in rough diamonds, and Al Qaida would find it hard to trade without bringing attention to itself. This contrasts with the more widespread network of cut diamond dealers, where controls are looser and monitoring less effective.

Al Qaida's use of diamonds and other commodities such as tanzanite and gold to hoard wealth and move it around—a centuries-old tradition—is not in doubt. Such transfers often work in tandem with the Hawala alternative remittance system (See Chapter 11). As formal banking channels are increasingly closely monitored, the calls to take control of all Al Qaida's hidden assets will grow louder.

A Sticky Source of Al Qaida's Funds

Supposedly legitimate businesses can act as a front for terrorist groups. The first example, the use of honey as a laundering commodity, is located in low-technology operations in the Third World; the second is hidden in the bosom of the West's sophisticated banking system.

The honey trade has a "dual use capacity." As one American official explained it, "The substance of honey makes it easy to transport drugs and weapons in it. The customs do not often check it—it is such a thick and sticky product." Similarly, Al Qaida runs fleets of ocean-going vessels that carry legitimate goods, such as food, oil, and clothes, as well as illicit goods, particularly weapons. Money is laundered through the accounts of legitimate trade, while arms travel unseen to wherever in the world the terrorist chiefs want to strike next.

Osama Bin Laden developed a commercial taste for honey after he left Saudi Arabia under a cloud in 1991 and moved to Sudan. His deputy, the Egyptian Dr. Ayman Mohamed Rabi al-Zawahri, apparently pioneered the exploitation of the honey distribution network when he was a leading light in the Islamic Jihad.

Honey shops in Yemen allegedly became fronts for Al Qaida and less than two months after 9/11, the United States blacklisted two such companies, Al-Nur Honey and Al-Shifa Honey, which have branches in northern Pakistan and throughout the Middle East.

Honey has also been tied to Al Qaida plots in the Far East. Khaled Sheikh Mohammed (KSM), operations chief of the group and third in seniority after Bin Laden and Zawahri, was arrested after a massive manhunt in Rawalpindi, Pakistan, in March 2003. KSM, as he is called, was also the genius behind the front companies Al Qaida uses to co-ordinate its war. In the early 1990s he set up a company in Malaysia called Konsonjaya (which means "big bang" in Serbo-Croat) to import honey from Sudan. Zawahri is in hiding and has a $25 million bounty on his head.

In fact, in the late 1990s, employees of the firm were planning to shoot down eleven U.S. airliners over the Pacific Ocean. Financing came from, or was laundered through, Konsonjaya. Although it was a legitimate company, said the Filipino Bureau of Immigration chief, Andrea Domingo, Konsonjaya's profits appeared to have been used to fund terrorist activities. One company director was Riduan Isamudin, better known as Hambali, the operational head of the Jemaah Islamiya terrorist network that was later blamed for the October 2002 Bali bombing.

The operation was exposed before it could be carried out but it set the template for September 11, another plot that KSM helped devise. Meanwhile, KSM's partner, Hambali, was arrested on Friday, August 15,

2003. He is said to have received a huge amount of money from Pakistan earlier in the year that may have been intended to fund the bombing of the Hyatt Hotel in Manila.

The Scapegoats and the Escapees

In the wake of September 11, American authorities targeted informal financial networks connected to the Islamic world for particularly severe treatment. One of these was called Al Barakhat, a cash transmission network that linked expatriate Somalis living in the United States with their impoverished home country. Al Barakhat had a long record of serving expatriate Somalis. It was founded in the 1980s by Ali Ahmed Nur Jamale, a Somali living in Dubai. Its initial customers were expatriate Somali workers living in the Gulf. An influx of Somalis to the West Coast of the United States in the 1990s led to its expansion.

Al Barakhat was closed down less than a month after 9/11, causing enormous stress to both the large expatriate Somali community in the United States and their families in Somalia.

The United States alleged at the time that Al Barakhat was a "quartermaster of terror" and closely linked to Al Qaida. It later claimed it was part of the "mosaic of a terror network." But the United States offered no evidence for its allegations, and no one associated with Barakhat was accused of terrorist financing.

Barakhat comprised nothing more than a group of grocery shops around the United States whose Somali owners accepted deposits in cash or cheques from their customers. These deposits were rarely more than $200. The individual grocers dispatched the money by bank, charging a small fee in the process, to a central bank account in Minnesota. This acted as a depository. The funds were then dispatched to Abu Dhabi, where they were converted from dollars to the Somali currency. A courier then picked up the money and took it to Somalia where another network of agents arranged for the money to be distributed round the villagers.

Somalia lacks a banking network and is largely off the map of money transmission services. Indeed, Somalia is widely seen as a failed state without financial or developed political institutions. Thus Al Barakhat serves an important social need. The damage done to the country's economy when

Al Barakhat was closed was recognized by the UN Development Program, which implemented changes to Al Barakhat's administration and constitution. In due course, Al Barakhat was revived with a more formal structure. Some local observers suggest the damage done by Al Barakhat's closure was reduced because enterprising Somalis used the opportunity to set up alternative cash remission systems.

In the wake of 9/11 some Al Barakhat grocer agents in the United States were charged with failing to disclose their money deposit or transmission systems to the state authorities. But these were minor offenses compared to the original damaging allegations. A senior investigator for banking supervision and regulation at the Federal Reserve System in Washington, D.C., says "We have had a fair amount of success with rounding up these ethnics but not one of them has been connected to terrorism. I have not seen the connection between any of these ethnic quasi-Hawalas and Al Qaida or any terrorist group."

Ali Ahmed Nur Jamale denies any links to Al Qaida, although U.S. department officials continue to maintain that he is part of Bin Laden's kitchen cabinet.

Western governments encourage the export of capital to poor countries because it relieves the pressure to provide state aid. But poor countries are the first to be suspected of using the money for purposes that Western governments rightly abhor, namely terror. The terrorist group has become part of an illegal economy in Ireland, Sri Lanka, Iraq, and Turkey. The following chapter shows how this wreaks havoc where their money is laundered through the trade in military supplies, drugs or machinery.

Chapter 5

The Many-Headed Hydra—
Ireland, Turkey, Sri Lanka

Political groups wedded to violence set up highly profitable local cartels to extract money to fund their campaigns. Their leaders understand how to control the brutal economics of the black market and launder the proceeds as we see in these examples from Ireland, Turkey and Sri Lanka.

The Irish Republican Army

THE IRISH REPUBLICAN ARMY (IRA) was born out of the resentment felt by Northern Irish Catholics at the creation by the British of a Protestant-controlled Northern Ireland in 1920. The IRA's central myth is the unification of the island of Ireland under its Catholic majority. The Provisional IRA (PIRA), a splinter group of the IRA, arose out of rioting and clashes between Catholics and Protestants in Northern Ireland in the summer of 1969.

The signing of the Good Friday Agreement by Sinn Fein, the PIRA's political wing, and the British government in 1998 was intended to signal an end to the violence. The PIRA's character changed in July 2002, when it startled its sympathizers and enemies alike by offering "sincere apologies and condolences" to the families of its civilian victims. However, two IRA splinter groups, the Real IRA and the Continuity IRA, still practice terrorism and utilize money laundering to fund their terrorist activities.

Drugs, Arms, and Real Estate

Irish terrorism is dependent both on crime and money laundering. Weapons are invariably bought on the black market with money released from drug sales, illegal commercial activity, or charitable giving. Black money moves around in terrorist organizations dedicated to achieving a political goal by violence just as it does inside criminal gangs.

But when terrorist groups lose the will or capacity to commit large-scale violence, where does the black money go, and what happens to the terrorists who managed the trade? Ireland's peace process has not turned swords into ploughshares as in the biblical vision. Rather, peace (or what passes for peace in a society riven by low-level sectarian violence) has fomented an outbreak of commercial crime and money laundering that threatens the society's harmony in quite a different way than terrorism.

This was dramatically demonstrated in 2004 when a group strongly suspected of having links to the IRA and its political wing, Sinn Fein, stole £26.5 million from the Northern Bank, based in Northern Ireland. This was an audacious bank robbery, involving the kidnapping of bank officials and an old-style heist. The lesson the UK authorities have drawn for this is that perpetrators of political violence are now turning their hands to commercial crime with ominous implications for the well-being of Irish civil society.

Ireland's terrorist groups have converted themselves into organizations that acquire riches for their operatives by financial crime. But rather than crime serving the cause or an ideology, it now serves to enrich a few men. Some 78 organized crime groups play the Irish field, and police believe that around half of these are linked to terrorists.

The stakes are high. According to one local observer, "At one time there might have been upwards of a few hundred Irish Republican Army members, and annual payouts could, at the very least, amount to anywhere from £12,000 upwards . . . One leader of the PIRA's southern command based in Dublin was said to receive a figure close to £6,000 one Christmas during the 1994–96 cease-fire 'to keep him happy.' It was seen as a form of control over those who dissented from the continued cease-fire."

Money laundering by the PIRA can be traced back to a meeting in Donegal in 1980 when the Republican leadership is reported to have told a number of senior people in the Republican movement to improve its financial situation. This was the trigger for a systematic and organized effort to launder funds, involving the acquisition of public houses and other leisure facilities across the whole of Ireland. The police now believe that this policy was extremely successful and say the PIRA has no less than £30 million tied up in property assets in Southern Ireland. According to the observer mentioned above, "'the Provisionals supposedly have 20 pubs in the Republic of Ireland. In Northern Ireland, it is likely that they control, or at least have influence over many more. But what does that actually mean? Does it mean that they are laundering money in them? Or does it mean that they just use them as private meeting places? Is it both? You don't know." According to an article in *Harper's Magazine*, entitled, "Making A Killing," "Whatever 'dirty' money raised from the Belfast protection and extortion rackets that is not needed for immediate operating expenses is smuggled into the Irish Republic, laundered through one of the estimated three dozen PIRA-owned pubs around Dublin, then deposited in legal bank accounts. All of which means the Provisionals no longer have to live the hand-to-mouth existence of most guerrilla groups; through prudent financial planning and entrepreneurial acumen, they have achieved long-term fiscal security, a solid base of assets and investments to draw on—the estimates range to as much as $60 million." It is also estimated that the PIRA needs some £5 million annually to meet its costs.

According to an Autumn 1997 article in *Terrorism and Political Violence*, entitled "The Provisional Irish Republican Army: Command And Functional Structure," the PIRA's substantial portfolio of investments includes not just pubs but also hackney services in Dublin, a security firm, guest houses, courier services, video shops, and a haulage company.

Catholic and Protestant groups pursue financial objectives in different ways. Catholics have the reputation of being slicker at criminal endeavors than the Protestants, who are regarded as more violent and thuggish. Catholics also profess to distance themselves further from the drug trade than Protestants. One academic observed wryly that, "The PIRA seems to be two or three steps removed from their financial criminal activities. The PIRA are undoubtedly involved in extorting money from drug dealers, but they themselves are not involved in the drugs trade. If they were involved in it, the PIRA's public image would not survive. Despite all the changes in this country (Southern Ireland), we are still a pretty conservative people. People who would support individual atrocities by the PIRA, would regard drugs as a step too far!"

Yet the groups have shown little of the sectarian purity they profess when it comes to devising money-making opportunities. So when the authorities seized a shipment of cigarettes at Warrenpoint, a coastal town on the border of Northern Ireland and Eire, they found that Protestants had used the PIRA to fund the purchase of £50,000 worth of cigarettes that they then intended to sell on the streets. Presumably, the two organizations would have split the profits. When examined by the House of Commons Northern Ireland Affairs Committee into the financing of terrorism in Northern Ireland in 2001, Raymond White, the former assistant chief constable in the Customs and Excise department of the Police Service of Northern Ireland, said, "Partnerships can spring up in the strangest of places where profit is the only motive . . . "

Protestant terrorist leaders have periodically acted against drug dealers in their midst, following media exposés. A key perpetrator was even killed to deflate one group's embarrassment. But the allure of the easy money available from drugs remains and observers believe that the Protestant groups have again become major participants in the local drug and drug money laundering industries. Hard drugs and hard men make good bedfellows.

Republican money laundering was exposed in detail by Veronica Guerin, an Irish investigative journalist who was shot dead by criminals linked to the drug trade. Her revelation of laundering activities in guest-houses and video shops had touched a raw nerve in the Dublin underworld. The war of ideology is now waged on the commercial battlefield, but many of the victims in both are innocents.

The really guilty parties are the Irish crime kings who are now the targets of the Criminal Assets Bureau, set up as a result of the outrage that greeted the journalist's death. But the Irish government's crackdown on money laundering has been knocked sideways by a series of financial scandals within its own ranks. The Ansbacher scandal exposed secret investments by Irish politicians in Cayman trusts and damaged confidence in their integrity.

Terrorists spend "much time and energy lining their own pockets. They're not using funds for the organization," says David George, an academic researcher into terrorist funds and behavior. He knows two leaders of the PIRA who "started out without a penny in their pockets and now are millionaires." When Irish Gardai [police] arrested Liam Campbell, a former PIRA operative for terrorist-related activities, they found numerous magnums of champagne at his home. They subsequently investigated his bank accounts and unearthed considerable private wealth. Just as arms manufacturers grow rich during wars, so too are terrorist leaders able to exploit their own battles.

British criminal gangs have admitted terrorist organizations, flushed with cash, into their substantial black markets. One police officer told the House of Commons Committee referred to above, "We now see the terrorists almost self-sufficient on the mainland using contacts with English criminals on the mainland to launder diesel . . . With regard to hand-rolling tobacco and cigarettes, we have seen terrorist organizations making bulk purchases from warehouses on mainland Europe and using Great Britain as a route to take them back beyond Ireland. We have also seen evidence of terrorist groups using haulage companies' drivers . . . The richest source of hand-rolling tobacco and cigarettes that we can identify at the moment would be the Baltic States and South East Asia." Scotland Yard also identified a ring of PIRA sympathizers in the United Kingdom organizing the import of cigarette lighters for sale on the streets. This activity was stopped when the UK government removed VAT (value added tax) from cigarette lighters reducing the price of a legitimate purchase.

Responding to the new acquisitive focus of the terror gang, law enforcement authorities have scaled down their use of military intelligence and upgraded the importance of financial intelligence. The evidence of Raymond White to the House of Commons Select Committee on Northern Ireland gives much insight both into terrorist money laundering and into the difficulties the British authorities have in pursuing the financial war. This committee gave a remarkable exposé of money laundering by terrorist groups, while indicating the authorities' lack of preparedness to respond and curtail it. White told the Committee, "we are still very much focused on the intelligence stage. I would not come before the Committee and hold out any great hope that money laundering investigations will leap to the fore, but they are very much there in terms of an output to be achieved."

Collusion between PIRA operatives and international terrorist groups unearthed in 2003 confirms the new PIRA strategy of acquiring wealth. The PIRA were believed to be selling their skills as bomb makers to the

FARC (the Revolutionary Armed Forces of Colombia) and Palestinian groups, applying a commercial approach that the private sector would call technology transfer. Nevertheless, three PIRA men charged with involvement with the FARC were acquitted by a Bogota court in April 2004.

As a result of its interest in the Colombian drug trade the FARC is cash rich. The PIRA, on the other hand, must have some concerns about its future financing opportunities. Its adherence to a cease-fire is hurting charitable and voluntary donations, largely from people in America, who are roused to dig deep by news of high-profile terrorist acts. So the PIRA is having to seek new funding possibilities, and one of these is transferring its unique expertise, built up over a long time, in bomb making and munitions. It is now believed that at least fifteen PIRA terrorists traveled in and out of Colombia since 1998, and the PIRA is said to have received at least $2 million in drug proceeds for training members of FARC.

The discovery of the PIRA involvement in Colombia provides strong evidence that cash from the drug trade has funded the presence of terrorism and organized crime in Ireland and on the British mainland, however much the Catholic godfathers would deny it.

PIRA activities in Israel and Palestine were uncovered by Paul Collinson, a British explosives expert working with the Red Cross. He identified hundreds of explosive devices found at Jenin on the West Bank and noted at the time that "the pipe bombs I found on Jenin are exact replicas of ones I found in Northern Ireland." The *Daily Telegraph* quoted a U.S. government official as saying in response, "If there was clear and convincing evidence that the PIRA has been training Palestinians in bomb-making techniques, then we are facing a grave and grievous situation for the PIRA. It would surely lead to a reassessment of whether the PIRA should be put on the designated list of terrorist organizations with a global reach." The incident came hot on the heels of a shooting spree of ten Israelis with a bolt-action rifle, perpetrated by a single sniper who left his rifle behind. This technique of mass killing by a single individual was also identified as a PIRA trademark.

The Secret Financiers

Trusted and wealthy supporters of terrorists groups, especially those based around an established community, lend their accounts to the terrorist organization to serve as repositories for their illegal funds. These funds are kept in anonymous deposit accounts and can be made available quickly when the organization needs them. Given law enforcement's lack of financial sophistication, terrorist groups appear to have been able to move their money between accounts, and to withdraw it from banks presumably as cash, with impunity.

Raymond White, the assistant chief constable in the Customs and Excise department of the Police Service of Northern Ireland, told the House of Commons Select Committee on Northern Ireland:

> The money does not rest in any financial institution such as a bank or building society under a recognized title which is 'Provisional PIRA.' The money that they raise is actually given to people who are in business; if you were an individual businessman with Republican sympathies, anything up to a quarter or half a million pounds, depending obviously on the size of your business, could be lodged with you with the view that as and when required it can be drawn down. You would simply need to raise a false invoice to receive £100,000.

> They are still one step ahead of us in the sense that the money is outsourced to legitimate businesses. So rather than walking in through the bank door, they are walking in through the pub at the side, or the launderette, or into somebody's businesses premises and money's deposited there. It can be put into the individual's personal account; it can go into the company account. It just sits there and they can draw down or hide it as part of the profits of that business for the year, so it is tremendously difficult financially to detect. Obviously there must be bankers or accountants or other financial institutions that must be aware of these large transactions.

> It is not a matter of just taking the illegal proceeds of one particular operation. With the money raised in terms of the fuel smuggling, they cannot very well walk down the road and lodge it in an interest-bearing account, so it gets itself rolled over into perhaps cigarette purchases the next time, or it will get itself invested in property purchase. The PIRA at the moment run a fairly substantial fleet of vehicles, which are given out to their members. In that sense, monies get turned over and poured into legitimate businesses. Certain pubs and clubs that come up for sale will get themselves purchased.

> You do not see the money passing through the financial institutions. It will pass through in the purchase of a property into which some clean individual will be put so it is that churning that goes on. Obviously where they

need to come up with fixed sums of money, they can draw that down having made the deposit with certain businesses. If they need it for arms purchases or anything else, that money can be very quickly found and taken in that sense. Or it can be cleaned in the sense that it can be put through a bureau de change, moved on to another country, and then brought back on false invoices.

The challenge to the authorities in every case is to distinguish terrorist money, which is money destined to fund terror, from criminal money, which is money acquired from crime or destined to be part of a financial scheme. One police officer commented, "Seizing the monies that are there that belong to the paramilitaries will be extremely difficult. We just go after the individual and we go after the monies that they have and if the paramilitaries lose out in the process then that is a benefit, but stripping it down to finding out what sums of money come from them (that is, the paramilitaries) would take years of backtracking."

Extortion

Mafia-like practices such as extortion are an established part of the fundraising activities of terrorist groups in Northern Ireland. While both communities practice extortion, the Protestant community is more ruthless in its pursuit of non-payment and more vicious in its execution. Extortion is prevalent in communities where violence is endemic and where law and order is weak and challenged. The elimination of extortion rackets is made particularly hard for police, who say trails lead almost invariably to the heads of terrorists groups. Raymond White said, "the godfathers of the rackets are almost coterminous with the godfathers of the paramilitaries."

Exact figures of extortion are flawed by virtue of the secrecy with which it is employed, and law enforcers believe no more than 10 percent of extortion is reported. White says, "legitimate businesses pay paramilitaries a substantial sum of money. These can range, if it is a multinational company, from anything in the region of £200,000 a year down to £20 or £50 a week from a small retail outlet. When all that is aggregated it is big sums of money." Police believe more than £4 million is raised annually by extortion and other terrorist rackets.

Terrorists have been extorting money from companies for decades in the long-running Irish war, and well understand the economics of their communities and of their extortion targets, say the police. White goes on to say, "The paramilitaries are smart. They do not bleed their host source. They live off it. They will tailor their financial demands to the financial profile of the business so they do not damage its capacity to keep producing."

Terrorists' Cash Economy

The black economy in Ireland is controlled by the terrorist groups. Their cash resources, acquired from extortion and other criminal activities, make them substantial players in the local economy. Law enforcers have tried in vain to follow their cash when it is spent on expensive cars. Garages have been under no obligation to report cash purchases of cars, although this is changing the UK's Proceeds of Crime Act of 2002. Raymond White said, "We are not short of examples where paramilitaries have walked into certain key businesses on the Boucher Road and have walked out with two Mercedes or two BMWs having just paid in cash."

The Republican terrorist community has long been involved in the illegal import of agricultural diesel fuel from the Republic of Ireland. Duty is not paid on the smuggled fuel, which can then be treated to appear like fuel for commercial vehicles and sold in Northern Ireland at a discount to the heavily-taxed, legally acquired fuel. The British authorities have watched as a mere cottage industry has expanded into a sizeable and well-organized business. Initial proceeds of the smuggling were used to buy up garages to sell the illegal fuel. The terrorists have even made deals with mainland British local authorities to supply them low-cost fuel.

One of the prime operatives in this trade is Slab Murphy, and the business has made him a multi-millionaire. Murphy's house straddles the border, making it a pivotal point for the cross-border transfer of goods. Says David George, a British analyst of terrorism, "He is not an intelligent man but he has a little farm, which straddles the border (between Northern Ireland and the Republic) and they drive in the diesel fuel at one end, in the Irish Republic, and then it pops out on the other side of the border, which is again all part of his farm. So he has not made his money by doing anything other than smuggling diesel fuel."

According to Raymond White, "Fuel laundering has moved substantively to the mainland here (the mainland of Britain). One Scottish council has engaged in purchasing fuel, which was coming to it at two or three pence a liter cheaper. The fuel arrived in tankers that were unmarked in the late hours of the night and the early hours of the morning. It was saving them money but when they looked a little deeper they became a wee bit worried. By that stage something in excess of a quarter of million pounds had been paid to a certain company in Donegal. Needless to say, the contract has been cancelled."

White continued, "Smuggled fuel is not being brought over just in one or two simple plastic containers, it is in liners with 13,000 liter tanks put into the back of them and shipped on through . . . You only have to look at the RIRA (Real Irish Republican Army) bottling plants in relation to illegal alcohol or to some of the fuel laundering plants that are there in terms of the volume of turnover, to see that once they get a taste for the money . . . "

White claimed the British authorities have been caught off guard by the fuel launderers' audacity at entering into long-term contracts. "It shows you the step-by-step process that these people are prepared to undertake, moving simply from one tanker of illegal fuel now and again, through to the business of the retail outlet, and now into what you would call whole-sale supply . . . This is indicative of the entrepreneurialism that is there amongst the paramilitaries, amongst the organized criminals," said White.

According to David Veness, the then assistant commissioner of the Metropolitan Police, "Great Britain is now a market place and a process-ing center, particularly in respect of diesel washing. That primarily relates to the activities of the Real IRA as opposed to the Provisional IRA . . . " Veness argues that the terrorist involvement in diesel smuggling should not be exaggerated. He said, "It is nine-tenths smuggling and one-tenth terrorism . . . The routes that allow you to smuggle the constituent elements of your contraband activity allow you very easily to move home-made explosives, timer power units, and other terrorist paraphernalia from the island of Ireland to Great Britain. The exploitation of smuggling routes is a real concern for Great Britain and a significant terrorist advantage."

David Veness was asked by the House of Commons Committee how para-militaries transferred money between the mainland and other overseas sources and Northern Ireland. He replied, "Our view is that it is relatively unsophisticated in so far as we have anything like a comprehensive handle on this . . . in RIRA, operating on the mainland at the moment, the need to move money is relatively limited because they are making very significant amounts of ready cash, particularly by the exploitation of diesel laundering, and it is not too much of an exaggeration to say that they can pay for their terrorist activities almost out of the marginal profits of the other criminality. It serves that third purpose." Veness confirmed that terrorists operated on a cash basis.

Between 2000 and 2001, Irish Customs and Excise seized 120 percent more fuel (an increase from 1.5 million to 3.3 million liters) and the number of vehicles seized rose by 220 percent. Seventeen laundering plants were disrupted during the period and one plant that operated secretly from the north of England was seized.

Irish police also broke up two laundering plants in South Armagh, one of the heartlands of Irish terrorism and lawlessness. Each of these plants had the capacity to produce up to five million liters of laundered red diesel each year worth £2.5 million in lost duty. Large quantities of fuel and acid were seized along with vehicles and laundering equipment.

British authorities refer to a scam perpetrated by terrorists to make money. This provides evidence of recently acquired financial sophistication. The fraud showed how bogus invoices were created to give the impression that companies created by the terrorists were large buyers of Coca Cola. Raymond White describes this over-invoicing fraud by saying, "An awful lot of Coke was being drunk in certain areas. The Coke never moved in the form of bottles but the invoices came through. For anybody auditing the books, it looks as if it is money legitimately received for services rendered. They will do that through setting up bogus companies and then perhaps letting that company go bust and move on and set up another one."

Irish Loyalist Terrorism in Business

Financial manipulation is a feature common to the Protestant Loyalist terrorist groups as well as the Catholics. Protestants have been found to make money by setting up pirate factories to counterfeit CDs and video playstation games. Here, they are regarded by law enforcers as "fairly sophisticated in relation to cigarette smuggling. Long gone is the white van. Now you are seeing shiploads of the stuff brought in cords of timber, where purposely within the cord of the timber there is constructed a concealment . . . ."

Cigarette smuggling is a massive activity, say the British authorities, although their figures are somewhat historic. They say that by the end of October 2000, some 44 million cigarettes were confiscated, double the amount that was confiscated in 1999. Cigarette smuggling has not proved as successful as fuel laundering, and a number of cigarette operations have been intercepted.

A facility for producing and bottling illegal spirit drinks based on industrial ethanol was found at Coalisland, County Tyrone, in September 2001. The plant, including a generator, compressors, and a 30,000-liter tank, was seized. A total of 26,300 liters of a counterfeit brand of "Vvodka," and nearly 600,000 smuggled cigarettes were also seized. The discovery of eighteen pallets of empty one-liter bottles indicated that the product of this operation was intended for distribution to the public.

Terrorist groups in Ireland are extensively funded by money gained either from crime or from the charity of well-wishers and ideological sympathizers. Whichever is the case, the money cannot be given openly to the terrorist groups, so it has to be hidden and laundered. Hence, terrorist money provides an important route to finding and quashing the terrorist groups, whatever their religious affiliation.

Other Terrorist Groups
PKK: The Kurdistan Workers' Party

The Partiya Karkeren Kurdistan, or PKK, was founded in 1978 by Abdullah Öcalan, a student leader. It was a Marxist group dedicated to the establishment of a Kurdish homeland in Turkey. The hostility of the Turkish government forced the PKK to leave Turkey in 1980 and set up in the Bek'a valley in Lebanon under Syrian control. Following the 1991 Gulf War the PKK moved into Northern Iraq, where Iraqi Kurds had established a de facto state.

Early funding and political backing came from Libya and Iraqi Kurds. But the PKK quickly adopted criminal laundering tactics. These include extortion, drug trafficking, arms smuggling, human smuggling (which is illegal immigration), and the abduction of children. Such racketeering is particularly prevalent in western Europe.

The PKK carries out its foreign activities through its front organization called the ERNK, the Kurdish acronym for the Kurdistan National Liberation Front. The PKK changed its name in December 2003 to Konga-Gel (KGK).

PKK and the Heroin Trade

In 1995 Bulent Cevik picked up 36 innocent-looking rolls of cotton waiting for him at a northeast London warehouse. His visit seemed perfectly innocuous; after all, he had taken twelve such deliveries over previous months. Unfortunately for Cevik, on this occasion two loading assistants were undercover officers with the UK Customs and Excise service.

The agents' suspicions were soon proven correct: the rolls had been hollowed out and stuffed with 190 kg of heroin, worth about £17 million at street prices. Drug traffickers from Istanbul had smuggled the heroin through Dover aboard a truck, and deposited it disguised as cotton rolls at the depot. Although Cevik's trial in January 1996 revealed no proof that the narcotics had actually been sold, Customs concluded that vast quantities had already been distributed around the country. Cevik was sentenced to twenty years in prison.

The Cevik case is one example among hundreds of similar transactions carried out each year in Britain, reported *The Independent* newspaper. Turkish and Kurdish gangsters control up to 70 percent of the United Kingdom's drug trade. Another earlier report suggested that fully 40 percent of the United Kingdom's heroin money found its way into PKK coffers. The PKK was reported in 1996 as responsible for carrying out extortion in London to raise funds for guerrilla warfare in Turkey.

The PKK have concentrated on heroin to avoid competing with traditional Kurdish family gangs, who lack the international contacts to import the drug. However, they are said to be customers of Turkish heroin traders. Many of the families have invested in nightclubs, drinking dens, and restaurants in areas such as Green Lanes in North London.

The PKK runs an intricate protection racket in Green Lanes where many restaurants have to pay an "insurance fee" or face retaliation. The area's smoky dominoes clubs are nerve centers for heroin selling.

In September 1996, the Belgian police force initiated "Operation Sputnik," a concerted series of raids on the Kurdistan Committee, the bureau of the so-called Kurdistan Parliament in exile. Some 60 people were detained for questioning. The police found a list that contained the names of Turkish businessmen and companies in Belgium from whom the PKK had extorted some 300,000 francs every month.

Simultaneously, German police searched homes and offices belonging to members and supporters of the PKK in North Rheinland Westphalia and in Lower Saxony. It is estimated that the PKK extorted approximately 250 million deutsche marks monthly throughout Europe. Belgian raids discovered that the group conducted activities through 15 different establishments that laundered their money. In 1996, UK police specifically targeted a money-laundering racket run by the PKK.

In mid-November 2002, the London Metropolitan Police dedicated 100 constables to fight the Kurdish drug threat. They carried out at least twenty raids that month, seizing an AK-47 assault rifle and intercepting a hit squad.

Belgium and France inaugurated "Sputnik II" in 2002 and the following year charged a Paris-based company with "money laundering, preparing fake documents, and corruption in its tax payments." It was also reported that a member of the group, confessed under police interrogation that pro-PKK businessmen gave money to the terrorist organization through an institution under the name of the "Kurdish Foundation Trust." "The trust is reputedly based in the British-controlled Jersey islands—an offshore haven for international money laundering," stated Turkey's Anatolia News Agency. It has been reported that large sums are collected from this institution to finance PKK activities.

The United States began waking up to the perceived threat from the PKK and similar organizations with its Antiterrorism and Effective Death Penalty Act of 1996, best known as the AEDPA. Two U.S. citizens and six organizations were put on trial for aiding the PKK and Tamil Tigers, and their attempts to plead innocent on the grounds of the First Amendment were fiercely contested. U.S. Secretary of State Madeleine Albright put the PKK on the list of 30 proscribed "foreign terrorist organizations" (FTOs) in 1999; her successor, Colin Powell, reinforced the ban on PKK activities, including raising money, in 2001. Although the PKK seemingly reinvented itself in April 2002 as a peaceful political entity named KADEK, the United States added KADEK to its list of FTOs in December of that year.

Yet for Turkey, this was apparently not enough. On September 22, 2003, Turkish Foreign Minister Abdullah Gul insisted that the United

States take stronger measures against PKK rebels massed on the Iraqi-Turkish border. He wanted the United States to get the rebels to agree to a new amnesty from Ankara, aimed at disabling the PKK forever. Gul tied Washington's reaction to this plea to Turkey's willingness to assist U.S. forces in the region, particularly in Iraq.

According to Raphael Perl, a specialist in international affairs, "The PKK is widely reported to be involved in the Balkan heroin trade, with activities ranging from brokering heroin deals between other parties, to controlling and owning laboratories and drug transhipment." Perl was addressing the U.S. Congress Committee on Senate Judiciary on May 20, 2003. Increasingly, Europe is turning into a propaganda battlefield between the Turks and the PKK. Ankara publicizes PKK links to drug running, money laundering, and extortion. At the same time, the "Kurdish information office," based in London's Barbican, counters with brochures showing horrific photographs of the Turkish suppression of the PKK and human rights abuses against Turkish Kurds generally.

Certainly, a brutal real war has gripped eastern Anatolia, where most of Turkey's Kurds live. At least thirty thousand have died in terrorist attacks and military retaliations since August 1984. Ankara only lifted its state of emergency in 2000. This effectively ended the overt conflict, and resulted in part from massive European Union (EU) pressure. Many Europeans are wary about challenging the PKK head on. One out of every seven Turkish citizens is said to be Kurdish, but their distinct ethnic identity is disputed by successive Turkish governments. They are misleadingly called "Mountain Turks" and their language, culture, and customs cannot be openly taught. Europeans also dislike reports of some 380,000 mainly innocent Turkish Kurds who have been displaced in a conflict where there are few angels on either side.

Yet Europeans are paying a price, too, in the form of growing numbers of addicts drawn to the PKK's cheap heroin. British police used a warrant under the Prevention of Terrorism Act to raid two community centers in London in September 1997. They followed a money trail to terrorist command centers, and sought "evidence of contributions towards acts of terrorism; money, accounting records, computer records, and other documentation." Since then the United Kingdom has introduced laws to ban fund-raising for foreign terrorist groups.

At least seventy thousand Kurds live within Britain's borders, though these are divided into separate and often antagonistic groups: some forty to fifty thousand from Turkey, another ten to fifteen thousand from Iraq, and a smaller number from Iran. By and large, the Turkish Kurds are the most militant, and they are the only ones who back the PKK. Said one London-based Kurdish source in 1999: "The PKK are extremely active among the Kurdish population here. Through intimidation and active organization, they control most of their people."

The fact that Kurds are predominantly Muslim does not mean that the PKK associates with Islamic fundamentalism. Only the *Ansar al-Islam* Kurdish group of northern Iraq has close ties with Al Qaida; its expatriate supporters are currently under surveillance in Denmark and Holland. The PKK, by contrast, is militantly atheist and Marxist-Leninist in ideology. That said, it has few qualms about generating money. Apart from drugs, the PKK is also said to generate huge funds through "people smuggling" by subverting the tough restrictions on migration into European countries, by forging passports and providing transport, and by charging exorbitant fees for assistance.

More bewildering, there were allegations in a U.S. civil lawsuit of ties between the PKK and R.J.R. Nabisco, which manufactures leading brands of cigarettes. In particular, it was alleged that between 1990 and 2002, R.J.R. Nabisco consorted with Audeh Trading and Consultancy Service and IBCS to smuggle millions of cigarettes into Iraq via the towns of Dohuk and Zakho. R.J.R. Nabisco has denied these allegations and the suit was dismissed.

PKK units located in Iraqi "Kurdistan," northern Iraq, profited by imposing a transit tax on all cigarettes smuggled south, towards Baghdad and the rest of the country. Before the end of his regime in April 2003, Saddam Hussein entrusted his elder son, Uday, to run the Arab Iraqi recipient and redistribution side of the business. All parties allegedly reaped immense earnings, all the more so as most normal trade between Iraq and the outside world was effectively blocked by successive UN resolutions from 1991 to 2003.

A civil case in October 2002 against R.J.R. Nabisco, R.J. Reynolds Tobacco Company, and a number of other related companies in the U.S. District Court in the Eastern District of New York brought by the European Community alleged that R.J.R. Nabisco, "devised a scheme or artifice to

defraud and/or to obtain money by means of false pretenses, representa-
tions, or promises, and used interstate and international mails and wires,
[communications] for the purpose of executing the scheme." Wire transfers, it was said, expedited the secret payments to the R.J.R. Nabisco
defendants "of funds that constituted the proceeds of criminal activity."

The European Union, itself, was one of the parties who are accusing
R.J.R. Nabisco of gross fraud. According to the allegations, "The motive for
committing fraud is plain: the acquisition of criminals as additional
customers by laundering their criminal proceeds meant increased profits
and market share for R.J.R.." The charges specifically related numerous
incidents when the PKK carried out hits and bombings on European soil.
Thus PKK terror, it stressed, is not merely something that takes place in
some faraway country, but is something that affects their own backyard,
and endangers their own citizens. EU's case against all defendants was
dismissed and allegations brought by the EU must be interpreted with this
in mind. For further details of this case, see Chapter 8.

PKK leader Abdullah Ocallan was arrested in Kenya and taken back to
Turkey in 1999, where he was put on trial. As part of an apparent plea
bargain, Ocallan called for a moratorium on the war against Turkey that
same year.

The Ocallan case reveals aspects of fraud, with possible ties to laundering. When arrested, Ocallan was travelling on two fictitious passports, both
in the name of Greek Cypriot citizens. Unsurprisingly, Ankara jumped on
this embarrassing discovery to argue against the Mediterranean island's
pending admittance to full European Union membership. Turkey has
alleged, moreover, that the officially recognized Greek republic of Cyprus
(by contrast with the unrecognized northern third of the island) is awash
with laundered millions—from the Milosevic regime, the PKK, sundry
drug dealers in southern Europe, and even Osama Bin Laden. Ocallan's
possession of two convincing Cypriot documents suggested official
complicity.

Turkey also contends that many European countries are naïve in
supporting the group, and turn a blind eye to its abuse of European financial institutions. In October 2001, Ankara sent an information note to the
North Atlantic Treaty Organization (NATO) countries regarding the PKK's
financial resources and press activities in Europe. It alleged that the PKK

gathered some 20 million deutschemarks in donations in Germany alone, and then laundered these sums through Greek Cypriot, Swiss, British, Swedish, Belgian, and Danish banks. It further charged the PKK's approximately thirty press organizations centered in Europe with complicity in the laundering scam.

Sonay Cagaptay, coordinator of the Turkish Research Program of the Washington Institute think tank, recommended a four-point action plan to crush the group. Point four was the familiar "cut off the group's financial pipeline." Cagaptay charged the European Union with complacency when it only placed the PKK on its list of proscribed groups in April 2003. By this stage, he noted, the PKK had officially disappeared, only to re-emerge as KADEK. Cagaptay did take aid, however, from the precedent of the European Union's "historic" decision in September 2003 to ban the Palestinian *Hamas* group, both its political and armed wings. But as to specific punitive financial measures, he remained curiously reticent.

Tamil Tigers

The Tamil National Army, also known as the Liberation Tigers of Tamil Eelam (LTTE), was founded on May 5, 1976, by Velupillai Pirabakaran. Its goal is to wrest power from Sri Lanka's Sinhala government which, it says, neglects Tamil grievances.

LTTE's power base remains Tamil's economically deprived agricultural workers, whose families lost their livelihood due to economic reforms in the late 1970s, as well as Tamil's unemployed urban youth who face economic and social discrimination.

Different Indian administrations have been responsible for training and arming the Tamil rebels in the past in different parts of the Indian sub-continent. The international wing of the LTTE has used its bases in London and Paris to acquire sophisticated weaponry. Most of the supplies are from the countries of the former Soviet Union. They have also captured large quantities of arms from the Sri Lankan security forces.

For many years the LTTE regarded India as its natural safe haven, enjoying the support of local Tamil radicals and the acquiescence of New Delhi. When it entered a separatist struggle in India after October 1987, the Indian and Sri Lankan governments signed an accord to join forces and crush the Tamil Tigers. The group was accused of masterminding the suicide bomb assassination of Indian Prime Minister Rajiv Gandhi in May 1991.

The LTTE were pioneers of money laundering. Years before the "Afghan Arabs" became a recognized phenomenon, expatriate Sri Lankan Tamils set up front companies throughout Europe, North America, and the Far East.

Expatriate Tamil activists in the West are reported to raise money using extortion, illegal trade, and front organizations. Partly as a result of frequent expulsions from their island homeland, they have become adept at managing transportation, and they have exploited the commercial possibilities of shipping as well as the military opportunities.

Tamil Trafficking

LTTE began building up a vast fleet of deep-sea ocean-going vessels to maintain contacts with these bases. LTTE ships, owned by front companies and registered in Liberia, Panama, and Honduras, ostensibly plied a legitimate trade, exporting South East Asian hardwoods around the world. Crews were generally non-LTTE members, and were paid regular wages, but profits were ploughed back into LTTE coffers.

In fact, LTTE was also transporting heroin to developed countries. The proceeds enabled them to acquire arms that were imported back to LTTE bases.

Rohan Gunaratna, an academic and one-time investigator for the UN's terrorism prevention branch and the author of the book *Inside Al Qaeda,* said, "The Tamil Tigers were the leading mover of narcotics before the PKK took over. But narcotics is a high-risk business, so once they have made their initial money, they intelligently invest it in legitimate businesses. If they continue through narcotics the police will target the organization and destroy them. They prefer to quickly move on." Gunaratna said the Tamil Tigers had ploughed the profits they made from drug cultivation in Cambodia and Myanmar, formerly Burma, into legitimate businesses in neighboring Thailand.

LTTE controls a diverse range of businesses, including jewelry, hardwood, videos, restaurants, fruit canning, gasoline retail, and travel. Gasoline stations in Britain, small businesses in Spain, and travel agencies in Canada have been named as money laundering fronts for the LTTE. Lord Michael Naseby, Joint Chairman of the All Party Sri Lanka Group, told the British House of Lords in October 2001 that some twenty thousand illegal Tamil immigrants in London alone run LTTE front companies. Lord Naseby said, "They run petrol stations in London and are involved in extortion, drugs, and money changing rackets . . . and other sources of moving money around . . . Asian and Arab terrorists, indeed, all terrorists, have enormous patience, great cunning, great skill and, on the surface, incredible plausibility. We must be on our guard. We must be equally patient, very thorough, and a little creative in rooting out the financial mechanisms that fuel terrorism. The tap of funding must be turned off."

Some eight thousand guerrilla-trained Tamil Tigers currently living in Canada assist the LTTE in carrying out human and arms trafficking, passport, credit card, and bank fraud. They also extort money from expatriate communities, import and sell heroin, and then launder the proceeds. LTTE front organizations in Canada channel between $1 and $2 million per year to their comrades in Sri Lanka. This amount can rise to $10 million if there is a "special need." And, as ever, funds donated to humanitarian appeals often get diverted to the terrorist group's coffers. The LTTE's global network raises about $2.75 million a month.

Many technically illegal immigrants residing in the big cities of the West are ready victims of extortion by those threatening to expose them to immigration authorities. The LTTE makes much of its money from "protection," or from threatening the lives of the relatives of potential donors "back home."

Tamil Tiger Links

Links with Al Qaida were claimed by Rashmee Ahmed of *The Times* of India who, on September 22, 2001, reported that the chief LTTE procurement officer, Tharmalingam Shanmugan Kumraran, alias Kumaran Padmanadhan or "KP," visited Afghanistan via Dubai and Karachi in May 2001. This represented strong circumstantial evidence that KP, who is normally based in Thailand, was visiting Al Qaida. Interpol, the International Criminal Police Commission, certainly felt as much as they imposed a Red Notice apprehension warrant on KP in July 2001. Meanwhile, East Asian intelligence agencies, Ahmed wrote, have demonstrated that the LTTE helped train two Al Qaida–affiliated Filipino Muslim groups, the Moro Islamic Liberation Front (MILF) and the Abu Sayyaf Group (ASG).

The alliance between LTTE and Al Qaida has more to do with military efficacy, which Al Qaida learned, and money, which the Tigers earned. The LTTE were an early exponent among terrorist groups of the practices of suicide bombing and money laundering.

Section III

Black Markets

Chapter 6

Diamonds:
A Launderer's Best Friend

Diamonds are converted into cash, which is used to buy arms, which are used to steal and conquer land to acquire more diamonds. And so the money-go-round proceeds in Africa.

THE PRIME GOAL OF THE MONEY LAUNDERER is to disguise the source of his criminal wealth. There are many hurdles to achieving this objective. Cash often has an ownership trail, and stolen goods have the taint of criminality. But no one has yet found a way to trace precious stones, and especially diamonds, back to particular owners, countries, or mines. They are, in short, the launderer's Mephistopholean gold. They are valuable, portable, and hugely desirable, and there are many miners, traders, and dealers who want to sell them.

The diamond trade is built on fantasies and bluff. The fantasy that diamonds are scarce was created by De Beers which controls the supply with an iron grip. The bluff involves the bargaining between dealers over every deal, the leap into the unknown taken by every cutter when he buys a diamond that the polished diamond will turn out to be a good color and quality, and the vanity by which a good stone that a dealer has managed to get known by a distinctive name has millions of pounds added to its value. The dream means lives are lost and livelihoods are made to bring tiny, useless stones from remote riverbeds to the ring finger of the majority of married women in the West.

The more that diamonds have become the criminal's best friend, the more they have served the goals of corrupt politicians and terrorists in countries where they are mined. Diamonds are, in short, Africa's favorite currency for buying the weapons that have prolonged wars. Wars have even been started to win control of diamond mines. Much of the information in this chapter is drawn from the official reports of the United Nations Monitoring Mechanism on Sanctions against Angola that summarize its investigation into the illicit diamond trade in Africa.

Until recently, diamonds could easily be sold to diamond dealers with no questions asked, providing instant cash. The diamond industry is traditionally secretive, operating across borders and frequently in corrupt and malfunctioning states, so it is very difficult for law enforcement agencies to verify their accounts. This makes diamond companies a prime vehicle for money laundering, even if the diamonds being exported, typically from Africa to Antwerp, are obtained legally. These factors also make it easy for diamond companies to feed illegally obtained diamonds into the legitimate trade, that is, to launder the diamonds.

Many of the world's richest diamond-bearing regions are in politically unstable regions of Africa that during the 1990s were controlled by rebel militias left over from the Cold War. When they were at each other's throats, America and Russia had tended to provide their proxies in the Third World with arms and supplies gratis, or tied to long-term loans. But when Russia disintegrated and the Cold War ceased, African governments and rebel movements such as the National Union for the Total Independence of Angola (UNITA) had to become self-financing. They did so by exploiting the wealth of natural resources, especially diamonds, in the regions they controlled. The diamond sales financed the rebels' war machines and the reign of terror they inflicted on the populations of these regions. They either used the profits of diamond sales to buy weapons or directly traded the diamonds for the arms. These illegal diamonds have become known as conflict diamonds or, more graphically, blood diamonds.

On a continent strewn with corpses from the conflict diamond trade, Angola was one of the worst affected countries. Its citizens had not known peace and security since 1975, when the Portuguese administration fled from an insurrection against colonial rule and the country descended into civil war. The main factions were the Popular Movement for the Liberation of Angola (MPLA), led by Dos Santos and supported by Cuba and the USSR, and UNITA, led by Jonas Savimbi and supported by South Africa and the United States. The brutal fighting continued until 1991 when the Soviet Union collapsed and the superpowers withdrew from the Cold War chessboard, abandoning the armies of proxies they had created to fight it out alone. There was a brief spell of peace in Angola leading up to multi-party elections in 1992. However, when the elections were won by Dos Santos and the MPLA, Savimbi rejected the result and relaunched his war against the now internationally recognized government. The fighting continued intermittently until Savimbi's death in February 2002. The war was funded by diamond mining. Angolan diamonds, renowned for their quality and colors, are among the most valuable in the world. It is a cruel irony of Africa that the mineralogically richest areas have suffered the greatest devastation and hardship as a result of this wealth.

In an attempt to reduce UNITA's military capacity and force the rebels back to the negotiating table, the UN Security Council voted in 1993 to impose an embargo on the sale of arms to Angola. Sanctions against dealing in UNITA diamonds followed, belatedly, in 1998. However, the implementation of UN resolutions by member states is notoriously deficient. The demand for arms was met by criminal entrepreneurs from all over the world who, violating the embargo, flocked to Africa to supply the rebels and get a slice of this wealth. The big players were mainly Russians. Some had been involved in supplying arms for the superpowers during the Cold War, and there was much continuity in the networks and routes from that time. Planes landed on hidden airstrips in the dead of night, after flying convoluted routes from the country where the arms were obtained in order to throw law enforcement agencies off the scent. (See Chapter 3 'Merchant of Death.')

The arms were old Soviet weapons stolen from Eastern European army warehouses, the officers in charge usually bribed by the arms dealers. A Ukrainian parliamentary commission found that between 1992 and 1998 a third of the Ukraine's weaponry, worth $32 billion, was stolen. Most appears to have gone to Bulgaria, where it then was flown to Africa. Oxfam estimates there are 50 million illegally obtained weapons in Africa, half of all the weaponry on the continent. The arms dealers created a maze of short-lived companies registered in different countries to obscure the nature of the trade and obstruct investigation. The purpose was evidently to ensure that by the time anyone got to the bottom of what had taken place, the arms dealers and their booty were far away and untouchable.

In one such deal in 1999, the arms were sourced from a Romanian company called Rom Arm (National Company for Military Technique).

The broker was the East European Shipping Corporation, registered in the Bahamas. Half a million dollars worth of arms, predominantly cartridges, were involved. In this instance they were not flown but were shipped to Africa aboard a Panamanian registered vessel, the *Kuraka*, with the port of discharge for the cargo, described as technical equipment, recorded as Lomé, Togo. In the deal involving Rom Arm, a UN panel investigating sanctions violations found that the Togo End User Certificate presented to the Romanian authorities was a forgery. The East European Shipping Corporation was supposedly represented in Europe by a company called Trade Investment International, registered at an address at Cumberland Mansions, London. On paper, the directorship of the East European Shipping Corporation was originally held by another company, T.I. Engineering Corporation. It then passed into the hands of a Mr. Samuel Sieve, of the same address in London as Trade Investment International. Clearly, Trade Investment International was more than a mere representative of the East European Shipping Corporation, as it was from the former's account at the Republic Bank, New York, that the $594,420 was transferred to the account of Rom Arm at the Union Bancaire Privée, Geneva. In May 2000, when the UN panel uncovered this information and asked Sieve about his involvement, he claimed that the East European Shipping Corporation had closed and he had retired. By January 2001, Trade Investment International officially ceased trading. However, another company called Trade Investment, with Sieve as director, continues to exist.

If that seems hard to follow, it's because it's supposed to be. The purpose of the setup is to present an impenetrable smokescreen to law enforcement agencies. The journey of a stone from the sediment of an African riverbed to the neck of a society hostess in New York is likewise convoluted. Many of the same players are involved in both the illegal arms and diamonds trades. Evidence of the presence of diamond appraisers on some arms-smuggling flights suggests diamonds were transported out on the return flights at the same time arms were brought to rebel groups. The proximity of most UNITA airstrips to a mine similarly demonstrates the strong link between their logistics and its mining.

UNITA started mining diamonds in the 1980s, but it was only when they took control of the Cuango Valley, the location of rich diamond deposits, in November 1992 that mining on a large scale was begun. The Cuango Mining Corporation was established, a partnership of UNITA's so-called

Ministry of Natural Resources (MIRNA); an Antwerp diamond merchant, David Zollman; and an entrepreneur, George Forrest, who was involved in many consortiums in neighboring Zaire, including construction and various types of mining. UNITA needed the external partners to provide the technical expertise to run such a large project. At the time UNITA controlled about three-quarters of Angola, and between 92 and 96 percent—almost the entire diamond output of Angola—was in the hands of UNITA.

The mining conducted by the Cuango Mining Corporation was labor intensive and low tech. There was some heavy equipment brought in, such as a plant for concentrating gravels and large-capacity pumps to divert small rivers. Pickaxes and sieves were the main pieces of equipment used, as miners scoured the sediment deposits at riverbanks for diamonds. By 1996, 100,000 miners were working for UNITA. A large contingent were Zairean, the result of an agreement between Savimbi and the then President of Zaire, Mobutu Sese Seko. These workers are young men known as the Bana-Lunda, a name which translates as mine children. They are drawn from the Bandundu area of the Democratic Republic of Congo. They are paid for their work in diamonds. Typically the miners worked in groups of six, each group controlled by a UNITA soldier.

The Cuango Mining Corporation made close to $3 billion for UNITA. Without this mining the war in Angola during the 1990s could not have taken place. At its peak in 1996, its annual output is estimated to have been worth $800 million. This is against an estimated figure of $1.2 billion for the entire Angolan output (much of the remainder was black market as opposed to officially licensed, albeit not mined by UNITA). UNITA also operated smaller mines, with other foreign partners. When it withdrew from the Cuango Valley at the end of 1997 during an uneasy truce, it left with a stockpile of diamonds worth at least $250 million.

The loss of the Cuango Valley and other mines marked a change in fortunes for UNITA, and a corresponding change in its structure and the nature of its mining operations. Despite relaunching the war in December 1998, after a clandestine rearmament, UNITA was slowly losing its grip on much of the country. By the end of 1999, UNITA's nerve center, Andulo, was captured by government forces, and UNITA entered its "guerrilla war" phase, unable in its reduced condition to engage in conventional war as before. UNITA militias roamed the jungle, launching raids on government towns and villages. The command structure became typical of guerrilla organizations, with few horizontal links between units. Instead there was a vertical chain of command leading up to Savimbi, who passed orders down to the militias on a need-to-know basis, keeping them in the dark about the activities of other units. Savimbi himself traveled through the countryside with a phalanx of twenty guards, four wives, and suitcases of valuable diamonds, communicating with the various units by satellite phones.

Foreign companies had pulled out of the mining consortiums with UNITA, and UNITA had lost virtually all its heavy equipment. Nevertheless, under these conditions mining continued. The military groups travelled with teams of approximately 50 miners, usually Bana-Lunda. They engaged in "hit-and-run mining," arriving at a location, mining it for a few days, digging a large square pit, and then moving on. This mining was on the lowest technological level, using only pickaxes and sieves. Sometimes they attacked other mines, massacred the miners, and pillaged their stocks. Non-UNITA mines had to be heavily fortified and guarded. Often when UNITA needed diamonds quickly, men, women, and children from villages under their control were flown in and forced to mine. Most of the diamonds mined by the military bands were collected by a roving five-man team and brought to Savimbi. Savimbi and one of his wives, Sandra Saikata, ultimately handled the movement's diamond trade and finances.

The diamonds collected by UNITA were sold in a number of different ways; as with the mining, these changed according to the changing circumstances of UNITA. The initial sales systems were established and organized by a former South African army officer, Fred Rindel, and two diamond-dealing brothers, the De Decker brothers. The best prices were obtained through selling by tender to diamond dealers at auctions that took place in neighboring countries. This continued while UNITA had a strong hand and its activities were little scrutinized, but as these practices were documented and exposed by UN investigations, neighboring authorities were cajoled into cracking down on them. The loss of the major mining regions to the Angolan armed forces and a decline in diamond production also meant it was less worthwhile organizing large auctions. The last known sale by tender took place in October 2000.

Diamonds that weren't auctioned were sold directly to dealers, or traded directly for arms and supplies. The De Decker brothers supplied De Beers' buying offices in Antwerp and Tel Aviv. Although there were no sanctions against trading in the diamonds at the time, since UNITA had no legal mining rights, this was, as the UN said, "effectively the world's largest diamond smuggling operation." UNITA generally sold diamonds in large packets of 30,000 carats worth $1 million, whereas the normal size in the trade is around the $100,000 mark. A carat is a unit of weight for diamonds, a metric carat is equivalent to 200 milligrams.

When the Cuango Mining Corporation ceased operating, Rindel and the De Deckers parted company with UNITA, but by that time they had trained many in UNITA to appraise diamonds. Important UNITA "ambassadors" traveled extensively to arrange diamond sales. Following the imposition of sanctions, it became somewhat harder to trade conflict diamonds on the open market; so many of the sales were arranged with cutters or their agents. This way the diamonds went straight into the cutting factory and out to the polished diamond trade, which had not come under general scrutiny.

At the end of UNITA's military struggle there were small opportunistic sales to passing dealers, sometimes of Jonas Savimbi's central stockpiles, sometimes of diamonds held by UNITA cells. In addition to these methods of selling UNITA diamonds, UNITA brought in revenue by licensing and taxing small-scale diamond traders. These traders traveled through regions UNITA controlled and bought diamonds mainly from miners. Miners in the region were allowed by UNITA to keep a proportion of what they produced as payment.

The packets of diamonds that had been traded and sold were transported to an international diamond market and laundered into the legitimate trade. A myriad different smuggling routes were used. Those that have been uncovered by investigators are thought to represent only the tip of the iceberg. Most were destined for the markets of Antwerp or Tel Aviv; a smaller quantity went to South Africa. The point in the supply chain to the international centers at which the conflict diamonds join legally mined diamonds and get the same rubber stamp of officialdom that the legal diamonds get is the point at which they are laundered. The legal and illegal packets are indistinguishable after that; an official export stamp, for example, endorses their legality. The nature of the diamond trade and the anonymity of rough diamonds meant laundering could take place all along that supply chain.

It became increasingly difficult to feed large quantities of UNITA diamonds into the official Angolan trading system, as the government monitored the trade to try and ensure diamonds from rebel regions weren't being exported. Therefore, most diamonds were smuggled into neighboring countries where the markets did not come under such scrutiny. The Democratic Republic of Congo (DRC) was a major smuggling and laundering center for UNITA diamonds, as it was for diamonds smuggled from other countries. This was true for both the government and the rebel-held regions. The 2,400-mile open border with Angola meant smugglers could operate with ease. Once in the Democratic Republic of Congo, illicit dealers might smuggle the diamonds to another country, or launder them into the official DRC system. It was found in 2000 that a number of Belgium companies had offices in the Democratic Republic of Congo, just over the border from Angola. UNITA representatives took the diamonds to the offices of the Belgian companies, purporting to have bought them from *garampeiros* (artesian miners) operating in the DRC, and legally exported them to Antwerp where they were recorded as DRC diamonds.

Until very recently, most of the diamonds taken from the DRC to Antwerp were not legally exported, but smuggled. They may have been sewn into clothing—a typical modus operandi used even by legitimate traders to transport diamonds—hidden under the false bottoms of attaché cases or inside the soles of shoes, swallowed, or concealed in body cavities. These techniques mirror those of the money or drug smuggler. Many diamonds so carried were declared on entry into Antwerp, and thereby laundered. No paperwork showing legal export from the declared country of its source was required by the authorities. Import and export statistics, a vital, if imprecise, tool for monitoring diamond smuggling, indicate how extensive this laundering was. In 1999, $261 million worth of diamonds were legally exported from the DRC, but $751 million worth were officially imported into Antwerp. Smuggling from the DRC explains the anomalies in these figures. But some diamonds may indeed never have gone through the DRC at all, but come straight from other countries, even from Angola, and were simply falsely declared.

By 2001, diamond smuggling from the DRC was being more heavily monitored by authorities, and the suspected proportion of smuggled diamonds dropped to about half of the total. The figure may be partially attributable to a reduction in illegal mining, but it also represents smugglers adopting less observed circuits. As exports from DRC fell there was a corresponding rise in diamonds exported from the neighboring and similarly war-torn state of the Republic of Congo (aka Congo-Brazzaville). The country produces practically no diamonds itself, yet between 1999 and 2000, the official export figures jumped from none to 1.5 million carats. There was evidently a little smuggling in 1999, as the Antwerp import figure was 72,000 carats, but by the next year this jumped to 3 million carats. The entire amount represented smuggling from the DRC and Angola. Zambia was another smuggling center. Although it only legally exported a small amount of diamonds of industrial quality, one Antwerp importer in 2001 declared $13.5 million worth of high-quality diamonds from Zambia. Some countries, like Liberia, had no desire to combat the trade. In 1996, it produced an estimated 150,000 carats of diamonds from its mines. However, it exported to Belgium 12.3 million carats, more than the entire production of South Africa.

Passing diamonds through tax havens was another route favored by diamond smugglers, as it is for launderers involved in finance. There was no scrutiny of imports or exports, and usually the authorities didn't even record a declared country of origin for imports. The diamonds may be mixed with clean goods and re-sorted, then exported to Antwerp, where the source is legitimately declared as the tax haven. In 1999, the source of $5.6 million of diamonds that entered Antwerp was recorded as the Cayman Islands. The Swiss *freilagers*, or tax-free zones, were another major smuggling route. Forty diamond companies at Zurich and Geneva airports mix, sort, and re-export diamonds. De Beers also passes all its diamonds, worth over $1 billion a year, through the zones to its sorting offices in London, so for years the origin of virtually all the diamonds imported to the United Kingdom was recorded as Switzerland, although this has now changed. Some illicit goods from the arms-for-diamonds trade were probably smuggled via Russia.

The problem was that the minimum requirement to legally trade diamonds at the international diamond exchanges was simply an unverified declaration of origin by the buyer. No documentation relating to the diamonds' origins and movement history was needed; the boundary between the legitimate and black market trades was so porous, nothing in particular had to be done to move diamonds across it. The diamond industry has traditionally had a very relaxed attitude to taxation, with smuggling seen as a time-honored form of tax evasion. Most dealers take part in the legal and illegal trades. One former diamond dealer said that when a client came in, one of the first things he asked was whether the deal would be done under or over the counter; most were under. Even today analysts estimate the black market in Antwerp accounts for 30 percent of the trade there. Because of the extremely secretive nature of the diamond trade, the use of vast quantities of cash, and the fact that deals are often sealed on trust with no paperwork involved, any such figures are highly speculative. Of course, a large proportion of stones are not laundered on import to Antwerp but are smuggled in and circulated on the black market there, eventually reaching cutting factories where they are sold when polished. So they remain black market for their entire existence as rough diamonds. Most of the black market does not involve conflict diamonds. It consists of diamonds stolen from official mines or diamonds bought from the local alluvial miners or *garampeiros* and smuggled to Antwerp to evade taxes. Non-governmental organizations (NGOs) and human rights organizations are far less concerned about this than about the use of laundering to fund regional wars and terrorism. However, it is generally recognized that the only effective way to target the conflict diamond trade is to stamp out the unregulated black market that conceals it. At the end of the 1990s, scrutiny of diamonds imported to Antwerp was increased. Smugglers responded by importing into other European Union (EU) countries where there was less scrutiny. Once in the EU the diamonds are not, of course, subject to any import procedures whatsoever to get to Belgium.

Meanwhile, in the official trade, the Diamond High Council, the industry's self-regulatory industry body, happily recorded vast quantities of top-quality diamonds from Zambia, which only produces industrial diamonds, and Togo, which doesn't produce any diamonds at all. Everyone knew the figures were a fantasy but few were bothered by it.

Moshe and Israel Fisher are the directors of Limo Diamonds in Antwerp and Tel Aviv. They bought their diamonds from a mysterious middleman, Carl Van Tures, whom they paid mainly in cash. He bought them from an Angolan smuggler, Jose Francisco, who went under the name of "Chico." The diamonds were Angolan diamonds, although it is not known whether they came from UNITA. Between January and September 2000, Limo Diamonds of Pelikaanstrasse in Antwerp imported $18 million of diamonds, recording the country of origin as the Central

African Republic. Between December 2000 and June 2001 another 24,000 carats worth $12 million were imported; this time they were registered as coming mainly from Zambia, with some coming from Côte d'Ivoire.

The average carat value of the diamonds was a high $360. Diamonds from the Central African Republic are much less valuable than this; their average carat value is only $140. Zambia, as we have seen, only produces small quantities of industrial diamonds. When UN investigators confronted the Fishers and suggested the diamonds might have been smuggled, the Fishers said they had only ever spoken to Van Tures over the telephone, and he was only an occasional supplier for them. In fact, over the period in question, Van Tures was Limo Diamonds' main supplier. UN investigators found no evidence Van Tures had ever been in Zambia, Cote d'Ivoire, or the Central African Republic. He certainly hadn't legally exported any diamonds from those countries. The UN report stated, "The paper trail was a series of elaborate fakes emanating from a middleman whose existence could not be proved." The existence of Francisco, the Angolan smuggler, could be verified, however, because a visit by him and another Angolan smuggler to the office of Limo Diamonds on the Antwerp Diamond Bourse had been recorded in their reception books. The Fishers have subsequently denied any involvement in diamond smuggling.

The fact that there was a paper trail at all makes this case unusual, and is indicative of the increased regulation the diamond trade was subjected to at the beginning of the twenty-first century. In contrast to the involved smokescreens of companies and documents that had to be set up for the arms-smuggling operations, diamond smuggling was still very easy. Despite those smokescreens, far more has been uncovered about batches of smuggled arms than about particular parcels of conflict diamonds. Exhaustive investigations have not managed to trace a single packet of UNITA diamonds all the way from the source to the markets. The trail runs cold every time and the diamonds, small and anonymous, just disappear. The exasperation of the investigators is evident from the tone of a UN report of October 2001:

> No diamond dealer has claimed to have witnessed Angolan gems being traded on any diamond bourse. These diamonds seem to vanish into thin air after leaving Angola. How is this even possible, given the magnitude of the trade, which is close to the value of the output of Australia or Namibia? Perhaps more importantly, why is it possible for diamonds to vanish?

As with the UNITA diamonds, so it is with conflict diamonds from other wars. The total absence of any requirement of a paper trail to buy diamonds on the world diamond exchanges nullified any security advantages control mechanisms like import and export records would have conferred.

The UN sanctions make it the responsibility of importers like Limo Diamonds to ensure they are not importing conflict diamonds. They could be violated with such impunity because, although they made arms trading with UNITA illegal, the UN has no powers to enforce Security Council resolutions. Enforcement and determination of penalties is left to member states, which are supposed to enshrine UN sanctions in national law. Countries had little incentive to mount complex international investigations to uncover sanctions busting when it was really only a problem for unimportant African states like Angola. In the early 1990s, the United States kept a few officers in the Central Intelligence Agency monitoring the illegal arms trade in Africa, but in 1995 they stopped bothering. It was decided, in the words of one U.S. official, that monitoring the illegal arms trade was "a part-time job at Interpol."

Furthermore, various leaders in Africa supported the rebel groups and used the cover of political instability to plunder the natural resources of neighboring countries. The arch example of a country suffering from this form of plunder by neighboring governments is the Democratic Republic of Congo (formerly Zaire). In what has been called Africa's First World War, troops from Uganda, Rwanda, Namibia, Zimbabwe, Angola, and their proxies decimated the country and ensured it had no chance of stability. Rwanda and Uganda have also been condemned by a UN investigative panel for aiding both UNITA and the DRC rebels. The investigation showed Uganda, Rwanda, UNITA, and the DRC all used the same diamond-smuggling circuits.

Not only did certain African governments turn a blind eye to sanctions-busting, they subverted the apparatus of the state to protect and support the criminals. Victor Bout, the head of the largest arms-smuggling organization, apparently operated in Kigali, Rwanda, under the protection of the authorities there. (For further information on Bout, see Chapter 3, 'Merchant of Death.') In 1996 he even traveled to Europe with a Rwandan diplomatic delegation, although the Rwandan government told the UN panel that he wasn't an official member of it. It was and probably remains common for arms and diamonds dealers to travel on diplomatic passports issued by African countries. Charles Taylor, the notoriously corrupt Liberian president, received enormous payments from both arms and diamond dealers and the RUF rebels undermining Sierra Leone, in return for organizing a meeting between them and allowing them to use Liberia to conduct their trade. The dealers, who included Al Qaida operatives (see Chapter 4), were flown around in helicopters of Taylor's so-called "anti-terrorist unit." Taylor even sold Victor Bout the right to register planes on behalf of Liberia's civil aviation authority. This Liberian "flag of convenience" was invaluable to the arms smugglers. Taylor's contribution to undermining regional stability was so notorious that the UN put sanctions on Liberia.

The full extent of the cooperation between corrupt leaders and the criminals may never be known. The instances that have come to light paint a depressing picture of Africa's endemic corruption. Active cooperation between authorities and arms smugglers was not limited to Africa, though. Many examples have come to light at the other end of the supply chain, of Eastern European leaders and officials abetting the criminals. The ease with which they were able to obtain stocks of arms suggests to many observers that cooperation must have been widespread. Probably the highest profile case of sanctions-busting involved Elf Aquitaine, the French state oil company. Information that came out during the court cases in Paris revealed the company had been providing Niger with arms in return for lucrative concessions. (For further information on Elf Aquitaine in Africa, see Chapter 9.)

Governments in Africa concerned about the arms-for-diamonds trade were faced with a powerful alliance of states and criminal organizations. If not wracked by civil war, like Angola, they were typically impoverished and could do little to combat it without the aid of the international community. The lack of will to take real steps to stop the illegal arms trade ensured the wars dragged on, and the tyrants and criminals became richer.

In the case of Angola, it took until 1998, after a failed truce and the resumption of fighting, for the UN to try and tackle the trade from the other end and impose sanctions on anyone who dealt in UNITA diamonds. Financial sanctions were imposed at the same time. It was part of a heightened recognition of the financial significance of multinational criminal networks and a shift of focus towards tackling them by "following the money." Above all, though, it was the result of a shake-up of the diamond industry brought about by the revelations of a hitherto obscure organization called Global Witness.

Global Witness is a United Kingdom–based non-governmental organization that investigates and exposes links between natural resource exploitation and human rights abuse. In 1998 it turned its attention to conflict diamonds and launched a highly effective campaign that brought the trade to the attention of media, politicians, and the general public. The trade had long been an open secret within the diamond industry and a small community of international observers, but was little known elsewhere. Now it was being discussed in newspapers, on radio shows, and within governments. The role of De Beers in smuggling blood diamonds was highlighted in the report entitled *A Rough Trade*, which Global Witness produced. At the time a diamond mining industry was emerging in Canada that was challenging De Beers's century-long virtual monopoly of the world's rough diamond supply. De Beers knew that selling diamonds was all about public perception. They were terrified of a boycott of their diamonds in favor of "clean" diamonds from Canadian companies, or of a boycott of the entire diamond industry.

The company acted decisively. It stopped buying diamonds on the open market in Angola, and subsequently pulled out of the official Angolan trade, which was rumored to include illicit stones. Public statements expressed De Beers' commitment to human rights. Eventually the company closed all its open-market buying offices, and only sourced diamonds from mines it either owned or was in partnership with. This was an extremely radical step for De Beers, which had always controlled the world's supply and bought the rough diamonds not to sell but to stockpile and so maintain high prices. De Beers is an organization that uses its muscle to control the entire diamond industry. It operates supply and demand a bit like an old print union. De Beers chooses what stones you buy from them. Diamond dealers who help De Beers to keep an eye on the activities of their competitors are rewarded with Christmas bonuses of stones worth hundreds of thousands of dollars; those who fall out with De Beers are impeded from buying stones from them and might as well close their businesses. As Matthew Hart, veteran observer of the industry, said,

"Only De Beers could have galvanized the trade into action." It was the start of a process that positioned the industry against the conflict diamond trade, leading to the establishment in July 2000 of an industry body, the World Diamond Council (WDC), to regulate the trade and keep out conflict diamonds. The WDC says its mission is to develop, implement, and oversee a tracking system for the export and import of rough diamonds to prevent the exploitation of diamonds for illicit purposes such as war and inhumane acts.

In March 2000, De Beers placed notices in all its sales boxes guaranteeing none of the diamonds had been purchased in contravention of UN resolutions. Many in the industry doubted this could be true, believing its stockpiles must still contain diamonds purchased from rebel groups. Hart said, "that doubts persisted . . . shows how completely the broader trade had been compromised by illicit goods, to the point where knowledgeable observers could not believe that the mass of goods . . . was not hopelessly contaminated."

That June, Nicky Oppenheimer, chairman of De Beers, wrote to all diamond stock exchanges urging them to expel any members found dealing in illicit diamonds.

The renewed efforts in early 2000 by De Beers to distance the industry from the conflict diamond trade corresponded to another development that once again thrust the trade into the limelight. The campaign by Global Witness and the sanctions of 1998 had changed the diamond industry, but they had not provoked much action on the problem by governments. As before, governments everywhere paid lip service to these sanctions, but did little more. During the 1990s, no one was prosecuted for violating sanctions on Angola or any other African country, and the illegal trade in both arms and diamonds flourished. Conflict diamonds continued to get through with ease. While the top end of the diamond industry operated differently, activity at the lower end was much the same.

The UN Reports on Angola

In the year 2000, the UN took a new approach to the problem of black diamonds. It began investigating sanctions-busting itself. The UN established a panel of experts to monitor and report on the effectiveness and breaches of UN sanctions on Angola. Frustrated by the lack of progress by UN member states in combating the arms and diamonds smuggling, activists and UN officials proposed bringing into the public arena hard evidence on sanctions violations that would stand up in court and force countries to act (the UN itself, of course, has no powers to prosecute anyone). This was a Promethean task for the investigators, who had nothing akin to a search warrant or right to view any documents. They could merely request them from governments, organizations, and companies and hope for cooperation.

In spite of these obstacles, the report of the Panel of Experts on Angola, called the "Final Report of the UN Panel of Experts on Violations of Security Council Sanctions Against Unita," came out in March 2000. The bulk of the information on the conflict diamond trade has emerged from this investigation and the others that followed. The UN panel adopted the brave and controversial strategy of naming and shaming those who were violating the sanctions. It also made specific and hard-hitting recommendations of steps the international community should take to enforce them, such as mandatory UN sanctions against persistent sanctions-busting countries. Most sensationally, it introduced to public scrutiny the enormous arms-dealing network of Victor Bout, who operated the largest fleet of cargo aircraft in the world. The controversy, though, stemmed from the fact that governments were used to a soft approach from the UN, which didn't disturb them. Leaders and governments mentioned unfavorably in the report were greatly annoyed. Many vehemently denied the charges and accused the UN of bias. The governments of Rwanda, Togo, and Burkina Faso all denied allegations made against them in the report. France immediately rejected many of the recommendations and accused the panel of unfairly singling out Francophone countries. But there was as much support as condemnation. The strongest support came from Peter Hain, Britain's Foreign Office Minister. He told the UN, "taking no action while citizens in our countries make money out of misery . . . is simply hypocrisy . . . The full force of law must be brought to bear on those responsible . . . public censure must now be followed by decisive action . . . We have a duty to act."

In seven reports on Angola released between October 2000 and December 2002, when hostilities in Angola had ceased, the Monitoring Mechanism on Sanctions against UNITA, the successor body to the Panel of Experts on Angola, continued to report on compliance with the sanctions and expose those who violated them. Other panels that were established to monitor the effectiveness of UN sanctions on Sierra Leone and Liberia adopted the same practice.

The naming and shaming was complemented by "quiet diplomacy" to encourage parties to cooperate. Meetings were held, often secretly, with government officials and other individuals who were "firmly urged to stop being a part of the problem and to become part of the solution." As one of the UN reports points out, often "quiet diplomacy was not conducted 'quietly,' but in hotly debated meetings with government officials who, even when presented with conclusive proof of violations, had to be emphatically reminded of the legal and moral obligations of their Governments under the Charter of the United Nations. In those instances, the Mechanism's reports to the Security Council became powerful instruments for exposing non-compliance."

The UN panel recorded that on many occasions, after such meetings, sanctions violations ceased. Notwithstanding their protests, governments, threatened with international embarrassment, realized they had to clean up their acts. The panel also met with international bodies such as the EU, the Economic Community of West African States, the South African Development Community, the World Customs Organization, the Waassenar Arrangement (a multinational diplomatic committee to limit the circulation of small arms), the International Civil Aviation Organization, and many others to try and persuade them to take steps to stop sanctions-busting.

The investigators had three approaches they could use to monitor the conflict diamond trade. They could try and trace links between illegal traders in African countries and diamond dealers on the markets (as in the case of Limo Diamonds), they could attempt to trace individual parcels of diamonds, and they could look at diamond import and export statistics to try and interpret smuggling trends.

Tracing links between diamond dealers required information like telephone call records and bank transfers. Investigators usually came up against the wall of "commercial confidentiality." Tracing parcels was even more difficult. Parcels of diamonds left rebels in Africa and suspected illicit parcels arrived in Antwerp, but they disappeared in between, and without a paper trail giving technical details of the composition of the parcels it was impossible to prove a link. Neither method conclusively identified traders who were dealing in UNITA goods.

The information from diamond statistics gives the best picture of the trade, but also the least specific. The large number of factors in play and possible causes of statistical discrepancies mean it is not possible to track the trends very accurately this way, but they do give many useful indications. Statistics of the number of carats exported and imported, rather than the value, are more reliable, as the values of African exports are often systematically underdeclared to reduce taxes.

The UN reports on Angola caused significant improvements in compliance of member states with sanctions. Regulation by the authorities was increased in Antwerp and elsewhere, laws were passed in several countries to uphold the sanctions, and UNITA, already in a weak condition, was squeezed. The tide was beginning to turn. But the actions fell far short of what the reports had recommended and the investigators had hoped for. Life was made more difficult for illegal arms and diamond dealers, and those named undoubtedly didn't welcome the publicity, but their activities were not curtailed. States frequently did not act on the information exposed by the UN panels' reports, and even where they did, their sluggish and incomplete workings allowed the arms criminals to rearrange their operations before any measures taken affected them, such as the freezing of bank accounts of certain companies or the outlawing of companies. Indeed, the majority of the countries to which the UN wrote during their various investigations to request information didn't even respond.

The attacks on September 11 changed all that. In the aftermath, America was determined to tackle head-on the entrepreneurs who go around the world selling weaponry to anyone who will pay. They began to pay acute attention—especially in Africa—to the lethal alliances that had emerged and been ignored between international criminal organizations, terrorists, and rogue states like Liberia. The arms smuggler, Victor Bout, who had allegedly supplied the Taliban with weapons, was a high-profile public enemy and had to flee from the United Arab Emirates, where he had been operating, to Russia. His network was paralyzed. The Americans also believed diamond-smuggling circuits were being used to launder terrorist money. Previously they had only expressed lukewarm support for regulatory initiatives. They now put their full weight behind the ultimate scheme to fight the conflict diamond scheme: a global certification system.

The idea of a certification scheme is to end the anonymity of diamonds by attaching a certificate of origin to packets of diamonds as soon as they are mined. The certificate has an unalterable serial number and must travel with the diamonds all the way to the cutting factory. It has security features to make it difficult to forge, and the issue of the certificate is registered in a local office administering the certification scheme together with technical details about the diamonds in the parcel, and logged on an international database. When the diamonds are sold, exported, or imported, the code on their certificate of origin is recorded, so a paper trail for all diamonds is created. An international body is set up to monitor the system. Tight regulation of the activities of dealers ensures diamonds that are illegally mined and therefore do not have certificates can not be traded, freezing conflict diamonds out of the system. Or that's the theory.

Such a scheme exceeds the various other possible ways to regulate the diamond trade. Lighter alternatives, which were already being introduced, included requirements that importers retain copies of export documents, receipts for purchases, airways bills, and the passports of diamond couriers. However, supporters of a full-scale certification system argued that without it, these are measures determined smugglers could always find a way around.

The blueprint for certificate-of-origin schemes already existed on the ground in Angola, Sierra Leone, and a few other countries. In Angola serial-numbered certificates were introduced in January 2001, and a state company, the Angola Selling Corporation, was established, with the sole right to buy diamonds in Angola and export them. It was not possible to issue all certificates at the mines, as the mining is done by *garampeiros* in extremely remote locations. Middlemen purchase the diamonds from the *garampeiros* and take them to the regional buying offices of the Angola Selling Corporation, where they are issued with the certificate. If the official buying the diamonds suspects the diamonds have a dubious provenance, he is supposed to refuse to buy them. The intention is to license all the middlemen in stages and eventually even the hundreds of thousands of *garampeiros*. Of course, such a scheme is of little use if diamonds can be easily smuggled into neighboring countries where they will not require certificates.

The response of the American authorities set the international agenda. At a meeting in Botswana in November 2001, the Kimberley process to create a global certification scheme was set into motion. By early 2003 the

basic form of the system was up and running. All the major diamond wars
had ended anyway as a result of various factors, including the pressure of
sanctions, before the scheme came into effect, and it is probably too early
to judge the results. Observers say there is still a very healthy black market.

Other more hi-tech solutions to control the diamond trade have been
proposed. The lack of scientific procedures to determine where a particular rough diamond came from has always been a problem for law
enforcement. In the recently established diamond fields of Canada they
are experimenting with identifying rough diamonds by analyzing minute
impurities in the diamonds. These vary from location to location. Another
possibility is to chemically analyze the water content in particles of soil
adhering to the rough diamond. The problem with such methods is that to
identify the provenance of a diamond thus analyzed, a database would be
needed of the chemical profile of every mining location in the world. Even
legitimate companies would be reluctant to give samples from their mines,
as this information is a valuable commercial secret.

Diamond sanctions resulted in a lot of smuggling straight into cutting
factories, and this is likely to be further amplified by the Kimberley
process, as the regulatory tentacle of the Kimberley process does not
extend beyond the point at which the rough diamonds are polished. So
attention has turned to attempts to regulate the polished trade in a way
that differentiates smuggled diamonds and legitimate goods. Hi-tech solutions have been brought to bear on the problem. Canadian diamonds
taken under totally controlled conditions from mines to a polishing factory
in Yellowknife, a Canadian city in the Northwest Territories, have a polar
bear logo lasered on the diamond to prove it is a genuine Canadian Arctic
Diamond. But forgers started lasering polar bears onto diamonds. To
tackle this, a revolutionary technology has been used. Designed by the
Gemprint Corporation, Toronto, the polished diamonds in Yellowknife are
bombarded with laser light; the reflection back is recorded and represents
a unique fingerprint of the surface of the diamond. This information is
encrypted in a Gemprint certificate issued with the diamond and recorded
on Gemprint Corporation's database, so the origin of every polished
diamond mined in the Canada Barrens can be verified.

De Beers has likewise started branding diamonds. A unique mark invisible to the naked eye but visible through special viewing machines available

at retail jewelers is inscribed on certain De Beers goods. The company hopes a De Beers branded diamond, certified clean of the blood diamond trade, will become the status symbol of choice in a market fueled by vanity. Some commentators are starting to think that the whole issue of conflict diamonds will only benefit De Beers. Meanwhile, it remains to be seen if a commodity can be as tightly controlled as groups like Global Witness hope, and whether such intense regulation will prevent future diamond wars and frustrate the designs of the criminals waiting in the wings to profit from death and destruction.

The laundering money-go-round involves complex swaps of precious goods for lower-value items like arms and cigarettes. But behind every trade there is likely to be a drug dealer looking for a home for his illegal proceeds, as we shall now discover.

Chapter 7

Colombia's Half Trillion

The illegal narcotics industry is the principal source of black money.
From drugs flow terrorism, corruption, and political instability.

THE PROCEEDS OF ILLEGAL DRUG SALES support a global laundering industry, which penetrates every sector of the world's economy. Narcotics are estimated to be worth between $500 billion and $1 trillion a year, an amount according to UN Secretary General Kofi Annan in remarks to a United Nations General Assembly session in June 2003, that is greater than the global oil and gas industry, and twice as large as the overall automobile industry. Some of that money is reinvested in the narcotics industry, and much finds its way into the black markets of arms dealing and terrorism. The rest is smuggled back into the legal economy to maintain the lifestyles of the industry's global kingpins; the profits of its multitude of dealers in the West; and the survival of its subsistence farmers in Latin America, Afghanistan, and the other countries where the coca plant and poppies are cultivated.

The Center for Strategic and International Studies of Washington, D.C. reported in 2004 that "the criminal narcotics industry ranks among the wealthiest and most powerful multinational business conglomerates in the world. . . . The effects of this worldwide, highly integrated industry have been felt from Colombia to Thailand, from Afghanistan to Sudan, and from Russia to the United States. No country has been impervious. Transnational drug networks have exploded in response to the new conditions in the former Soviet Union. Particularly menacing are the connections that have been identified between networks in Latin America, Central and Eastern Europe, and the Soviet successor states."

Countries where workers are paid low wages and where investment in the soil is a low national priority are easily seduced by the massive returns available from the production of opium and coca. Drug growers offer to fund the development, saving poor countries' national exchequers (caretakers of the national revenue), the cost of growing legal produce. The U.S. State Department has shown how the cost of a kilo multiplies 200 times between cultivation and the retail market. The coca leaf, required to produce 1 kilo, costs some $650 when it is grown in Peru. When the leaf is exported to Colombia for production into cocaine, it costs $1,050 per kilo. When the cocaine is imported into Miami, its price has risen to $23,000. By the time it enters Chicago's wholesale market, it is worth $33,000, and on the streets of Chicago the price has risen to $188,000 per kilo. These are indeed frightening statistics, and explain the desperate greed, often resulting in violence, that accompanies the making and selling of drugs, not to mention the enormous ingenuity that goes into the laundering of the proceeds.

That violence has also bred terrorism. Expansion of the drug industry has put money and weapons into the hands of warlords, who pose a threat to law and order. George Henry Millard, a special adviser to the Commissioner of Police in Sao Paulo, Brazil, said in 2003, "The irregular armies in Colombia have become a serious threat to the government with the increase of illegal drug activity. In 1980 there were about 1,000 men in the Colombian FARC (The Revolutionary Army of Colombia). By 1999 illegal groups had grown to 21,000. As a reaction, by the end of the decade there were also about 10,000 men in the illegal auto defense forces."

Mr. Millard also said, "It has become impossible to collect taxes in areas where the FARC and the paramilitaries are active. Another effect of the violence in Colombia has been to make the government more reluctant than usual to carry out economic reforms through fear of generating further violence."

Cartels based around the Colombian agricultural centers of Medellin and Cali, were established over the 1960s and 1970s to capitalize on this illegal industry. The first chiefs of these cartels were gangsters, and in due course the Medellin cartel imploded in violence. Their greed was not sustainable, in spite of the fortunes they amassed. Cali did it differently. Instead of Cali's leaders squandering their profits, they spent them on developing organizations that they wanted to endure. Founded in the 1970s, Cali was the world's leading money laundering organization. But their cartel began to unravel in 1995 when Colombian forces swooped down on the cartel's leader's Cali apartment and reportedly found him in a wardrobe. Another leader was arrested a year later. By 1996 the cartel's seven leaders were either dead or behind bars.

Cali's founders, brothers Gilberto and Miguel Rodriguez-Orejuela, and Jose Santacruz-Londoño, understood the first law and lore of laundering, namely that the best way to hide dirty money is to mingle it with clean money, so they invested their profits in legitimate businesses. They also bought large amounts of land in Colombia.

Gilberto liked to describe himself as an "honest drugstore magnate," a reference to the chain of pharmacies owned by the family. Gilberto, called the "chess player," was known to be the more cerebral of the brothers, with a passion for Colombian poetry and football. He was said to be responsible for the strategic, long-term planning of the organization. Miguel, known as "the Master," ran the day-to-day operations. In 1995, the U.S. Drug Enforcement Administration (DEA) estimated they had annual profits of $8 billion. The brothers' combined fortune was estimated at $205 billion. The Rodriguez-Orejuela brothers are also said to have gained the respect of other traffickers, who used the honorific term "Don" when addressing them. By 1995, the DEA believed them to be responsible for 80 percent of the world's cocaine trade. They were also thought to be making inroads into the heroin trade.

Drawing on management techniques used by terrorist groups, Cali's chief operating officers separated their workers into cells, with each small group knowing little about other employees. They also adopted a scientific approach to analyzing their enemy and resisting it. Technology was used to design communications equipment that could not be bugged while leading lawyers were hired to study the moves of the DEA and its prosecutors. The cartel invested heavily in political protection. In the past ten years, the former president of Colombia, Ernesto Samper, and hundreds of congressmen and senators have been accused of accepting campaign financing from the Rodriguez-Orejuela brothers.

Cali had a strong sense of their consumers' needs so they increased shipments into Europe and Asia when cocaine use in the United States began to drop. One observer plotted the growth of the cartels and the expansion of their laundering activity. The observer said, "As their drug distribution started to become more and more sophisticated, so too did the money laundering side. It ended up that in the early years, again in order to maximize profits, they needed to maintain the lowest possible overhead. So if I am sending a courier from South America to New York with 10 kilos of cocaine, I have to end up bringing him back to South America. Well, why not let him come back in with the same false bottom suitcases laden with U.S. dollars and bring my drug profits back to me in South America? The profitability and the market became so huge that it became harder to smuggle money back into South America than cocaine into the U.S."

Careful management of costs was a hallmark of the more sophisticated Cali cartel. A pilot may be paid as much as $500,000 for flying a plane with 250 kilograms on board, no less than 2 percent of the retail price of $25 million. If the plane has to be abandoned after one flight, $2,000 will be added to the price of each kilogram.

Heroin smuggling is not so efficient. Because most of the low-cost producers, Afghanistan for example, are very distant from the United States, dedicated vessels cannot be used. A great deal of heroin travels in small bundles carried on individual couriers. Couriers carrying drugs and money have been replaced with small airplanes making covert trips to the United States. Over time, the proceeds have been reinvested in more sophisticated laboratories, better airplanes, and even an island in the Caribbean where the planes can refuel.

In the mid-1990s, the Cali went the way of all cartels when their chiefs were arrested. The Colombian government would not extradite them and DEA agents believe they continue to run their empire from their prison cells.

One of the Cali cartels' operatives was Franklin Jurado. The Colombian looked like every other American MBA student. He was middle class, clever, and smooth. He would have comfortably found a job as a finance executive at an American corporation and moved swiftly through the ranks. Instead, in the early 1990s, Jurado was seduced into laundering the money of the Cali cartel's co-founder, Jose Santacruz-Londoño. An above average salary paid by money laundering organizations enticed the recently graduated student to work for the notorious Colombian cultivator.

Jurado passed some $65 million through accounts with fictitious European names before it was channeled into front companies registered in offshore tax havens like Antigua and the Isle of Man. Jurado attempted to legitimize the money—the so-called placement stage of the laundering process—by transferring it into Santacruz's legitimate Colombian businesses, such as restaurants, construction companies, pharmacies, and real estate holdings.

Jurado wired this money from a Panamanian bank to Europe through the offices of Merrill Lynch and other financial institutions. In Europe, it went into more than one hundred accounts, many of which were held in the names of Santacruz's relatives and mistresses. Jurado had accounts at no less than 68 banks. Jurado was a master at "smurfing."

This form of laundering, first encountered by New York police officers investigating a banking scam, involves breaking up large sums of money into amounts that are small enough to be deposited into the American banking system without arousing suspicion. The cartels knew that any bank deposit of more than $10,000 would automatically generate a Currency Transaction Report (CTR), which would alert the authorities. Thus those holding very large sums of dirty money would hire people to make deposits of under $10,000 dollars in, say, twenty different branches of a bank or banks on the same day. If the cartel hired just twenty people, then it could easily place several million dollars into the banking system in a morning. This money could subsequently be transferred back to Colombia through perfectly legitimate channels.

Jurado's activities prompted the U.S. Financial Crimes Enforcement Network, part of the Department of the Treasury, to introduce a Suspicious Activity Report that made it incumbent on banks to file a form to notify the government when they merely suspected that someone was attempting to evade the CTR. The cartels were already looking at alternatives to labor-intensive smurfing techniques and they now started to devise more complex schemes, such as the use of offshore corporations as fronts through which they could launder their cash.

The high-powered young financier was ironically caught out by a low-technology glitch that rendered all his clever schemes worthless. Jurado, it appeared, had a noisy money counting machine that, given the amount of money involved, was being used almost continuously, often at anti-social hours. Irritated neighbors told the police who began an investigation. At the same time, the Luxembourg police put Jurado's name through their system and found that it cropped up in connection with the collapse of a bank in Monaco. He was convicted in Luxembourg and then extradited to the United States where a New York court found him guilty of the same offense and sentenced him to seven and a half years in prison.

Jurado had sought to acquire anonymity by creating numerous "cut-outs" between himself and the underlying business. Dummy companies kept his name away from the corrupt organizations where his money was sourced and destined. These layers of disguise made the money launderer a financial player who was only identifiable with great difficulty. In fact, the canniest money launderers aim to put their money in the most legitimate and established institutions, like London or New York banks, to leech off their reputations. They are masters of smoke and mirrors.

Younger lieutenants have taken over from the cartel founders, and now control the cocaine industry in South America. They run smaller, more compact groups than the Medellin and Cali cartels, compartmentalizing their responsibilities, so one group smuggles the drugs from Colombia to Mexico, another group controls the jungle labs, and a third deals with transportation of coca base from the fields to the laboratories. Colombian Marxist guerrilla groups work with cocaine trade cartels, protecting the fields and the laboratories in remote zones of Colombia in exchange for a tax that the traffickers pay to the organization. Colombian right wing paramilitary groups are also thought to control the fields, laboratories, and some of the smuggling routes.

Over the last three decades, the cartels' laundering experts have created a system of exchange of currency for goods, called the Black Market Peso Exchange (BMPE). This is of fundamental importance to an understanding of how drug money is handled, transported, and spent by the South American gangs. The drug dollars are used to buy equipment in North America, which is then exported to South America for apparently legitimate purposes such as farming or manufacturing. The importers of the equipment pay the drug barons in South America with their legitimate money. The middleman in the trade is an agent who reconciles the transactions and takes the risk of handling dirty money. The BMPE is explained in greater detail in the last section of this chapter.

The DEA and the Colombian National Police believe there are more than three hundred active drug-smuggling organizations in Colombia today. Cocaine is shipped to every industrialized nation. Colombia's narcotic industry employs around 200,000 people and generates between $2.2 and $5 billion annually, roughly 3 percent of the country's gross domestic product.

Today's drug organizations are financially driven, in some respects not unlike a conventional corporation. An officer in the financial operations section of the U.S. Department of Justice, Drug Enforcement Administration (DEA), in Arlington, Virginia, commented, "The head of the organization is likely to be in South America, but he has cell heads in the U.S. handling his affairs in New York or in the principal markets. You should think of crime and drug trafficking as globalization of the economy."

Colombians have proved they are global citizens by meeting with crooks from many countries over the years. Indeed, their global reach contrasts with the ultraconservative national bases of law enforcement officers. Drug money laundering requires collusion between cartels and opportunistic crooks and terrorists. The collapse of Communism brought a new wave of launderers and customers into the international marketplace. Colombians met with Russians, Italians, and Cubans to plan a route for moving the drugs from South America, through the United States, and on into Russia.

The launderer handles cultural and linguistic problems by bringing in local operators who know the territory. The need to blend into a business environment is paramount, whatever the terms or purpose of trade. A senior money laundering expert at OIPC- Interpol at its headquarters in Lyon, France, said, "Colombians want to sell cocaine in Russia and in Italy, but they need someone to arrange the business because they can't send some Colombian person to sell the drugs on the street because they would stand out and they need a local network."

A spokesman for the UK Metropolitan Police also reported a close connection between the Colombians and the Jamaicans. The two groups forged early links in the United States in the 1950s and 1960s, and today Colombians use Jamaicans for producing crack out of cocaine, for handling smaller amounts of drugs on the street, and for trading. An officer from the Metropolitan Police said in London in 2003, "Once the Jamaicans have sold their cocaine, they take the cash back to the Colombians and buy more kilos of cocaine." Colombians also use Jamaica as a stopping-off point for drugs and cash on their way back and forth between Europe and the United States. Nigeria is another important trans-shipment point for Colombians, as Nigerians have strong links with Germany and the United Kingdom. Nigerian merchants assist Colombians trucking drugs and cash to Myanmar (formerly called Burma) and Turkey.

The law enforcement community produces "typologies," or analyses, of the way these drug organizations work. These are abstractions based on a few germs of information and a lot of speculation, devised to help identify the men and their means. An investigator with the DEA commented to the author in 2003, "Hundreds of money launderers offer an unknown quantity of people these services. There is no way of knowing exactly how many; this is an illegal activity and they don't license people to do it. This financial advisor has the ability to know three or four different bankers who will be friendly and open up bank accounts because of the façade that they create."

Drugs on his fingers connect a dealer to a drug gang, but the drug money launderer is only linked by the money chain. Top money men cut themselves off from drug operatives or get cut off themselves. Winning respectability and acceptability is their goal and they use chains of companies and layers of false identities to achieve it. In fact, the launderer is likely to present a face of super-respectability to the world. He looks just like everyone else, but more so. The Interpol officer already quoted commented, "They are good people in the society and you don't know that they are members of the organization. They have the best university degrees; they have the best skills and managerial functions. Everyone regards them as good people until you can demonstrate, through the investigation, that there is a link between this level and that level. But that is almost impossible because the professionals take huge trouble to ensure there is no link."

The DEA officer says, "The launderer tells anyone who approaches him with drugs, 'I don't want to see cocaine, I don't touch cocaine, and I don't have anything to do with the stuff because I am in no way involved in drug trafficking.'"

He continues, "If you have anyone involved in drug trafficking, then don't have him or her involved on the money side because you will have the authorities looking at them for suspected cocaine trafficking. They are going to find out that they help launder the money. You want someone of respectability who could come in and open up the accounts above reproach, which can sustain the due diligence or the know-your-customer type of inquiry made by the financial institution before the account is opened."

The authorities aim to catch drug financiers by linking them to someone dealing in drugs, said Interpol's officer, speaking at the agency's headquarters in Lyon. He also said, "You need a link between a white collar and a criminal operator before you can bring a case before the courts. We have to put the two in contact and that is the difficult part. A store-front operation or an undercover (sting) operation allows you to operate in the name of the boss of the organization. You need a special link!" This officer has particular expertise in the field, having served most of his career as an undercover agent in Italy.

He cited an instance when Argentinian police helped him bring together a white collar launderer and a top Bolivian cocaine producer. The cartel chief was lured to Italy to meet the man whom he understood to be capable of laundering the proceeds of his drug sales and transferring them back to Bolivia. The Interpol officer said, "I put him in contact with the criminal level. That was the scope of this meeting and they fell into the trap. We photographed him on the criminal side with other people and that was enough to prove it in the court. They stay very closely connected to the profits. They are not going to trust them to anyone else."

Management structures in laundering operations are tight, hierarchical, and ferociously controlled. Cartel chiefs rule by fear from on top; greed is the main motive. Professional managers with untarnished backgrounds, in particular lawyers or accountants, supervise "hoods" who work the streets, perform basic tasks, round up drug money from many dispersed sources, arrange couriers for money and materials, perform smurfing around banks, and enforce discipline among the troops. Managers subcontract tasks, or indeed work with another gang that is powerful in a territory. An approach based on competence to complete a task has replaced the self-sufficiency and ethnic or geographic trust that characterized the Italian or New York-based Cosa Nostra.

Opportunism, not strategy, is the lower-level drug launderer's message. Service businesses, in particular those in the catering trade like hotels and restaurants, are similarly exploited for financial manipulation of unaccountable drug money. Saunas, launderettes, and sun-tanning shops create cash flows with minimal documentation or paper trails. These outlets are routinely acquired by those with drug money to launder.

Colombia's footprint is routinely found in the retail sector of the West. One British police officer watched a Colombian gang around the jewelry shops of London's West End buying every Rolex watch that was available.

A certain opportunistic launderer set up a bogus car rental outlet to serve as a "shadow business" with substantial profits and overheads. According to a UK Metropolitan police officer, new cars were bought and parked on a small Greek island, yet no car ever left the parking lot. The business was low key and local police ignored it; checking and tracing the business's activity would be complicated and time-consuming. Invoices, ostensibly paid by those renting cars, and bills submitted by mechanics for crash repairs that never occurred, created a paper trail to offset move-ments of the dirty money. When the cars, which remained pristine, were depreciated down to zero, they were sold.

Drug dealers with large quantities of illegal cash need ingenious schemes to hide their money. For example, Ibrahim Marrat Karagozlu, a Turkish drug baron, thought he could mix up his drug money in the duty-free takings. He bought a second-hand Tri-star jet from the Dutch bank, ING, for $2 million cash. ING later acquired the collapsed bank, Barings. The rickety plane became the sole carrier for the grandly named IMK Airlines, a name representing nothing more than the initials of his name. His goal was to run a holiday company carrying tourists on international travel that would give rise to large amounts of foreign currency.

The travel company never got off the ground, and Karagozlu's plane sat on the tarmac at Manchester Airport in the UK for nine months. Then he took some £12 million over a period of time to Thomas Cook, the British bureau de change (currency exchange), and travel agent, with his prepared tale about the airline. The incredulous bureau de change reported it to the police. Collin Phillips, a police investigator with the UK's National Crime Squad, explained in 2003, "They were looking for a legend, some kind of respectability as to why they should be handling so much cash." The police later found that the bogus airline, which had been moved to Sweden by British aviation authorities already concerned about its bona fides, had sold no more than £1,750 worth of duty-free sales.

Karagozlu displayed his imaginative skills at his trial, when he sought to refute a prosecution claim that he had been in London on a critical date by claiming that he had been in Turkey, bedridden in an Istanbul hospital. X-rays of his lungs were said to prove it until the Crown showed they belonged to an elderly woman rather than a man in his forties. In 2002, Karagozlu was sentenced to twenty years in prison. Ibrahim's brother, Hasan Murat Karagozlu, was also part of the scheme and was sentenced to seven years in prison in 2003 for large-scale importation of heroin to the United Kingdom.

Karagozlu undoubtedly scored high marks for ingenuity, but none for common sense. Indeed, Collin Phillips, the detective constable investigating the case, commented, "As a drug trafficker you are limited only by your imagination. As long as you have the imagination and the financial resources to do it then any system, any venue, is a possible money-laundering venue."

The gambling industry is a well-established hideaway for the drug barons. Al Capone, one of the senior members of the laundering industry in the 1930s, pioneered the art of putting money through casinos in Cuba. Meyer Lansky, an ally of Capone, and Lansky's business partner, Salvatore "Lucky" Luciano, took interests in casinos in the Bahamas and in other centers around the Caribbean. Lansky understood the importance of having a well-disposed political regime in the locations where he had made his investment. According to R.T. Naylor in his book *Hot Money* (1994), he was part of a "carefully concocted scandal" that discredited the incumbent regime and brought the Progressive Liberal Party to power in Bahamas under its leader, Lynden Pindling. Naylor writes, "The casino boom coincided with the boom in Bahamian offshore banking activities, and the subsequent growth of legitimate banking transactions provided cover for a similar increase in money laundering."

The opportunity to mingle large quantities of cash of all currencies and sources turns the casino into an ideal vehicle. Gambling regulators in the larger financial centers have wised up to the launderers' threat and now demand evidence of the sources of funds. But casinos continue to open in small and corrupt drug centers like Cambodia, exposing the country to inevitable risk.

Wealth gleaned from laundering may be hidden or dissipated around companies or in offshore hideaways. Launderers use the same tax loopholes as global companies and wealthy individuals. This has led John Moscow, a prominent lawyer in the New York District Attorney's Office who led the American investigation into the Bank of Credit and Commerce International (BCCI), to make very explicit public demands that tax havens be curbed, or even closed down. BCCI came to be known as the Bank of Crooks and Conmen International. The abuse that occurred under its roof was legendary, turning BCCI into the iconic laundering institution of our age. BCCI was founded in 1971 by expatriate Pakistanis who claimed to be building a bank for the world's Muslim community. But BCCI proved to be little more than a vehicle for those seeking to launder black money, including the money earned from drug sales of Panama's General Noriega. The bank was prosecuted for money laundering in 1989 in Tampa, Florida, and closed down in 1991.

Two of laundering history's most famous cowboys pioneered the exploitation of offshore loopholes to hide gains made from drugs and other illegal activities. Bernie Cornfeld and Robert Vesco were notorious American financial manipulators and tax evaders. Bernie Cornfeld's company, Investors Overseas Services, collapsed amid fraud and financial abuse in the 1960s. Cornfeld was one of numerous financiers serving the ends of the U.S. government and its Central Intelligence Agency. Vesco set up companies on the Caribbean island of the Bahamas, humorously dubbed the "Switzerland of the Americas" by its investors, and lined the pockets of politicians in the Bahamas, Panama, Haiti, and Costa Rica, who had earlier enjoyed his largesse.

The drug trader who successfully smuggles cash out of a country will still need to convert it into another currency and place at least some of it into the financial system, preferably before it leaves its country of origin. The drug industry's requirement for financial services is very similar to that of any other wholesale or retail operation. Law enforcement officers compare the drug industry with conventional businesses. Collin Phillips has investigated the activities of Turkish heroin-smuggling gangs and likened their operations to those of the giant British supermarket, J. Sainsbury, when he said, "The whole system was like Sainsbury's but bigger. When you go to Sainsbury's and you take a loaf of bread from the shop and you take it to the checkout, somewhere, a lorry is on a motorway with a load of bread on board to restock the shelf. What was most important to the heroin distributors was really the process of getting the funds from the UK back to Turkey to fund the next shipment."

This requires access to a financial system whose tests for acceptability and honesty are becoming tighter. One drug gang sent the proceeds of UK heroin sales back to Turkey to fund the supply chain, using a British bureau de change.

The scam started in 1995 when two Iranian political refugees, a father and son, set up shop as currency dealers, money remitters, and money dealers in a quiet and commodious mansion block, called Spencer House, in Marlborough Place in St John Wood, an area of London largely inhabited by diplomats and wealthy expatriates. Most of the team's customers were Iranian expatriates who wanted to move money between Britain and Iran without falling foul of Iran's strict foreign exchange controls.

But the combination of currency dealing and trust banking is easily abused, as will be shown in Chapter 11. So when some wealthy Turks, linked to Ibrahim Marrat Karagozlu, came to the Iranians with large volumes of cash to remit to Turkey, the Iranians had a working system. A police investigator noted that, "Several people were seen entering the premises with large heavy bags and then leaving empty handed."

The Turks paid the Iranians amounts in cash ranging between £100,000 and £350,000. The Iranians deposited the money into a sterling account in the London branch of the Bank of Kuwait and then, when the pound-to-dollar exchange rate was most favorable, transmitted it to a U.S. dollar account in New York. The funds' next port of call was the account of a money dealer in the Emirates Bank in Dubai.

Dubai, as we have seen, is one of the world's most lax financial centers. Money transmitters channeling cash flows of Asian workers back to their home countries are numerous, lightly regulated, and highly profitable. This entrepôt is also used extensively for Russian flight capital. The money went from Dubai in the form of wire transfers to the traditional heart of the informal banking network in the gold souks, or marketplaces of Istanbul. A Turkish money dealer based in the Grand Bazaar in Istanbul served as the last piece in this money movement chain. He paid the Turkish drug dealers the value of the first payment made in Central London. The Iranians in St John's Wood took a 5 percent commission on the deal as well as benefited from any exchange rate fluctuations during the procedure. From London to Istanbul in one swift and dirty move!

The scheme was closed down in 2001 by the British National Crime Squad after eighteen months of operation, and both the Iranians and a Turkish drug baron, Ali Tore, were arrested. They were estimated to have laundered £4 million through the system. During the course of the investigation, police say they found 65 kilos of heroin. Tore, the ninth man to be charged in the operation, was convicted in October 2002 for conspiracy to distribute drugs. He was sentenced to 26 years in prison on drug charges and twelve years for money laundering.

International money movements are such a critical part of the drug money laundering process that the largest cartels and groups have devised a system for mingling dirty money with legitimate trade to keep their intentions from the authorities' gaze. This is called the Black Market Peso Exchange.

The Black Market Peso Exchange (BMPE)

Over the last 20 years, as the U.S. drug industry has expanded, U.S. cash flows have been transported to South America by a quasi-barter system. This has been given the name the Black Market Peso Exchange (BMPE). The BMPE is said to total $500 billion a year. Those involved in setting up BMPE structures require sophisticated invoicing systems together with a knowledge of international law and regulation.

The BMPE is operated by currency dealers catering to the demands of Colombian black market importers. These currency dealers acquire a supply of dollars from drug dealers in American bank accounts. The Colombian importers' requirement for dollars abroad match the drug exporters' need for pesos at home. The black market peso broker services all parties to the transaction.

The scheme enables Colombian importers to evade currency controls and taxes and duty on imported goods. Colombian importers need an unofficial channel to buy foreign currencies, mostly U.S. dollars. Savings made by evading taxes and duties back home compensate for the premium charged over official rates. A DEA official expressed it in these terms, "A lot of the money was going into Panama because it was a tax haven. The secrecy provisions in its law meant that it could accommodate customers of all types and that includes criminals. We saw people depositing $100,000 today and immediately transferring it by wire to a tax haven country. That type of activity was suspicious because it couldn't be substantiated with some legiti-mate business rationale. The launderers had realized that the best place to hide a tree was in a forest."

The theory of the system is similar to that which underlies hawala bank-ing. Hawala banking is described in detail in Chapter 11. A Colombian importer who wishes to buy a number of American refrigerators, but wants to evade import duties, obtains dollars through a source that chooses not to alert his government to his intentions. A drug baron, on the other hand, is sitting on a pile of dollars in the United States but needs to make a payment in pesos to a Colombian farmer for his next consignment of cocaine. Clearly he too wishes to avoid the attentions of the authorities in both countries. A broker then matches the two parties.

The drug baron's dollars can be used to pay for the refrigerators and the refrigerator importer's pesos can be used to pay for the coca. The goods that have been purchased in North America are then shipped to a destination in the Caribbean or South America from where they can be smuggled into Colombia and delivered to the customer, while the Colombian coca farmer receives his pesos in cash or check, as he prefers. In this way, the transactions can be completed without any exchange of currencies or any movement of money across the national borders.

The peso broker has to overcome a number of problems to make the dollar payment for the American goods. A cash payment to the American supplier direct from the drug dealer's stash house is the least sophisticated route. Another is to "smurf" the money, that is, to break it up into smaller chunks that go below the bank's minimum reporting requirements, and put it into the peso broker's accounts in the United States or smuggle it into Mexico and smurf it there. This allows the broker to write checks or get a bank draft to pay for the goods. The cash can also be used to purchase small-denomination money orders which are then passed on to the American exporter.

This method appears to have been used by Colombian drug dealers involved in the purchase of a helicopter from Bell Helicopter, the large American company. The transaction started when a representative of Victor Carranza approached Bell in Colombia. Carranza owns emerald mines in South America, and is said by U.S. officials to have links to the drug trade and to right-wing political groups. Bell appeared to have had no scruples about dealing with Carranza, although the company later denied that it knew that it had received any drug money. The deal went ahead, but Bell was paid in a most extraordinary way. The company received no less than 26 payments totalling $1,029,000 from Americans who had no connection with the ostensible purchaser, namely Carranza. The DEA saw the unmistakeable stamp of a black market peso transaction and on August 4, 2000, seized the helicopter.

The BMPE involves apparently legitimate transactions as well as blatantly corrupt ones. The DEA officer explained, "The accounts we looked at before obviously attracted our suspicion because they were used to receive and transmit suspiciously large cash payments. The accounts we look at now are receiving and transmitting wire transfers, bankers' acceptances, and letters of credit from legitimate companies like Sony, Philip Morris, or General Electric."

The DEA's response to the suspicion of a BMPE deal is to mount an undercover operation to gain the drug dealer's confidence to see where he is sending his money. The DEA officer described the process by stating, "We would pose as money launderers in our own right and be able to tell the trafficker or the money launderer, listen, you let us launder your drug proceeds and we will collect your U.S. dollars here in the U.S. and wire it under your instructions to whoever you want, be it to an accountant here in the U.S., be it to an offshore tax haven, be it in payment for goods as yet to be shipped directly from the free zone or from the U.S. The only limitation to this approach is that when you are buying drugs undercover you can only work your way up so far within the organization. The highest echelons are not going to be involved with the drugs per se! Certainly not with multi-ounce or multi-kilo quantities, not even with 500-kilo shipments. They will end up separating themselves in order to insulate themselves from that kind of criminal activity."

The officer continued, "Peso brokers work for a multitude of drug traffickers. They will end up having perhaps as many as ten contracts to fill in the course of a week. They may have three contracts of drug cash to pick up in New York, three in Miami, two in Chicago, leaving two in Los Angeles—a total of ten. He is someone who goes around to various drops and picks up large quantities of cash. As an undercover operator, I may be dealing directly with Colombians. They say, ok fine, you pick up $300,000 in New York, well I want your courier to contact me on this particular telephone number and we will make the arrangements to pick up the money. The individual will bring the money. The undercover guys will engage them in conversation to identify that those monies that he believed he delivered were in fact from drugs."

The largest peso brokers juggle many deals of this kind at one time. They also work for many drug traffickers, and so have a range of currencies on their books which they trade like any currency exchange or commercial bank. The result is an industrial activity of quite enormous proportions, with some sources estimating it at over $500 billion.

One cross-border trading scam worked like this. A General Electric washing machine purchased in the United States and brought legally into Colombia attracts substantial tariffs and excise taxes that have to be paid before the shipment arrives.

Expert operators on the black market order 100 washing machines at $200 each, making a total of $200,000. The machines are then shipped out of a free zone, like Panama or Antigua, where they are not taxed or subject to any import or export controls. The order is placed in the United States and the payment made in the United States. The shipment will go from the free zones where there are no taxes and if smuggled into Colombia there are no tariffs or taxes.

Colombians in Colombia buy the machines, paying with pesos as Colombian law prohibits them from owning foreign U.S. currency. The broker must now pay General Electric the $200,000 with dollars.

The black market peso broker brings together the drug trafficker and an appliance wholesaler that deals in black market goods. The drug trafficker has $200,000 in the United States of drug proceeds and wants pesos. He pays the black market peso broker a 10 percent commission, so the broker pays the drug dealer $180,000 worth of Colombian pesos.

The remaining part of the transaction is the $200,000 payment to General Electric, or to an importer in Miami with its inventory in Panama's free zone. The broker arranges for the payment, charging the drug dealer a 10 percent commission on the U.S. dollars, a total of $220,000, to add to the commission he receives on the pesos. The broker makes that payment in U.S. dollars to allow the corporation in Miami to be able to send those goods.

Once the broker has lined up his $180,000 worth of Colombian pesos, he arranges for the dollars to be paid to the U.S. supplier and that triggers the shipment of washing machines into Colombia.

The scheme poses particular problems for investigators as it bypasses many of the standard money laundering red flags. Said one FBI officer, "You are now no longer looking necessarily at only cash transactions with wire transfers going to tax haven countries. In this case, wire transfers, bankers acceptances, and letters of credit issued from a suspicious bank account have been paid into reputable companies like Sony, Philip Morris, or General Electric."

Payments resulting from an international transaction need to be assessed for prudence and legality, whatever the prestige of the operating company or the size of the sale. The DEA official said, "What does that tell you if you receive a payment from two different entities, one in New York, one in Los Angeles for a total of $200,000 dollars for goods to be shipped to yet a third company? There is something suspicious! If you have a wholesaler in Colombia wishing to buy ten washing machines, they would simply set up a wire transfer payment for $200,000 from Colombia directly to your account. It would be more normal to have a letter of credit if they assume that they are going to be buying ten washing machines every other month. The revolving letter of credit affords commercial guarantees and assurance. Otherwise you leave yourself open to the possibility that the goods are never shipped or that the goods don't meet the specifications laid out in the original invoice."

An Afterword on Drugs

If people are prepared to spend so much of their money on something they know is deeply destructive to themselves and no one else, perhaps they should be allowed to do so legally and take the consequences. Legalization would have enormous consequences for the laundering sector of the economy. It would open up the market in drugs and introduce competition between suppliers. On the other hand, drug dealers would have to start paying taxes to their governments rather than to their cartel chiefs. The effect on the industry's revenue might well be neutral.

The effect on the law enforcement and the anti-money laundering industry would be catastrophic. For that reason, if for no other, legalization, even if it were desirable, looks a long way away, if ever!

Drug money gets converted into numerous other commodities as well as cash. Prime among them is cigarettes, of which no less than one third of a billion are smuggled every year. This dirty trade is analyzed next.

Chapter 8

Smoking Guns

Countries with less developed economies and rickety law enforcement structures are most vulnerable to manipulation by money launderers. These countries have been targeted by those involved in trading low-value objects like cigarettes and high-value objects like diamonds. The following chapter examines an instance of alleged cigarette laundering where the major manufacturer, R.J. Reynolds, is alleged to have an involvement.

CIGARETTE SMUGGLING HAS MUSHROOMED in recent times due to high levels of duty, transportability, light penalties relative to those for drug trafficking, and profits available to the smuggler. It is estimated that the importer makes around €1 million of profit on a single 40-foot shipping container.

Colombian cartels import, arguably with the connivance of multinational companies, large amounts of cigarettes and whisky into tax-free zones in Aruba or Panama where they are acquired for dollars. The trade suits the multinational company, which is persuaded it can only break into a market by playing to the local rules.

This case has been argued most strongly by the European Community, which brought a civil lawsuit in October 2002 against R.J.R. Nabisco, R.J. Reynolds Tobacco Company, and a number of other related companies in the U.S. District Court in the Eastern District of New York. R.J. Reynolds Tobacco Company is the second-largest cigarette maker in the United States, manufacturing about one out of every four cigarettes sold there. Reynolds Tobacco's products include Camel, Winston, and Salem. R.J.R. Nabisco is contesting the European Community's lawsuit.

Smuggling claims were dismissed by the District Court on a technicality in 2002, but the judge also confirmed that the European Community and EU Member States had the right to proceed with their money laundering claims in separate lawsuits. The EC appears to be determined to do so. "Fighting fraud and the illegal trade in cigarettes remains a top priority," said European Union Budget Commissioner Michaele Schreyer. "The Commission is not giving up on its battle against tobacco smuggling and money laundering."

One step along the path to eliminate cigarette smuggling was taken on July 9, 2004, when the European Commission reached an agreement with Philip Morris to settle claims that it was involved in cigarette smuggling. In the deal, Philip Morris International (PMI) agreed to pay $1.25 billion over 12 years. The agreement with PMI said that the company "incorporates and builds into a comprehensive contractual framework Philip Morris International's existing money laundering policies." The agreement states later, "PMI will mark certain packaging with information indicating the intended market of retail sale, mark 'master cases of cigarettes' with machine-scannable barcode labels and implement other procedures useful for the tracking and tracing of its products."

The European Community claims that it loses around €1 billion a year of tax revenues through the illegal cigarette trade, according to UCLAF, the European Community's police agency, in its 1996 Annual Report. Smugglers target consumer demand in markets where tobacco carries the highest taxes, in particular the United Kingdom. Many of the seized cigarettes are brands produced in the United Kingdom. A World Bank publication in 1999 estimated that around a third of all cigarettes exported are smuggled and reappear on the world's black markets. Approximately one trillion cigarettes are exported in any year, and 350 billion of these are illegal.

Seizures made in the European Union over the last few years indicate the scale of the business and its recent growth. Seizures are numbered in terms of "master cases," each of which contains 10,000 cigarettes. The reported seizures are as follows:

    1997 - 264,250 master cases
    1998 - 471,935 master cases
    1999 - 569,010 master cases
    2000 - 623,250 master cases

Cigarette smuggling cannot be detached from smuggling of other illegal goods, such as weapons, drugs, and humans. Networks and routes designed for one product can be converted by organized gangs to carry a different product according to consumer demand. Gangs have particular interests and capacities, so tobacco smuggling is most closely identified with organized crime groups in Naples, called the Camorra, according to the Italian Parliament Anti-Mafia Committee in its report on the Camorra.

Weak confiscation measures mean that no more than 10 percent of the contraband tobacco is seized on the black market, while low fines (no more than between two and ten times the amount of the tax evaded) are not a deterrent to would-be smugglers.

Berlin-based Vietnamese mafia and Italian, Montenegrin, and Albanian gangs throughout central Europe control the illegal trade. Violence is endemic. Criminal gangs offloading cargoes of smuggled cigarettes in the south of Italy take the precaution of having homemade armored jeeps waiting at the dockside to take receipt of the cigarette shipments. Several police officers attempting to intercept these convoys have been killed or injured.

Gangs use three modes of transport to bring the contraband into Italy: high-speed motorboats take cigarettes from the Adriatic coast of Albania and the former Yugoslavia into Italy; motorboats or fishing boats transship loads from "parent ships" stationed outside territorial waters to the Italian coast; and roll-on/roll-off ferries take containers of cigarettes, usually secreted in other cargoes, into major ports.

Smugglers employ many techniques to obscure the acquisition, movement, and sale of illegal cigarettes. The acquisition process is obscured by the establishment of "intermediary companies" in Switzerland, Liechtenstein, Andorra, the British Virgin Islands, Panama, and Belize. The handling of illegal cigarettes is disguised by unloading and reloading cargoes several times in different countries.

The illegal cigarette trade is funded with cash produced from the sale of drugs. The exchange process between the dirty cash and the smuggled cigarettes is managed through a series of complex transactions. When a Colombian drug baron sells products in the backstreets of Europe's capitals, he is left with a surplus of euros, which he needs to swap into pesos that can be used back at home. Meanwhile, a company importing cigarettes to Colombia from the United States has a surplus of pesos from their domestic sales, which they need to convert to U.S. dollars away from the scrutiny of any tax or regulatory authority.

A black market currency broker buys pesos from the local cigarette vendor (whose crime at this stage may just be tax evasion) in exchange for U.S. dollars. He then sells the dollars he bought to the drug dealer in exchange for euros. In turn, a separate cartel buying black market cigarettes from a European supplier might purchase the euros from the money brokering exchange for local pesos from a previous deal and so the cycle goes around.

Each of the parties has benefited from the exchange:

- The drug trafficker has converted the proceeds of his foreign sales into domestic currency that he can take as profit or use as investment capital.

- The U.S. and European cigarette suppliers have been paid in their local currencies, which helps them avoid the need to explain why they have such large reserves of Colombian pesos in their coffers.

- The currency broker has taken a percentage from each exchange in the cycle as his fee.

In theory, everyone is happy. In practice, the funds that make the black market exchange cycle work come directly from the sale of drugs. The cycle itself launders the drug money and allows its reinvestment by the cartels. People buying black market cigarettes around the world are unknowingly funding the trafficking and trade of illegal "class A" drugs. Ironically, the Colombian drug cartels have learned that black market cigarette trafficking is highly profitable while remaining less risky and carrying lighter sentences than trading in their core domestic products. The logical next step was to enter this market in force.

Trading in drugs and cigarettes differs primarily in terms of volume of the smuggled product. Where cocaine with a street value of several million dollars can be carried across a border by one "mule," cigarettes of comparable value require a container. The cartels learned how to transport bulky cargoes in secret from their criminal connections in the former Soviet Union and in China—the experts in trafficking people. These connections form the inextricable link between the illegal import of cigarettes and the smuggling of people into the West for prostitution and slavery.

The money broker in the transaction acts as a "cut-out" by creating a layer of activity between the participants and those receiving the proceeds.

A cigarette manufacturer sells its product to criminal distribution channels using wholesalers to reduce its risk of exposure.

Organized crime has long been involved in the distribution of cigarettes. As early as 1978, the U.S. Senate began to investigate links between New York's Colombo crime family and Colombian cocaine traffickers on the one hand and Russian heroin dealers and their distributors in Switzerland, Panama, the Caribbean, and Eastern Europe on the other.

In 1994, Colombian cocaine barons were shown to be using profits from drug sales in U.S. dollars to pay for cigarettes. These cigarettes were smuggled into Colombia, providing cocaine traffickers with a source of pesos as well as an alibi for the source of their wealth. Cocaine sales were facilitated through money laundering operations in Colombia, Panama, and Switzerland.

Cigarette sales, money laundering, and organized crime are linked, says Jimmy Gurulé, Under Secretary of Treasury for Enforcement in the United States. He argues money laundering takes place on a global scale and that the black market peso exchange, though based in the Western hemisphere, affects business around the world. Gurulé also has responsibility for tracking down Al Qaida.

The EU has made allegations of cigarette smuggling against Gilbert Llorens, Luis Garcia Manolo (also known as il Spanolo), Patrick Laurent, and Patrick Monnier, dubbed 'the fabulous four.' They allegedly bought their way into the top echelons of the government of Montenegro, at that time a country in a state of complete lawlessness, to set up a state vehicle called the Montenegrin Tabak Transit (MTT). MTT acted as an agency to transfer cigarettes to Italian crime groups through Montenegro. Their supporters were the Foreign Investment Agency and, allegedly, the Prime Minister of Montenegro, Milo Djukanovic himself. The local mafia killed the Montenegrin journalist who investigated this case of corruption in May 2004.

Dirty trade attracts corruption, so throughout the 1990s substantial sums were paid to public officials in Montenegro to protect cargoes of cigarettes as they passed through a country where war was raging and no streets were safe. Security came at a price, and Zetatrans, the official Montenegrin freight transporter that handled all the cigarettes passing through Montenegro, was paid around $30 for each case of cigarettes. This money was divided among the many Montenegrin officials who controlled licenses to ship the cigarettes. Beneficiaries allegedly included Djukanovic, as well as the former head of the Montenegrin Foreign Investment Agency.

According to the EU complaint, a money-transmitting organization called Intercambi, based in Lugano and owned by Alfred Bossert, served as the intermediary handling the Italians' bribes and payments. Bossert held accounts at Swiss Banking Corporation and ABN AMRO. The transmitters also converted currencies for some subcontractors hired by the Italians. Corrado Bianchi, one customer of R.J.R. Nabisco, allegedly used Intercambi to transfer payments to R.J.Reynolds and other cigarette manufacturers. A group of money couriers transferred the criminal proceeds from Italy to Switzerland and then allegedly handed them over to Bossert.

The "fabulous four" were among those who used two Swiss companies, Algrado and Weitnauer, to create an alleged laundering scheme. Mingo Finance, a British Virgin Islands company, was used to open a series of bank accounts at the Bank of Liechtenstein to hold payments of criminal money for Algrado. Algrado employees, Renato Meyer, Diego Luchessa, and Oscar Ivanissevich, allegedly "neutralized and decoded" marks and numbers on cases of cigarettes to disguise shipments to a group of criminal customers. These customers allegedly used ships called the *Tara 1, Ali B, Bleu Diamond II*, and *Wendy I*.

Criminal money from the sale of arms and drugs was washed through a series of accounts at Bossert's organization. Bossert was also allegedly used by Gerardo Cuomo, an Italian living in Switzerland, subsequently indicted by the Italian authorities and convicted. Cuomo used a company called Maxim in Lugano to distribute cigarettes through Italian front companies.

Cuomo also set up companies located in Cyprus, Belgium, and Switzerland to create fronts to supply and distribute cigarettes. Each company had a bank account in a mainstream banking center. For example, according to the EU lawsuit, Kyro Avia and Old Navy Trading, both of Cyprus, had accounts at Union Bank of Switzerland in Basel; Van Caem (of Holland) and Rowill International (of Belgium) had accounts at KBC Bank in Holland; and Namari Holdings of Jersey had an account at Harris Bank International in New York. The money that Cuomo put through these accounts allegedly went back to R.J.R. Nabisco. Cuomo was convicted of cigarette smuggling in July 2001 and sentenced to 10 months community service. He was also excluded from Italy for five years.

R.J.R. Nabisco shipped cigarettes to off-the-shelf companies based in the Colon Free Trade Zone in Panama where secrecy laws prevented police from identifying the cigarettes' origins. Between October 1995 and April 1997, the company also shipped large quantities from Panama to Entire Warehousing in the United Kingdom, from where they were shipped to Spain. A customer of R.J.R., provided the cigarettes through distributors in Panama, thus allegedly disguising R.J.R.'s role in the process.

R.J.R. allegedly accepted payment by checks payable to intermediary companies, often through cut-out companies to disguise the transaction. But payments were also made directly to the account of an R.J.R. subsidiary in Puerto Rico using a numbered account that did not name R.J.R, the EU has contended. Those paying R.J.R. for cigarettes regularly changed banks to escape detection by U.S. law enforcement—a process known within R.J.R. as "musical banks," the complaint stated. This is a reference to the children's game, "musical chairs," where players circulate round chairs and must be seated when the music stops.

The complaint published by the European Community against R.J.R. Nabisco and others, lodged in the U.S. District Court, Eastern District of New York, also alleges that known money launderers met R.J.R. employees and gave them large quantities of cash in return for cigarettes. R.J.R. people traveled to Colombia via Venezuela every month. They allegedly paid bribes to guards at the Colombian border to escape having their passports stamped and then traveled by car to places like Maicao, a notoriously lawless area in Colombia, where they allegedly met money launderers and drug traders. They received payments for cigarettes in bulk cash denominated either in dollars or Venezuelan bolivars. They were also paid with checks. On their return journey, they are said to have bribed border guards at the Venezuelan border to ensure they were not searched and found with large amounts of money on their person. On reaching a major Venezuelan city like Maracaibo, they allegedly transmitted funds back to R.J.R. in the United States.

At different times in the 1990s, R.J.R. bought financial instruments called Brady Bonds. These were named after the former U.S. Secretary of the Treasury Nicholas Brady in association with the International Monetary Fund and the World Bank as part of an effort to restructure outstanding sovereign loans into liquid debt instruments. Brady Bonds carried a coupon, for which the principal and interest were collaterized by the U.S.

Treasury zero coupon bonds and other high-grade instruments. Brady Bonds are transferable and can be bought and sold at various exchanges. When R.J.R. was paid in bolivars, the currency of Venezuela, it bought Brady Bonds and transferred them to an exchange in New York where they were sold for dollars.

In the course of an investigation by a group of private bankers in the 1990s into the way that Brady Bonds were used as collateral in South America, it was concluded that the bonds were being bought by holders of pesos who were seeking the legitimacy of a U.S.-backed instrument that they could then use to negotiate to buy dollars. The private bankers' report further observed that the principle holders of pesos engaged in this dubious trade were Colombian and Venezuelan drug dealers.

During the nineties, when trade with Iraq was embargoed, the European Community's case against R.J.R. Nabisco, which the U.S. courts dismissed, alleged that the cigarette company had a sales network dedicated to selling cigarettes in Iraq. Its vehicle was a Liechtenstein company, Tradinter Middle East Development Establishment, which was allegedly controlled from 1989 by Abedl Hamid Damirji and a former R.J.R. employee, Issa Audeh.

When Iraq invaded Kuwait in the autumn of 1990, the cigarette operations moved to Jordan. The sales in Iraq continued, and according to the EU complaint, R.J.R. delivered large quantities of boxes of cigarettes to Damirji. In June 1991, R.J.R. purportedly delivered to Damirji seven full air-cargo shipments consisting of 17,000 master cases, with 10,000 cigarettes in each master case. R.J.R. sold Damirji 600,000 master cases between March 1991 and September 1992, with most reaching Iraq.

Between 1993 and 1995, Damirji acted as the exclusive distributor through Damirji's Liechtenstein company. But Damirji dropped out of the picture in January 1997, and R.J.R. allegedly began selling through Akshimpex Trading, an Iraqi-owned company, with offices in Bucharest and Sofia. The cigarettes were delivered from Puerto Rico to Valencia and then off-loaded and transported to ships bound for Cyprus. The cigarettes were briefly placed in warehouses before being moved through Mersin in Turkey to Dohuk in Iraq, the EU contended.

The Turkish port of embarkation enabled them to escape international sanctions. The Iraqi government and ruling family were aware of this cigarette trade, but R.J.R. allegedly sought to conceal the sale of shipments to

Iraq by transporting a quantity of cigarettes between Turkey and Belgium, and then back to Turkey, for onward sale to Iraq.

Again, the EU's claims have not been proven. But, whether or not R.J.R. Nabisco colluded with South American money launderers, the EU's account of money laundering on a global scale suggests the extent of the launderers' skills. An agent who can arrange cash movements across borders for one client and deal in Brady Bonds and other financial instruments for another is a valuable asset to the company wishing to operate in dangerous and unstable areas. But such an agent is completely oblivious to, and careless of, national and international law. His only law is self interest and self preservation.

Cigarettes from China

Rolandas Sackavickas was a furrier in the import/export business from Lithuania whose biggest business, according to police sources, was importing falsely branded cigarettes from China. He had made a lot of black money and needed a UK bank account. He found someone in the United Kingdom who wanted to get rich quick.

The Reichwald family fur company had banked at Midland Bank, which later changed its name to HSBC, for some sixty years, ever since the family had set up business in London as refugees from Nazi Germany. The business had prospered and the father handed it over to his son, Stephen. They were a respectable Jewish family, and the bank knew them, their business, and the pattern of their bank accounts. Then, a cash payment went through of some £180,000 that made the bank blink. The money was transmitted through Benex (see Chapter 2) on to the Bank of New York, and then to a Lithuanian company. It was a red flag with devastating consequences.

The bank notified the relevant authorities, who in turn instigated a police investigation. This resulted in the humiliation of the Reichwalds, the destruction of their business, and the imprisonment of Stephen.

The Lithuanian accounts to which Benex moved the money were owned by Rolandas Sackavickas. Sackavickas was desperate for a bank account when he met Stephen Reichwald on business in Finland in 1995. The two men did some fur trading together, with Sackavickas offering Reichwald some very favorable deals over the next three years. Then Sackavickas made his proposition to Reichwald. If Reichwald would allow Sackavickas to use his bank account to transmit money to Lithuania, he could take at least 2.5 percent of the proceeds. Reichwald was looking forward to retirement, and succumbed to his greed. He may initially have believed that the money was from legitimate trade, but quickly would learn otherwise.

Sackavickas put hundreds of thousands of pounds into Reichwald's account. He initially did it in the suspiciously large sums that had alerted the bank, but over time became more sophisticated and broke the money into packages of tens of thousands of pounds. This was "smurfed," so he paid it into different branches, but on the same day, and into the same account. It was amateurish money laundering, and it was obvious.

Up until this point, the authorities knew little about those working with Sackavickas and Reichwald. But then the bank came up trumps. It had asked Sackavickas for evidence of identity when he was paying a large amount of money into the account. He gave them a fax sent to his London hotel room. The bank kept the fax, and gave it to the police. They then watched the hotel, tracked Sackavickas, and, importantly, found that Sackavickas had a regular visitor. This was Brian Eddishaw, a businessman from the British Midlands with an interest in transportation and containers.

An investigation of Eddishaw revealed how Sackavickas made the cash that Reichwald was putting into his highly valued bank account. Sackavickas and Eddishaw were in the cigarette smuggling business. The demand on the UK streets for a product that was tax free made this immensely lucrative. Eddishaw managed the logistics for the British end of the operation, while Sackavickas saw to it that smuggled and largely counterfeit brands, exported illegally to Lithuania from China where they were manufactured, made the journey to the United Kingdom.

The markup on these fake brands, especially when the tobacco is composed of the sweepings and discards from pure tobacco, are vast. A box of twenty cigarettes of this kind leaving the factory costs between 25 and 30 pence but is sold on the streets, in the bars and clubs of London or the North of England, for around £2.50. This contrasts with the £4.50 charged for a legitimate box of properly made and branded cigarettes.

Sackavickas also bought properly made and genuinely branded cigarettes produced by British American Tobacco from companies based in Cyprus and the Canary Islands. These acted as offshore "cut-outs" to disguise the identity of the original purchaser.

The method of transporting these fake cigarettes replicated that used by drug dealers and for some time the police thought they might be dealing with drugs. They sent some of the currency to a laboratory which concluded they had not been handled by drug dealers.

The cigarettes were carried from Eastern Europe in large trucks, stacked under great quantities of wood to give the appearance that the truck's cargo was timber. When they reached the British port for disembarkation, Eddishaw provided Customs and Excise with documentation that he had forged. He stole the identity of a legally constituted company called Mason Timber to provide Customs with an apparently genuine value-added tax number. Customs would check this number, find that it related to a timber company, and provide the necessary documentation for importing timber.

The trucks made their way to a warehouse, called in the business the "slaughter point," where they would be discarded. The massive consignment of cigarettes was stored there. Eddishaw met street dealers at a point on a motorway some distance from the slaughter point so as not to give away its location to his customers. Street dealers brought their vans to the pick-up point, then Eddishaw drove them to the slaughter point, loaded them up, and returned to the meeting point. The dealers checked the contents, handed over the cash payments, and drove their loads away.

When a large amount of cash had accumulated, Eddishaw and Sackavickas brought in Reichwald to transmit the cash to Lithuania. Sackavickas and Reichwald went together to a branch of his bank in Central London where Reichwald filled out the relevant deposit form. He then presented the money. The bank later said that the trademark of this operation was the immaculate packaging of the money. The notes were kept tightly bound together with elastic bands.

Reichwald then arranged for the money to be moved from his sterling account into his dollar account and then sent, via Benex at the Bank of New York, on to Sackavickas's companies in Lithuania. Reichwald sought to create a paper trail to explain these payments by making up invoices from bogus companies in Russia. According to one source, "if he received $200,000, he would want to see several letters from companies called Globus and Uniastra, purporting to be his customers, asking him to send these monies elsewhere in respect of payments for fur business. So for every lump of money he had numerous pieces of paper, which covered him—or he thought that they covered him."

Sackavickas did not, of course, know that the police had got permission from the appropriate judicial authorities to install bugging and filming devices covering hotel rooms he occupied when he visited London to collect the money from Eddishaw. On the evening of January 25, 2001, the police installed themselves in the room at the Hilton Hotel in Central London adjoining that occupied by Sackavickas and his Lithuanian girlfriend.

The couple arrived in the afternoon and spent the evening talking about the cash they were expecting to receive from Eddishaw the following day. When Eddishaw arrived at the room in the morning, he was dragging a large suitcase on wheels. It was stuffed full of cash which, according to one observer, "was in pretty crap order and they were very particular about the way the cash should be packaged."

As the three eagerly applied themselves to the task of repackaging the cash, wrapping elastic bands round each bundle to keep it tight, Eddishaw complained that he needed more consignments of smuggled cigarettes than Sackavickas could supply. The verbal evidence of their involvement in a major British cigarette smuggling operation was conclusive, while the visual evidence of dirty cash demonstrated their intention to launder the money. With more film and videotape than they could possibly need to gain a conviction, the police moved in.

The police slapped handcuffs on the three, then searched the room and found a total of £330,000 worth of sterling notes, some on the floor, some in a wardrobe. The profits of crime were noted, filmed, and confiscated.

But the police had arrested Hamlet without the prince. For Reichwald was not at the hotel. He was pursuing his fur business in Russia when his partners were raided. But the police went from the hotel to Reichwald's house in Highgate, searched it, and found some £30,000 under the floorboards. They then called him on his mobile phone and informed him of the recent events, and that he was under arrest. He agreed to return, and he was met at the airport, formally charged, and convicted on 20 March 2003. Sackavikas was sentenced to seven years in prison, Reichwald received six years and Eddishaw received an eighteen-month sentence.

Global banks facilitate laundering by scoundrels like Sackavickas and they now enter our drama.

SECTION IV

Bad Banks

Chapter 9

Cover-up! Bankers
and Their Corrupt Clients

Dictators and corrupt politicians are a primary source of black money. Their influence and power enables them to extort wealth from citizens, opponents, and business people.

Private Banking

WHEN YOU TAKE OUT A LOAN FROM A BANK, it is very likely the money you borrow will at one time have passed through a bank account belonging to a dictator or a major drug dealer. The bank account is the primary layering vehicle of the launderer.

Virtually every bank courts the wealth of the rich and powerful, and although the super-rich do not walk through the same branch doors as the average high street customer, they need the bank's services just as badly. For dictators and corrupt politicians and public servants need financial networks that they can trust to smuggle their ill-gotten gains out of their country and put it into secure offshore havens where they can access it either to pay bribes or to secure a refuge if they get overthrown and sent into exile.

In fact, commercial banks set up separate departments for their rich and famous customers, called private banking departments, with tax experts who are masters of the arcana of the offshore world. They know where the dictator's cash should be hidden or where the tax avoider's cash can be kept lawfully but out of reach of his tax accountant. In recent times, the former President Slobodan Milosevic of Yugoslavia was found to have secreted millions in Cyprus, the former Palestinian leader Yasir Arafat had large sums in Switzerland, and leaders of Qatar had money stashed in the British offshore island of Jersey.

Private banks can be found within large banking corporations like Citigroup and HSBC. They also exist as separate entities occupying anonymous private houses on the streets of Geneva, Mayfair, Vaduz (in Liechtenstein), Vienna, Luxembourg or Manhattan. They are owned by their partners and guard their clients as if they were family members. The most famous of these discreet private banks are Swiss. They are over 200 years old, and have been serving the same European families for decades if not centuries. Their reputation for obstructiveness and insularity has haunted Switzerland in recent years, although some attempts have been made by national banking regulators to smarten up their act. We shall see.

The world of private banking has expanded as banks have exploited the profits available from this occasionally quite legitimate activity. So during the course of the 1990s most commercial banks—high street institutions like Barclays—and most investment banks—wholesale institutions like JP Morgan Chase—have set up private arms to serve the so-called high net worth individual. These private banks advise the wealthy (as well as handle their money). They also set up trusts for their children and buy and manage their investments. The banks also provide exceptional financial services like moving their clients' cash around the world.

Private bankers can serve as mentors and friends to the private clients they service. Courtesy of private banks, dictators have the resources and facilities to travel around the world in bulletproof limousines, stay at the world's finest hotels or villas in Switzerland, enjoy private medicine, and ensure themselves a pension when their time is up. The high living of Zaire's former President Mobutu or the grotesque excesses of Ferdinand Marcos were a blot on the banks that feted them while they were enjoying power similar to that acquired from the other, more technical financial scandals of recent years such as Enron or WorldCom. The citizens of poor countries were the losers in the first set of scandals, while shareholders and employees in rich countries lost out in the second set.

The paraphernalia of private banking includes some technical privileges like the facility to create "private investment corporations" (PICs) in locations where strict secrecy laws apply. Banks in these jurisdictions are prohibited by law from disclosing information about accounts or clients to regulators in onshore jurisdictions. The Permanent Subcommittee on Investigations of the Committee of Governmental Affairs of the United

States Senate reported: "Private banks keep pre-packaged PICs on the shelf, awaiting activation when a private bank client wants one. Shell companies in secrecy jurisdictions managed by shell corporations which serve as directors, officers and shareholders—shells within shells within shells, like Matryoshka dolls, which in the end can become impenetrable to legal process." Banks have provided the mechanics of banking secrecy even when the client's financial activities were suspicious and attracting the attention of regulators and law enforcement.

Contrary to general belief, privacy nowadays no longer extends to the numbered account. A numbered account allows a wealthy client to own an account distinguished only by a unique number, thus restricting the number of bankers who know of his existence to a minimal number in the bank's top echelon. Pressure from banking regulatory agencies has largely outlawed this practice. Austria lags behind international standards by maintaining a numbered bank account system known as the "postbook" account.

The amount of money slushing around the private accounts, put there by con artists, corrupt politicians, and those hiding money from divorced spouses or business partners, is vast. Senator Carl Levin, the chairman of the Senate's Permanent Subcommittee on Investigations (referred to above), has estimated that between $500 billion to $1 trillion of international criminal proceeds are moved internationally and deposited in a bank.

Corrupt banking stains the societies where the banks operate. The financial servants of corrupt dictators participate in the subversion of the country's economic and political systems. When Citibank was used by Asif Ali Zardari, the husband of ex-Prime Minister of Pakistan Benazir Bhutto, to handle what was alleged to be a bribe paid by a gold importer, they ensured that gold would cost more on the streets of Karachi. This incident is described in detail below.

When intermediaries, allegedly linked to the oil company Mobil, provided bribes to officials and politicians in Kazakhstan to buy influence, they added a cost to the country that will be reflected in the price the government receives for its oil. The courts have yet to decide whether banks that act as the conduits of bribes are also its targets. They certainly should be. Mobil denies any connection with these middlemen in 'Kazakhgate.'

The Senate Report into private banking

The lid was taken off private banking most dramatically in 1999 when the Senate's Permanent Subcommittee on Investigations conducted a detailed examination of the workings of Citibank's private banking department. Its subsequent report, "Private Banking: A Case Study of Opportunities and Vulnerabilities" (2000), gives a unique exposé of the workings of a private bank. The committee's interviewees ranged from account managers who had day-to-day control of each account to the bank's then chairman, John Reed. Reed squirmed and shuffled in his seat as the senators, led by Senator Levin, interrogated him on television.

The report's basic facts have not been challenged, and it has been used to provide evidence for this chapter. But one caveat needs to be made. The committee focused on a single bank to the exclusion of numerous similar institutions that were involved in identical activities. Some material in this chapter, drawn from other sources, refers to other banks, but the bulk of the evidence of appalling practice is leveled at Citibank. A number of American investigative agencies examined Citibank's private banking behavior in the wake of the Senate report, but the bank was never charged. It says it has since upgraded its money laundering rules and replaced its head of private banking.

Citibank's Dirty Clients

President Sani Abacha

Citibank was one of the primary beneficiaries of the cruel reign of President Sani Abacha of Nigeria. The bank, along with many others, was used by him to transfer funds as he pillaged the national treasury and removing the proceeds to London, Jersey, Switzerland, and other centers. A few politicians and unelected cronies became extremely rich as a result. For the rest, it was grinding poverty. A country that was rich in oil became so impoverished that the majority of the citizens were reduced to living on an income no greater than a dollar a day. It became a sick joke that, despite its huge oil resources, Nigeria was forced to ration gasoline, creating a massive black market.

Abacha's five-year rule over Nigeria ended with his death in 1998. Banks that had grown fat on the proceeds wept crocodile tears. Abacha was big business for them.

The financial abuse started inevitably at the top. President Abacha was surrounded by a group of corrupt and greedy men who used his power and authority to steal an estimated $3.5 billion from the national Exchequer. The money went from the Central Bank in the form of cash, telegraphic transfers, or traveler's checks into a local Nigerian bank. It was then passed to a series of major Western banks, which handled it without compunction or even the semblance of due diligence. Some Nigerian participants have explained the process in great detail in the course of subsequent legal actions brought by the Nigerian government to retrieve the money.

They have told how President Abacha's sons or advisers took letters written by the country's National Security Adviser at the President's behest to the governor of the country's Central Bank saying that the President requested money for "security reasons." The money was to be paid out of the State's own account at the Central Bank. The Governor was a friend of the Abachas and allegedly arranged for the president's assistant, Zazzawa Zafara, to have the cash stuffed into a minimum of twelve bags and a maximum of 15 bags. They were then loaded onto a truck that, surrounded by armored vehicles, went through the streets of Lagos directly to Abacha's presidential home.

Abacha's national security adviser, Ismaila Gwarzo, took immediate charge of the cash. He had responsibility for exporting and keeping the money safe, but he needed commercial guidance to ensure that the financial protocol was completed formally and quickly. So he contacted Abubakar Attiku Bagudu, a member of Abacha's close coterie and a Nigerian businessman with numerous bank accounts and many companies. Attiku Bagudu allegedly arranged for the money to be deposited at one of Nigeria's two main commercial banks, Inland Bank (Nigeria) and Union Bank of Nigeria.

Bagudu arranged for one of his companies to issue the government a contract to give the appearance of a legal transaction. The money had then to be exported out of the country into accounts at international banks that corrupt Nigerian business people could access to pick up their bribes. The pretext for one major payment (of $5 million) from the Central Bank was to finance an international operation to improve the image of Nigeria by launching a campaign directed at opponents of the regime inside Nigeria. Another payment—a mixture of dollars ($30 million) and Sterling (£15 million)—was said to be directed at "aiding neighbouring countries."

Once the contract paperwork was in order, Gwarzo went to the Minister of Finance Anthony Ani, who allegedly gave the formal authorization. The country's strict foreign exchange controls required Ani to produce a piece of paper requesting the Governor of the Central Bank to permit the export of money.

This process, which was very carefully fulfilled to the letter of the law, resulted in many transfers of cash from Nigeria to secret accounts owned by the Abacha family and their corrupt coterie outside the country.

In the course of his evidence to the Swiss regulators, Bagudu described many of the fund transfers in great detail. He talked about fifteen sizeable payments from Inland Bank (Nigeria) to international bank accounts controlled by the Abachas and their circle; he referred to six transfers from Nigerian banks to the Morgan Procurements account, controlled by the Abachas, at Union Bank of Nigeria in London. He detailed five transfers, totalling some $10 million, from Nigerian banks to the Navarrio account (controlled by the Abachas) at Citibank in London. Other transfers were made to Nigerian accounts at London branches of Merrill Lynch ($3 million), ANZ Banking Group ($320,000), Commerzbank ($3.5 million), and ANZ Grindlays ($18 million).

This research only scratches the surface of Abacha's depredations as Western officials estimate that over $3.5 billion was looted during Abacha's five years in power. More than $2.2 billion of this amount was said to have been taken from the Central Bank of Nigeria in the form of cash or checks.

This licensed robbery was aided and abetted by some of the world's most prestigious banks. The fact that a country's leading family was willing to steal so wantonly from their country is of course reprehensible. The negligence of the leading international banks in accepting money that was deposited by individuals and companies whom they failed to examine for honesty makes them equally culpable. Ancillaries to the crime, in this case "fences" to a burglary, are typically punished even more severely than the burglars themselves. Regrettably, no bank or banker has been severely punished as a result of the Abacha robbery.

Citibank was far from the only bank to handle Abacha's looted billions without compunction. Investigations that followed his death resulted in the freezing of stolen money in five Swiss banks. Moreover some fifteen other banks, largely in London, were also censured by the Financial Services Authority for the way they handled the money. A total of 36 banks are named by lawyers working for the Nigerian Government seeking redress from Abacha's heirs. British authorities refused formally to name the individual banks based in the United Kingdom and, due to the FSA's lack of legislative responsibility at the time, the bankers were not punished with fines or other penalties.

The appalling behavior of the Abacha regime, which the country endured between November 1993 (after the military coup that brought Abacha to power) and June 1998, was well established long before its financial depredations were discovered. Human rights abuses were so serious that the country became an international pariah. When Abacha executed eight opposition members, the country was expelled from the British Commonwealth in November 1995. A 1999 Nigeria Human Rights Report describes the Abacha administration as involving "years of terror and brutality" in which "extra-judicial killings, torture, assassinations, imprisonment and general harassment of critics and opponents was commonplace."

The international community failed to enforce powerful economic sanctions against this regime, so the men around the president had complete license to pillage the country's treasury. The president led the way, according to one observer, who described his reign thus: "Locked inside the presidential villa, whilst pillaging state funds, General Sani Abacha seemed only to listen to his sycophants and witchdoctors who prided themselves on protecting him from his enemies." A country demonstrating so little concern for the rule of law could also be expected to treat its own treasury recklessly. Bad men let off the leash would seek not only unfettered power but also unimaginable wealth. Yet leaders of the world's financial community closed their eyes to the Nigerians' financial excess, their money considered too good to turn away.

The presidential coterie who took most interest in the country's finances were National Security Adviser Ismaila Gwarzo, Finance Minister Anthony Ani, and friend of the family Attiku Bagudu. But members of the family also had their fingers in the national pot. These included President Abacha's sons, Mohammed Sani and Ibrahim Abacha, and his wife, Mariam.

Citibank were the chosen advisers to Mohammed, Ibrahim, and Abacha's other son Abba Abacha, who opened up accounts at the bank's Nigerian branch in 1988. The sons may not have started their looting yet, but they had their eyes firmly fixed on self-enrichment. The likelihood that their father would obtain power in 1992 prompted them to go to New York in that year to beef up their banking arrangements. Using a false passport, they were able to present false names, and the Citibank managers did not know the correct identity of their new clients for four years. One of the managers said later, "In February 1992 [one of] the Abacha brothers, Ibrahim Sani Abacha, came to New York to pick up some cash from our tellers. I found out that he was—he told me he was a businessman, that he was in the process of establishing an airline company that would run flights between Lagos and New York and decided that there was a need for an account at the Private Bank. At that time, there was no reference to the name Abacha. Ibrahim Sani—the name that was referred to was Sani."

The Senate subcommittee reported that "it is unclear whether either (of the two responsible managers) realized they were managing accounts for the sons of the Nigerian head of state, until sometime in 1996." In fact, the bank had not known the full identities of the Abacha sons since they first used Citibank as their trading institution, which was in 1988. This was demonstrated during a further exchange at the Senate subcommittee's hearing: "Prior to opening the New York accounts, Mr. Alain Ober obtained two bank references for the Abacha sons and also asked Mr. (Michael) Mathews for a reference."

In an email dated March 3, 1992 , Mr. Mathews wrote the following: "Ibrahim and Mohammed Sani are the son and adopted son of Zachary Abacha, a well-connected and respected member of the Northern Nigerian community. He has given his sons power to operate his accounts, and for the last three years they have been trading commodities through us, and the account has operated entirely satisfactorily, although balances have fluctuated wildly. In contrast to other Nigerians we have dealt with, I have found Ibrahim and Mohammed unfailingly charming, polite and, above all, reliable. . . . They are clearly target market by association, and the section of the Nigerian community that we should be dealing with."

The Citibank manager overseeing the account said he was "unaware for the first three years he handled the accounts that Mohammed and Ibrahim were the sons of the Nigerian military leader. He said that they used 'Sani' as their last name, rather than 'Abacha,' and he believed them to be ordinary Nigerian businessmen, rather than relatives of a public figure." Until the two men's identity came to light in January 1996 (apparently by accident), the bank thought their client was Mohamed Sani, the country's youth and sports minister.

Massive amounts of cash flowed through the bank accounts from the moment they were opened. Citibank provided a secretive "special name" account called Navarrio and a shell corporation called Morgan Procurement Corporation to handle the Abacha sons' fortune. Initially, the Nigerian money was said to have come from an airline. But when U.S. carriers pulled out of Lagos airport because of safety fears, the Abachas needed to provide other explanations for their funds.

A range of other businesses was established that included commodity trading, pharmaceutical import/export, petroleum trading, as well as personal investing. Although their business was rarely straightforward, Citibank showed no curiosity until the Abacha brothers went to Libya—a country the United States had boycotted since 1985 after bombing it in retaliation for some terror outrages—and Citibank sought assurance that the bank would not be exposed to Libyan deals.

The Abachas gave the assurance, and the bank accepted it without question. In a memorandum headed "Source of funds/Libya," one Citibank manager reported, "Ibrahim assured us that he is not engaged in any political activity and all transactions are directly on terms of his business contracts. My concern is heightened with the knowledge that he was with the Nigerian Ambassador in Libya plus the recent increase in the flow of funds into the account. For the two months December 1994 and January 1995, we have received in excess of $21m."

The bank's passive attitude to the wily Abachas could not have been better demonstrated than in their response to a brazen attempt by the brothers to cheat Citibank out of millions of dollars. The scam involved Abacha shell company Morgan Procurement Corporation's purchase of Pasteur Merieux vaccines for $111 million. The contract was a cozy inside deal, signed by the materfamilias Mrs. Mariam Abacha on behalf of her Nigerian Federal Ministry of Women Affairs.

Trivial documentation (a mere two pages) and an inflated price (roughly four times the market price) alerted Citibank to the scam and it stayed out of the deal. But in the course of an exchange of emails, the bank instinctively assumed that its clients were victims rather than perpetrators of the scam. "The client is a prominent and longstanding Nigerian customer," said one manager, "and therefore we need to be specific, clear and diplomatic in the way we present our concern about potential money laundering scams to which we feel he may be at risk."

The reply from the manager inside the bank stated: "I just do not feel right about this deal, it has 'typical' characteristics of a 4-1-9 [the typical fraudulent Nigerian 'begging' letter]. A women's group in Nigeria apparently has $210m to spend on vaccines and is prepared to pay $55m up front against a guarantee issued by Citibank, the value of the guarantee will reduce as goods are shipped—sound like a rum one to you?"

Although the deal proceeded without any Citibank financing, the profits from the deal, some $28 million, were credited to Abacha-controlled accounts at ANZ Banking Group and Citibank. The Citibank account called Morgan Procurement was later found to contain no less than $60 million.

The mysterious vaccines deal brought into the spotlight a number of British business associates of the Abachas, including David Jones, a major shareholder in the British company Smith and Tyers. Jones was believed to be a long-standing family friend of the Abachas, and Mohammed Abacha was a shareholder in Jones's company.

Jones had power of attorney to act over at least one of the Abacha accounts in London, and he came to prominence when he was found to be involved in a $1.25 million bank transfer from Germany to a United Kingdom account. This transfer followed the launching of investigations by Swiss and British authorities. Smith and Tyers had already received £300,000 from one of the Abacha's Citibank accounts in April 1996. Jones is also alleged to have acted as an agent for the Abachas between 1995 and 1997 when they were soliciting (from Citibank and elsewhere) the $111 million required to buy vaccines for Nigeria's "Expanded Program on Immunisation (EPI)." Jones was interviewed by British authorities in connection with the Abachas, but the matter was not pursued.

Another key participant in deals involving British banks was Ismaila Gwarzo, the National Security Adviser. He would later be found to have arranged for the Nigerian Central Bank to pay a billion dollars and half a billion pounds sterling into correspondent accounts at British and American banks. The London-based banks included Midland Bank (later taken over by HSBC) in Golders Green, a suburb of north London, and Barclays Bank at its Belgravia and Knightsbridge Business Centre in central London.

The owner of the Nigerian *bureau de change*, Ahmadu Daura, was another key player in the Abacha funds exporting scheme. Daura's "Sunshine" bureau was used to "launder numerous misappropriations of public funds and other secret commission payments," according to one source. Daura later admitted that Mohammed Sani Abacha had put more than $50 million through Sunshine for dispatch abroad. Daura was arrested at London's Heathrow Airport in March 1998 carrying a mere £3 million, which British customs officials confiscated believing it to be the proceeds of drug trafficking. The British government later returned the money to Nigeria, once the truth about Abacha's activities was exposed.

The methodical looting of the Nigerian Central Bank proceeded efficiently until General Abacha's death in 1998. Then the gang that had run the show lost their pilot, and the source of their claim to legitimacy. The result was a desperate scramble to remove cash out of the country, helter skelter, before the new political masters and their appointees caught up with them. The reliance on paperwork went by the board, and they resorted to naked smuggling of cash and valuable certificates across the border. Nigerians were traveling the world loaded down with millions of dollars urgently seeking banks that would relieve them of it without asking questions.

The danger that the family's wealth would be seized by British authorities, in the wake of his father's death, sent Mohammed Abacha to Citibank in a desperate bid to remove some money to more secret jurisdictions before it slipped out of his control. Abacha wanted not only a $39 million check, he also wanted it free of the penalties that would apply if he removed the money before the time deposit, in which it had been invested, matured.

Despite the well-publicized search for Abacha's stolen money, and the global freezing order placed on their funds, an obliging Citibanker approved a $39 million overdraft, which allowed the Abachas to transfer their funds to Swiss banks and elsewhere. The overdraft was the subject of fierce questioning of Citibank's chairman, John Reed, when he was brought as a witness before the Senate subcommittee. Reed floundered in embarrassment as he sought to explain this wanton breach of protocol. Mohammed Abacha was later arrested for the murder of Kudirat Abiola, the wife of the late opposition politician, Moshood Abiola. He was acquitted of this charge, but other charges of money laundering are being investigated and Abacha has been released on bail.

The Nigerian government, under its new head General Abdulsalami Abubakar, doggedly pursued the money stolen by Abacha and his cronies, and within a few months it had recovered $750 million. Abubakar's government was replaced by a new government under President Abasanjo, and this regime placed further pressure on international agencies to recover the stolen money. A London court issued an order in a civil suit in July 1999, freezing all accounts related to General Abacha at several London banks, including Citibank. Then Swiss authorities issued orders on October 14, 1999, freezing accounts held by Abacha family members and associates at five Swiss banks.

Many of the orders concerned money sitting in accounts that had been quickly identified as belonging to the Abacha coterie. But one issue was more complicated. This was an extraordinary scam involving a $2.5 billion debt buyback transaction involving a steel plant commissioned by the Nigerian government. The Nigerian government had issued letters of exchange with a face value of five billion Deutschmarks to Tyajpromexport, the Russian builders of the steel plant. The steel plant failed to perform, and it appeared that the Nigerian government did not intend to honor the letters of exchange. But the Abacha sons bought back the letters of exchange from the Russian builders at 20 percent of their face value. Then, in what can only have been a high-level act of corruption, the Abachas persuaded the Nigerian government to pay their private company, called Mecosta Securities, 65 percent of the notes' face value, some 973 million Deutschmarks.

This money was transferred from the Nigerian Central Bank to the Abachas' own bank accounts using ANZ Banking Group before being transferred on to Mecosta. The profit made by the Abachas was 491 million

Deutschmarks, according to Bagudu, a member of Abacha's close coterie, who later admitted a role in the transaction.

The proceeds from this particular scam were frozen by a Luxembourg court, until the Abachas agreed with their creditors to repay 300 million Deutschmarks plus interest and costs. But the case took a further twist when the Abachas refused to honor their agreement. The Nigerian government then used English courts to get their hands on Abacha assets in London.

Attiku Bagudu was a particular target of the British authorities as they tried to tie down Abacha money in London. A British court order froze many of his accounts. These included: one account holding $6 million, in the name of Aicha Bagudu and Attiku Bagudu at Citibank in London; two accounts in Bagudu's name at (the Swiss) Banque Union Privee holding £3 million; an account in Bagudu's name at London's Midland Bank holding £400,000; two accounts at Credit Agricole IndoSuez holding $10 million; Mecosta Securities (the Abacha family private company) also had an account at Credit Agricole IndoSuez that held $9 million.

While the British belatedly imposed freezing orders on these accounts, the Attorney General of Geneva, Bernard Bertossa, carried out a major investigation of Abacha's money in Switzerland. In the largest exercise ever undertaken by a Genevan magistrate, he froze 130 bank accounts containing a total of $645 million. Investigations in France of Elf Aquitaine, the oil company, revealed that it had made corrupt payments to Abacha and his coterie.

The British Financial Services Authority conducted its own investigation of British banks' involvement in the Abacha scandal and unearthed one account of particular importance. The account, called Umbria, which had been established in 1996 at Union Bank of Switzerland in Zurich (UBS), was held in the name of Uri David, an Israeli citizen and businessman living in London's plush Hampstead district who was also a major donor to the British Labour Party. Umbria was found to contain $60 million thought to belong to the Abacha family.

This money could have been familiar to UBS as it is thought it had earlier been deposited by a company called Rigi Consulting in an account called Dihedral. Dihedral had been closed down when UBS, called at that time Swiss Banking Corporation, expressed concern about its source. Rigi was an intermediary for the German company Ferrostaal—the winner of a contract to build an aluminum plant in Nigeria—and the money was assumed to be commissions paid by Ferrostaal to the Abachas.

A later investigation following the Abacha scandal suggested that Uri David had merely switched the $60 million from Dihedral to Umbria to overcome the bank's restraints. The bank professed surprise, and then embarrassment, when the money was discovered.

David had told them that the money belonged to two Nigerian businessmen and he held full power of attorney on their behalf when the account was opened in 1996. He assured the bank that the two men had no political background. The bank took his word for this reference, and did not require a passport from the "businessmen." Later, the Swiss Federal Banking Commission fined Union Bank of Switzerland 750,000 Swiss francs for this breach. Three years earlier, UBS's rival, Credit Suisse, was reprimanded by Swiss regulators for failing to exercise due diligence when accepting some $660 million of money related to Abacha.

In the course of a general examination of British banking's role in the Abacha money laundering, the FSA found that 23 banks in the United Kingdom had accounts linked to the Abachas. It reported that 15 of these banks had "significant control weaknesses." Phillip Thorpe, the FSA's managing director, said, "the extent of the weaknesses identified is frankly disappointing. . . . Potential breaches of the money laundering regulations are being discussed with the appropriate law enforcement authorities." The FSA said that its investigation identified 42 accounts linked to Abacha family members and close associates in the UK. Total turnover on the accounts amounted to $1.3 billion for the four years between 1996 and 2000. Some 98 percent of the $1.3 billion went through the fifteen banks with significant control weaknesses. Despite these censures, the FSA was unable to bring charges as Abacha's laundering activities occurred before the Financial Services and Markets Act was passed (at the end of 2000) giving the FSA authority to prosecute for breaches of the 1993 Money Laundering Regulations.

The Abacha affair ended with some recriminations between Swiss and British authorities over the speed and efficiency with which they had moved to freeze and seize the stolen Abacha money. Attorney General Bertossa later said that the British failed to move quickly or effectively enough against the responsible UK banks: "There was or is still as much money in London as there is in Switzerland. The British authorities never started a single money laundering investigation. They cooperated in freezing money and they gave assistance to other countries but they never started any of their own investigations. They are not prosecuting anybody in England for money laundering. One thing that is sure is that among the main launderers involved in the Abacha case there is a friend of the Abacha family who is living in London."

British inefficiency was the target of a number of articles and editorials in the *Financial Times*. According to the one of those articles, the investigation was hampered terribly by the British: "The UK government has been asked to help trace the money deposited in London, but has failed to respond more than four months after the request was made. UK officials say they lack the power to freeze accounts and seize documents until charges have been brought in Nigeria . . . the Nigerian government . . . has collected more than 100,000 pages of documents to establish the routes used by the Abacha family and their collaborators to spirit funds out of the country . . . the trail has led to accounts at London offices of fifteen banks. They include Barclays, HSBC, Standard Chartered, Citigroup, Merrill Lynch and Australia & New Zealand Banking Group."

In another article, the paper stated, "More than $300 million flowed through London on its way to or from Switzerland. The total deposited in banks located in the UK is likely to have been far greater. But while ministers have lectured offshore financial centres on the iniquities of money laundering they have failed for four months to respond to a request to co-operate with Nigerian investigators."

Banks that handled the Abacha money were justifiably the butt of much criticism. But some in the City of London came to their defense. One lawyer commented, "Some of this money comes to them in the form of trusts, referred to them by very reputable firms of lawyers and accountants. It's not just an Abacha en famille, turning up on the doorstep with a bag of blood-stained dollars or squiffy Deutschmarks, it comes through a whole variety of respectable and quasi-respectable referrals."

A representative of the Serious Fraud Office also sought to minimize the banks' culpability: "The individuals concerned in Abacha weren't representatives of the country but they were family members and their wealth was probably not questioned! I cannot quite imagine Prince Charles going abroad and wanting to open an account in Liechtenstein, but he probably wouldn't be questioned because his physical presence would be enough for people not to question him. That's the bottom line."

A much less apologetic and compromising stance was taken by Nigerian President Abasanjo, the man who had to pick up the pieces, clean out the Augean Stables made filthy by the Abachas, and retrieve some of the money they had stolen from his country. "Bankers, go-betweens and wheeler-dealers gave their support to this criminal organization. No country should allow despots to use the Western system to hide stolen money." It is a message the Western banking system has yet to heed.

Citibank's culpability does not stop with President Abacha. The Senate Committee investigated three other instances where the bank was glaringly hand in glove with wrongdoers. These cases, like that of Abacha, continue to tarnish the image of the banks involved. They are described below.

President Bongo of Gabon—The Price of Democracy

Citibank watched Gabonese President Bongo's millions going into his bank accounts and coming out of his bank accounts. But neither the source of the money nor its destination concerned them unduly. As professional bankers, they provided merely the techniques that ensured it moved between accounts seamlessly and secretly.

The bank handled extraordinary amounts of money for the head of a tiny West African country like Gabon, which has a population of just 1.2 million and a GDP of $7.3 billion. In the course of one year, the bank allowed Gabon's president to deposit and move around no less than $111 million. Even allowing for the country's rich oil reserves—it is the third-largest oil-producing state in Africa—this was wealth far beyond the earning capacity of a single elected politician.

The fact that El Haj Omar Bongo (as he is properly called after his election as president) was an embezzler on a grand scale was not fully revealed until the Elf Aquitaine scandal broke in France, revealing payments from the gasoline producer to Bongo and other African oil tycoons.

Bongo employed Citibank to set up structures involving complex movements of money and name swaps to obscure the origin of the funds.

He was able to obtain multiple loans from the private bank, collateralized by his deposits, which were issued under an arrangement in which the private bank allowed President Bongo's accounts at Citibank Gabon to incur multi-million-dollar overdrafts. These were immediately covered by transfers from Bongo accounts in Paris, which were in turn covered by transfers from offshore accounts belonging to "Tendin"—the code name used by Citibank officers to refer to Bongo in internal correspondence.

Multiple transfers of this kind make little sense and are costly and slow, but Bongo wanted every device to ensure his staff could not discover the sources and whereabouts of his money, with the attendant risk of robbery, blackmail, or exposure. The price the bank charged for these complex arrangements was less important than the fact that the money was shifted efficiently and by a particularly untraceable route. Bongo had many options for the route his money could take as he had accounts at Citibank offices in Bahrain, Gabon, Jersey, London, Luxembourg, New York, Paris, and Switzerland. His many accounts had obscure names like Tendin Investments, a Bahamian shell corporation; Leontine; and OS.

The beneficiaries of these movements were Bongo's political appointees who ensured his repeated re-election, as the bank was well aware; an internal memo recorded that Citibank suspected that loans made to Bongo were "used to finance last re-election campaign," referring to President Bongo's successful re-election to office in December 1993. The winner of five elections, Bongo, born in 1935, has been the country's head of state since the mid-1960s. He is expected to obtain yet another term in 2005.

The internal Citibank document goes on to say, "The only risk really associated with this credit is the so-called 'political' one, i.e. the supposedly negative consequences which may result from a public knowledge of the credit transactions.... A stigma is more likely to be attached to the large deposits the client has with us overseas if this were to be known. A credit relationship does not have the same impact. ... The U.S. press would give political disturbances very limited coverage."

Bongo accounts were protected with lurid code names indicating perhaps the President's own preferences. He requested a code at one point to describe his account transactions based on the phrases "NEW YORK USA" and "Fort Knox Securities."

An almost paranoid obsession with security and secrecy kept Bongo's bank on its toes. One Citibank private bank official in Africa stated that he does "not have any problems with the large deposits held in New York by President Bongo, providing information concerning them is kept completely confidential." Another Citibank document stated, "This is a highly confidential transaction given the identity of the borrower. It is therefore recommended that this package not be circulated as usual by the Credit Department, but directly reviewed by" certain senior private bank personnel.

A slew of accounts were created in the mid-1990s in which Bongo's chief oil adviser, Samuel Dossou, was a signatory and had power of attorney. These had mysterious names, so the account called simply OS was launched with a $5 million payment from an oil company. This is now suspected to have been a payment from Elf Aquitaine, the French oil company. Citibank later justified secrecy, saying that oil revenues are a particularly sensitive matter in Gabon, because "oil revenues provide the largest source of government funds, and there are longstanding rumors of government corruption involving the oil industry, including government officials diverting oil revenues from the public treasury and receiving bribes from oil companies." The account was opened around the same time that the IMF (International Monetary Fund) completed a new loan agreement with Gabon imposing new restrictions on oil revenues and greater accounting controls.

The Federal Reserve took an interest in the source of Bongo's money in 1996 as part of a routine examination of U.S. private banking. Citibank's managers were forced to rummage through their back files when asked to identify the source of the initial $52 million deposited into the account. The rummaging was to no effect. They had not the faintest idea of the source or the destination of their client's funds as this revealing exchange of internal memos demonstrates.

One manager wrote to another, "The Federal Examiners are auditing the Tendin Account. . . . There is one major issue which remains unresolved. . . . You may remember that this account was opened in 1985 at [the Citibank private bank in New York] with $52m coming from a time deposit at Citibank Bahrain which was opened by Citibank Libreville on behalf of our client. . . . Bill indicated that the $52m were accumulated over several years at the Branch at the time you were there. Neither Bill nor myself ever asked our client where this money came from. My guess, as well as Bill's is that . . . the French Government/French oil companies (Elf) made 'donations' to him (very much like we give to PACs in the U.S.!). . . . Do you remember specifically where [the monies] came from . . . ?"

The email sent in response stated, in part, "Gabon resembles a Gulf Emirate in that Oil . . . accounts for 95% of revenues for a population of less than 1 million. It is clear therefore that Tendin Investments draws most of its wealth from oil, but we have no way of being more specific."

The managers made an indirect approach to the President, not wishing to arouse his concern, but he was less than forthcoming and the banker said later that he did not go directly to the President "for reasons of etiquette and protocol" and because he was "not sure what the reaction would have been."

The Federal Reserve examiners stated that they were not satisfied with the explanation for the source of funds and the use of loan proceeds. They also noted a comment by the private bank's legal counsel who said, "Citibank had considered ending the relationship . . . but they were concerned for the safety of the country officer in [Gabon], so the account remains open."

The Bongo account was still open and active in 1997, when the bank's profile accurately assessed the President's prime source of funds. "Self-made President of African oil producing country for 30 years. Wealth created as a result of position and connection to French oil companies (Elf) since country is major oil supplier to France. Wealth invested in real estate locally and in financial instruments overseas. It is believed that subject through affiliated [entities] retains ownership in many oil related ventures in the country which over the past 30 years resulted in significant accumulation of wealth estimated at $200m."

The Office of the Controller of the Currency (OCC), the U.S. government's regulator for domestic banks, began its own investigation of Bongo's source of wealth. This forced the bank to probe the accounts more assiduously. They interviewed "a Gabonese civil servant, a consultant to the President" about the source of his money. One Citibanker wrote to another about the interview. "I was pretty direct in my probing and the answers I received, although not comprehensive, give a better picture of

Gabonese public finances as they relate to the Presidency. . . . Every year, an overall allocation, loosely referred to as 'security' or 'political' funds, is voted into the budget across the operating and investment categories. Although not spelled out for obvious reasons, these funds are understood to be used at the discretion of the Presidency."

The President's personal entitlement was listed under four budget headings, according to the civil servant, with the sum of these entitlements amounting to 8.5 percent of the annual budget. That was no less than $111 million in 1995. President Bongo had "carte blanche" authority over government revenues, and because the $111 million in Gabon government funds was "sufficient to account for all of the monies in the Bongo accounts," the investigators did not press the private bank to obtain documentation of the President's oil interests or determine the source of particular and dubious deposits.

The OCC examiner noted, that "Citibank—Paris performed an analysis of Gabon's last published budget (1995) and found that President Bongo had approximately $111m, or 8.5% of the total 1995 budget of Gabon, at his disposal. 'It is the understanding of bank management that these funds are available to the Presidency, without limitation . . . ' President Bongo has substantial oil interests in Gabon and other African countries. When combined, these factors serve as support for the source of Tendin Investments funds."

The OCC examiner also noted, "Based on our review of the information in all related files . . . we conclude that this relationship and related transactions do not meet the level of suspicion expected for filing a Suspicious Transaction Report (STR) because . . . the transactions conducted through Citibank NA are the sort of transactions that the customer has historically been making and are normal for the Head of State of an African country."

This was later shown to be an extraordinary omission as the Senate subcommittee investigating Bongo's wealth concluded, after taking advice from academic experts, that the only subvention legally available to President Bongo from the country's budget was some $13 million rather than the $111 million. The experts reported: "The Gabon budget experts indicated that no recent Gabon budget authorizes the Gabon President to make personal use of government funds . . . . the assertion that these budget items openly authorized a $111 million set-aside for the President's personal use was inaccurate, implausible, and plainly contrary to Gabon's budget policy and actual spending."

The committee further picked over Bongo's accounts and found some most unusual payments. For example, a $30 million deposit into the Tendin account was undocumented. There was also plenty of evidence that Bongo's family used his Citibank accounts for their own purposes. They arranged for Citibank to transfer $1.6 million to the family for their visit to New York to attend the United Nation's 50th anniversary celebrations. Payments made to President Bongo's children were also made through Citibank. Citibank served not merely as a shadow Central Bank for the country, but also as the President's personal bank and the bank for all his family.

The OCC's complacency was blown open by the revelation in the course of five in-depth articles in *Le Monde* of murky details about millions of dollars in bribes paid by Elf to accounts at Citibank and two Swiss banks. One headline stated: "Omar Bongo Could Be Implicated in the Elf Affair." Bongo was now subjected to the full glare of international investigation. A shell corporation called Kourtas Investment and a special name account called Colette were linked to President Bongo through his oil advisor, Samuel Dossou. French criminal investigators requested Swiss authorities to freeze the accounts. The Swiss prosecutor defending the freezing of the Kourtas account declared in open court that President Bongo was "the head of an association of criminals." (August 6, 1997, *Le Monde*).

Many French politicians and businesspeople were exposed using funds belonging to Elf, an oil company owned until the mid-1990s by the French state, to make illegal payments to foreign politicians, many of whom were African. Those payments totaled three billion French francs, and were allegedly authorized at the highest levels of government to further France's political ends.

Bongo's paymaster at Elf was André Tarallo, a senior Elf executive, who was described as the oil company's "pro-consul for Africa." Tarallo is alleged to have presided over a system in which Elf profited from African oil, in exchange for providing political protection and secret offshore payoffs to African leaders. When bank statements were disclosed showing that 600 million French francs ($97 million) passed between Tarallo's Swiss bank accounts and accounts belonging to the president of Gabon, Tarallo was removed from the company.

Leaders from newly independent West African states with close ties to France particularly benefited from the Tarallo system. Other participants in Elf's African network were André Guelfi, who made a fortune with his African fishing fleet, and Daniel Leandri, a former policeman and Africa specialist who was a close aide to Charles Pasqua. Pasqua, the former French Minister of Interior, was found to have been heavily implicated in Elf.

President Bongo blamed the French government and in particular its President, Jacques Chirac, for the revelation of his role in Elf's activities. He sent an angry letter to Chirac on March 18, 1997, demanding that he put a stop to the investigation being pursued by Eva Joly, the legendary French investigative magistrate who exposed the Elf scandal. Bongo telephoned him late at night on March 29 to cancel a state visit to France planned for April in protest at the ongoing criminal probe. The (British) *Guardian* newspaper carried an article entitled "Gabon Chief Threatens Oil Deals After Fraud Charges" revealing that Bongo switched a contract from Elf Aquitaine to a South African oil company as a result of Joly's investigations.

While the brickbats flew, Citibank was desperately calming its client's feathers. Internal advice between bankers was to keep heads down. One manager said at the time, "I feel quite strongly that all of us need to be very thoughtful and selective about the press coverage we choose to interpret and share about our top customers. . . . I am unable to interpret the current press allegations insofar as they might touch upon the Bank but would not be tempted to try because of the doubts it could raise in people's minds about our own relationship with our customer. . . . We ought to be extremely careful about sharing such information with regulatory authorities, because we can't answer for it. . . . We should stay as far away as possible from this mess, unless and until any one of us has firm or verifiable evidence which would lead us to suspect the Bank's interests are at risk."

For some time, the bank assessed that Bongo's business was too good to lose. There also remained the risk that Bongo's friends and associates who live in Africa and in France might pull out of the bank alongside their patron. But in late 1998, the head of private banking started to weed out the more dubious public figures among its clients, and in 1999, Bongo was ejected. Elements within the bank were less than happy. Christopher Rogers, a Citibank manager, wrote to his head of private banking, Salim Raza in worried terms: "We ought to ensure that we face this issue and its possible implications with our eyes wide open. Whatever internal considerations we satisfy, the marketing fallout is likely to be serious. . . . Sam [Dossou] gets his marching orders from Tendin [Bongo]. . . . Tendin has been vitally instrumental in our franchise's success over the years. . . . Sam helped the Branch considerably over the last two years to obtain a more reasonable and rightful share of public sector deposits, with Tendin's blessing.

"Tendin and Mandela are the foremost African leaders today, and they are friends. Tendin's position in Francophone Africa, including Congo K, is pre-eminent. Although we can't measure how far the negative vibes could go, there is no doubt that they will spread, and that that will include France. Tendin's family and friends extend far.

"The probability of this support being reversed indefinitely should be weighed seriously. . . . The impact on [private bank] marketing in Francophone Africa will be serious. Beyond this, there would be legitimate grounds for concern in many people's minds about whether Citibank was abandoning this part of the Continent."

Sources in the bank tried to hold onto Bongo as a client. One thought he could engineer a (somewhat unrealistic) compromise. They said, "It is possible . . . we could induce Tendin to maintain a completely transparent relationship. . . . The idea of setting new target and acceptance criteria for top public figures who are whistle-clean and agree to total transparence in exchange for the privilege of banking with us might be compelling to Shaukat [Aziz] and others. We would be adapting to the times instead of jettisoning quality assets. . . . In extremis, we could demonstrate to anyone that our customer is not bleeding a poor country because all balances and sources of funds would have been vetted by us at the source."

Asif Ali Zardari—Fixer With a High Price

Citibank's branches in Dubai and Switzerland provided the offshore accounts and banking facilities that would allegedly enable Asif Ali Zardari to receive a questionable payment from a Dubai-based financier.

Zardari is the husband of Benazir Bhutto, the former Pakistani prime minister. He had served as special adviser to Benazir's first government from 1988 to 1990, and as investment minister in her second government between 1993 and 1996. During the three years when Zardari was out of government, he was in detention, charged with corruption.

Citibank opened three private bank accounts in Switzerland and a consumer account in Dubai for three corporations under Zardari's control between 1994 and 1997. Some of these accounts were allegedly used to disguise $10 million in kickbacks for a gold importing contract to Pakistan.

The money was paid into an offshore account called Capricorn in two $5 million chunks, one day after the other in 1994. The source was A.R.Y. International Exchange, a company owned by Abdul Razzaq Yaqub, a fabulously wealthy Pakistani gold bullion trader living in Dubai. Razzaq also owns interests in Pakistani media. Benazir Bhutto's government awarded Razzaq an exclusive and very valuable license to import gold just three months after the payment. Razzaq used this to import more than $500 million worth of gold into Pakistan. Razzaq has denied making any payments to Zardari.

Zardari approached Citibank in Dubai through Jens Schlegelmilch, his Swiss lawyer and a friend of the Bhutto family. The lawyer told Citibank that he was working for the Dubai Royal Family and he wanted to open an account at the Citibank branch office in Dubai. The account, domiciled in British Virgin Islands, was called M.S. Capricorn Trading. Schlegelmilch had a Dubai residency permit; a visa signed by a member of the Dubai royal family gave credibility.

The account manager did not know the beneficial owner. He was not required by Dubai law in force at that time to ask who was behind the account, and the lawyer did not reveal who owned it. In fact, the account manager later said that he assumed the beneficial owner was the member of the Royal Family who had signed the visa. The account, which would receive and transfer money to Switzerland was opened in early October 1994—one day before the arrest of another Citibank client, Raul Salinas.

Citibank was sufficiently impressed by the funds deposited in its Dubai branch to encourage their new client to open an account the following year at its Swiss private bank. Zardari completed "Swiss Form A," which required the ultimate holder of the account to identify himself, but this information stayed within the Swiss branch. The Dubai account manager at Citibank was never told who stood behind Capricorn and continued to think the account's beneficial owner was a member of the staff of the Dubai Royal Family—some indication of the standing of Dubai within the Citibank hierarchy, perhaps.

The bank responded to the crescendo of concern about Zardari's honesty (especially in Pakistan, of course) by putting his accounts under a special regimen. He was told that the accounts were not supposed to be the "primary accounts" for his assets, that the funds deposited in the accounts should not exceed $40 million, and that they were to be used as "passive stable investments, without multiple transactions or funding pass-throughs." Zardari ignored the restrictions, and the bank retained the money. They also helped him buy some property in London. The matter attracted some publicity and when the bank involved went to his lawyer to inquire the source of the money, they were told it came from the sale of some sugar mills.

Accusations of corruption and graft in the run-up to Pakistan's 1997 general election, followed by the claim that he had murdered Benazir Bhutto's only surviving brother, Murtaza Bhutto, led to an investigation of Zardari's accounts. The accounts were closed in January 1997 on the pretext that he had infringed the restrictions imposed the previous year.

The existence of the accounts, and the way they were used to handle bribes, was disclosed in an article in the *New York Times*, and Citibank had to shamefacedly admit its role in the squalid affair. The bank reassured critics that the rules governing disclosure of beneficial ownership at its Dubai branch had been tightened up. Citibank's chairman John Reed later wrote to his directors saying that he was "inclined to think" that the bank had "made a mistake" in taking on Zardari.

A Suspicious Activity Report (SAR) on the Zardari accounts was hurriedly prepared and filed with the Financial Crimes Enforcement Network (FinCEN) at the U.S. Department of Treasury. The bank's sluggish response to Zardari's exposure was transparent and reprehensible. The filing was made fourteen months after the Zardari accounts were closed, thirteen months after Zardari was arrested a second time for corruption in November 1996, and nearly two months after the Swiss government had ordered four Swiss banks (including Citibank Switzerland) to freeze all Zardari accounts.

The shockwaves from Zardari's business transactions continued to be felt in 1998 when Zardari's Swiss lawyer (among others) was indicted for money laundering in connection with kickbacks paid by Swiss companies for the award of a government contract by Pakistan. The lawyer had benefited greatly from Zardari's largesse, receiving a fifth of the funds deposited as a

commission. Zardari and Benazir Bhutto were themselves indicted for violation of Swiss money laundering law in connection with the same incident.

Zardari's business dealings were investigated by the Pakistani
Accountability Bureau, which alleged that he had plundered government
funds, raked in kickbacks on aircraft and submarine deals, and obtained
commissions on the import of gold and fertilisers. An investigator further
claimed that Zardari was "involved in narcotics." Another claimed he
diverted tax revenues and skimmed funds from power project deals. A
Western arms dealer (admittedly, not likely to be the most reliable source)
was quoted as saying that "when Benazir was in power, everything went
through Zardari." Western banks that held accounts for Zardari's companies included Union Bank of Switzerland, where Zardari's Bomer Finance
company had an account. Zardari spent his very considerable fortune on
UK property, owning a 131-hectare (1 hectare is 2.47 acres) estate in
Surrey called Rockwood and eight other British properties.

Pakistan charged the greedy couple with accepting kickbacks from the
two Swiss companies in exchange for the award of a government contract.
They were sentenced to five years in prison and fined $8.6 million in 1999,
after a long and bitter trial. Both were disqualified from holding public
office. Pakistani authorities also froze an estimated $300 million in prop-
erty and assets, including agricultural land, twenty bank accounts, and five
sugar mills. Benazir Bhutto, who now lives in London, denounced the
Pakistani government's disqualification decision. Zardari remains in jail.

Citibank was left to face public and internal recriminations. Chairman
John Reed told a meeting of the Senate subcommittee that the bank
manager who took Zardari on "must have been an idiot." Reed said he
knew about Zardari's reputation, and he was aware of "troubling accusations concerning corruption surrounding Mr. Zardari, that he should stay
away from him, and that he was not a man with whom the bank wanted to
be associated." By that stage, the damage had been done. The accusation
of money laundering would attach itself not only to the client, but also to
the bank that had handled his money.

Raul Salinas de Gortari—Señor Anonymous

Raul Salinas de Gortari was one of the strongmen of Mexican politics. He was
known as a "tough guy who knows how to raise $20 million over a weekend,

how to fight with the toughest guys on the other side." Salinas was adept at raising money for himself as well as for his brother, Carlos, the country's President. Over the course of the 1980s and early 1990s, Salinas accumulated no less than $132 million.

One of the banks looking after Raul Salinas's fortune was Citibank, the American flag carrier in South America. Citibank salted away the Salinas fortune overseas, until the chickens came home to roost for Raul. He switched, almost overnight, from client extraordinaire to alleged murderer, and a huge embarrassment. None of this stopped the bank from pocketing a tidy $2 million in fees from the account.

Raul Salinas was trained as a civil engineer and for five years during the late 1980s he earned some $190,000 as director of planning for Conasupo, a state-run agency that regulated agricultural markets. From 1990 until mid-1992, Salinas was a consultant at a government "anti-poverty agency" called Sedesol. These positions gave him enormous opportunities to access the country's most powerful business people for graft and embezzlement. The huge sums of money he was depositing and his comparatively modest salary should have quickly alerted the bank to question the sources.

One important source of Salinas's money was the drug trade. Carlos Salinas, president of Mexico from 1988 to December 1994, ushered the country into a "narcocracy" that aligned drug barons with politicians. The politicians got massively rich, and the drug barons were left to their own corrupt devices. Twenty-one billionaires were created in the course of the Carlos Salinas presidency, while the general standard of living sharply declined.

Carlos Hank Rhon, a prominent Mexican businessman and longtime client of Citibank private bank, introduced Raul Salinas to Citibank's manager Amy Elliott in early 1992. Hank Rhon was a friend of the Salinas family and acted as powerbroker to ensure Carlos Salinas's election to the country's presidency. Hank owned the Laredo National Bank in Texas, as well as a shipping company called Transportation Maritima Mexicana (TMM). Hank had his own problems with the authorities, and TMM would later be accused by the National Drug Intelligence Center of moving cocaine to the United States, and laundering millions of dollars in drug money. Carlos Hank Rhon has denied all allegations.

Within a few months of Hank's introduction, Raul Salinas was signed up with Citibank, and Elliott was bragging about the millions that he would be putting through the accounts. Salinas had "potential in the $15 million to $20 million range," she speculated in an internal Citibank report. Even at this point, there were hints about the sources of the Salinas family wealth as Raul Salinas's cousin had been sentenced to seventeen years in jail in the United States for drug trafficking.

No less than five accounts were quickly opened in New York to absorb the Salinas money. Another one appeared in Switzerland, where a banker wrote in June 1992: "The client requires a high level of confidentiality in view of his family's political background. . . . This relationship will be operated along the [same] lines as Amy's 'other' relationship [with Carlos Hank Rhon]; i.e. she will only be aware of the 'Confidential accounts' and not even be aware of the names of the underlying companies. . . . Please note for the record that the client is extremely sensitive about the use of his name and does not want it circulated within the bank. I believe Amy's 'other' client has a similar arrangement."

Citibank went into overdrive to develop the panoply of secret companies in secret havens that would ensure Salinas stayed anonymous. It created a shell corporation called Trocca Ltd in the Cayman Islands, and three other shell, or "nominee companies," were created to serve as Trocca's board of directors. A year later, Cititrust also established a trust, identified only by a number (PT-5242), to serve as Trocca's owner.

By now Raul Salinas was Señor Anonymous, and his famous name did not appear anywhere on Trocca's incorporation papers. As far as the American bank was concerned, he was just "Confidential Client Number 2" or "CC-2." The code "CC-1" was used to refer to his patron Carlos Hank Rhon. The Swiss requirement to have the name of a beneficial owner of an account forced the only chink in Salinas's armor of anonymity. But the Swiss reputation for discretion would more than take care of any risk of disclosure.

Accounts called Trocca started to mushroom, appearing in London and Switzerland. But secrecy was golden, and bank managers in London were not told who owned the account. The next Salinas family account was set up in Switzerland, this time in the name of Bonaparte, an indication, perhaps, of how Raul Salinas saw himself.

From the very opening of the Trocca account, Amy Elliott appeared to have some suspicions about Salinas's account, in particular about a

$2 million payment to Salinas from Carlos Hank Rhon in the form of two wire transfers. Elliott challenged Hank about this and he explained that the funds had been given to him by Salinas for a business deal that did not go forward. The money launderer who lodges a deposit with a lawyer with a view to buying a house and then pulls out of the transaction employs a similar technique.

In fact, the funds were paid into the Salinas accounts in New York. The money was then moved to the Trocca investment accounts in London and Switzerland. Later Hank Rhon's own bank, Laredo National Bank, would be suspected of acting as a conduit for the transport of Salinas money to Switzerland.

If Raul Salinas was twitchy about his secrecy when he opened the account, he was positively quaking with concern as Mexico's general elections loomed in 1994. He professed to Elliott that he was concerned about the impact of the elections on the strength of the currency, and thus on the value of his massive deposits held in Mexican pesos. Another explanation for the need to export his money at breakneck speed is that he saw the writing on the wall for his brother's presidency, and knew that his replacement would move against him to regain the money. Raul Salinas's fears were realized on both counts. Carlos was ejected from the presidency, and the currency was devalued.

In any event, as a last-ditch effort, Salinas persuaded Citibank to set up a new system, arguably even more foolproof than the last, to move his money out of the country. His fiancée, Paulina Castanon, would pay cashier's checks, drawn on Citibank itself, into his account at Citibank's Mexico City branch. Castanon used her middle names, Patricia Rios, when she took the checks to the bank to guarantee her own anonymity. Over a period of less than three weeks in May and June 1993, Castanon presented seven cashier's checks, totalling a massive $40 million, far exceeding Elliott's expectations. The greedy banker wrote to a colleague in Switzerland: "This account is turning into an exciting, profitable one for us all. Many thanks for making me look good."

The funds continued flooding in, and over two weeks in January 1994, Castanon used the system to export no less than $19 million from Mexico through New York accounts to Trocca accounts in London and Switzerland. The total funds in the Salinas accounts originating from

Mexican cashier's checks had reached $67 million by the end of June 1994. Yet another $20 million reached Salinas's accounts from other banks. In less than two years, the secretive Salinas had removed from Mexico a grand total of $87 million.

The funds were still flowing in 1995 when Salinas transferred $5 million through a Citibank account in New York. The money was then moved to the Zurich-based Julius Baer Bank's correspondent banking account at Chase Manhattan Bank in New York. Traces of Salinas's dirty money were later found at Baer and at another Swiss bank, Rothschild.

Raul Salinas's need for secrecy became obvious to the bank in February 1995, when Citibank discovered he had some very serious enemies. Indeed, he was wanted for the murder of his former brother-in-law, Ruiz Massieu, a leading Mexican politician. Salinas sought to reassure Elliott that the allegation was politically motivated, and he denied any involvement. But on February 28, 1995, Salinas was arrested and imprisoned in Mexico on suspicion of murder. This was a man with a dark past, of which the bank was either unaware or culpably forgetful.

The bank reacted cynically to their client's plight. On the day following the arrest, telephone conversations took place between private bankers in New York, London, and Switzerland. Recordings on an automatic taping system indicate that the private bank's initial reaction to the arrest was obstructive rather than helpful to the police. In fact, Hubertus Rukavina, the head of the private bank, suggested that the money could be moved out of London and deposited in Switzerland without leaving a trail back to Salinas. London bank records would disclose the funds transfer to Switzerland and Rukavina's scheme was abandoned.

Mexico's press was understandably very excited by Raul Salinas's arrest, and the story hogged the headlines week after week. Citibank's executives could only take so much revelation and embarrassment, and four weeks after the arrest, they decided to ask Salinas to close the accounts and move the funds elsewhere. Elliott resisted the decision, but she eventually agreed to speak to Castanon. Elliott did not tell Salinas about the bank's decision to have the accounts closed until early October 1995.

The Mexican investigation of the sources of Salinas's money inevitably led to Switzerland. Many accounts linked to Salinas were found at the leading Swiss private bank, Pictet et Cie., under the false names of Juan

Guillermo Gomez Gutierrez, Juan Manuel Gomez Gutierrez, and Margarita Sanchez Nava. The Swiss in due course froze no less than $84 million found at Pictet. Castanon herself was picked up by the Swiss authorities at Banque Pictet where she was trying to gain access to Raul's safe deposit box.

With Castanon's arrest, the Swiss police went into action. They immediately issued an order freezing Salinas accounts at several other Swiss banks, including Citibank. Approximately $132 million was frozen, including about $27 million at the Citibank private bank offices in Switzerland. A British court later froze the Salinas accounts in London.

Castanon was detained in a Swiss prison for just a month while the authorities investigated the origins and destinations of the Salinas fortune. Castanon disclosed to Elliott that much of the money did not belong to Salinas at all, but was given to him for safekeeping. Mexicans with money from dubious sources had apparently used Salinas to give them access to accounts at leading banks, like Citibank. Citibank performed its part in this laundering exercise by failing to ask any questions about the sources of Salinas's money. The bank's embarrassment was reinforced by reports in the *New York Times* in 1997 that cited accounts from U.S. officials. These alleged that Raul Salinas received suitcases full of cash from drug traffickers to distribute to Mexican government officials at a meeting that took place in 1993.

The Swiss brought the full panoply of their investigative and prosecutory procedures down on Salinas. The Swiss Attorney General conducted a three-year investigation and in October 1998, a Swiss federal court ordered the forfeiture of $114 million frozen in the Salinas accounts, as illegal proceeds related to drugs trafficking. This order was later revoked on procedural grounds.

Various investigations were launched in the United States. Following Salinas's conviction, the U.S. Attorney for the Southern District of New York investigated the roles played by Citibank private bank or any of its employees in Salinas's money laundering. No indictments followed, and the five-year statute of limitations has since elapsed.

The Senate subcommittee also took up the case, and brought Elliott in as a witness. She was asked whether the private bank was aware of the origin of the funds used to obtain the cashier's checks Castanon had paid into the Mexico branch of her bank. Elliott indicated that no one had made the necessary inquiries. The committee's report concluded that Salinas used the device of the cashier's checks to "effectively disguise the funds' source and destination, thus breaking the funds' paper trail."

Elliott described three ways in which cashier's checks were used to launder the Salinas millions: first, the cashier's checks named only banks as the payer and payee; second, the cashier's checks were handled by Citibank in Mexico for a non-account holder using an alias; third, the funds passed through the private bank's concentration account in New York, bypassing any specific client account and further obscuring the true source and ultimate destination of the funds.

The committee also pressed Elliott on the due diligence that Citibank had gathered about Salinas's funds. She said that Salinas had told her that he was thinking of selling a construction company. She checked this with Hank who told her that the sale had gone through and Mr. Salinas had "done very well."

The committee found that she did not know some critical details about Salinas's story, including the company's name, to whom it was sold, when the sale took place, the amounts involved, or the profits realized. She did not even know whether the company or its projects were genuine or real.

In January 1999, Salinas' murky past came back to haunt him. Following a lengthy trial in Mexico, he was convicted of murder and sentenced to 50 years in jail. This was halved on appeal.

Raul Salinas de Gortari remained Señor Anonymous to the end as far as Citibank was concerned. Carlos Salinas, the one-time Mexican president, still seeks anonymity, holed up in exile in Dublin, Ireland. An unlikely end for a family that pursued bad money as the ill-advised route to building a dynasty.

Has Citibank Learned Anything?

While each case brings dishonor upon the bank, Citibank's 30-year-long relationship with President Bongo of Gabon is particularly extraordinary. The bank assisted the African leader in extracting hundreds of millions from his country's annual budget, for what Citibank strongly suspected (by the admission of its own local bankers writing private memos) was the corrupt purpose of political bribery. The American bank connived at the undermining of democracy—its client's unspoken aim and routine political practice. Banks operating in the United States are required by their constitutions (as well as the federal statutes that govern them) to operate free and open markets. But, given the power that Bongo held over Citibank, the bank could not have served the country's president and his local opposition at the same time, in the unlikely event those individuals had the wealth to make it worth the bank's while. Banks that collude with politicians in perpetrating corruption are also players in the countries where they have branches. They should be vulnerable to statutory redress.

The relatively light treatment of Citibank by American regulators in the wake of the Senate investigation indicates a degree of coziness at the senior levels of the American financial establishment. This is little different from the sort of coziness the bank was able to exploit in the top echelons of the developing countries where it made such a mark. Citibank, or Citigroup as it now likes to be known, is not alone in escaping scot-free from the exposure of corrupt banking practices. Although national regulators have become more confident at "naming and shaming" banks—consider, for example, the restrictions placed by the British Financial Services Authority on the 23 banks associated with Abacha—few banks have materially suffered for handling a corrupt dictator's wealth. The government that replaces a corrupt dictator may decide that the best role for the bank that assisted the theft—in the jargon, "fenced" the dictator's stolen proceeds—is to assist in the recovery of the looted funds. An element of self-preservation or compromise may also be at work as successor governments are likely to have benefited from the earlier theft, and an investigation of the bank will turn up yet more corrupt politicians among the new gang in power.

Has the Banking Community Learned Anything?

Private banks were hugely embarrassed by the findings of the U.S. Senate's Permanent Subcommittee on Investigations' 1999 report "Private Banking: A Case Study of Opportunities and Vulnerabilities." Its findings shamed them into acting on their practices in handling politicians and those close to them. A series of standards emerged that were intended to protect them from accepting money from dictators and other dubious individuals. The Wolfsberg Principles on Private Banking dub people in the public domain "Politically Exposed Persons" or PEPs. Banks are now required to investigate the bona fides of a PEP before it gives him or her a bank account. Wolfsberg defines PEPs as "individuals holding or having held positions of public trust, such as government officials, senior executives of government organisations, politicians, important political party officials as well as their families and close associates."

Changing attitudes to banking ethics, exemplified by the wide acceptance of Wolfsberg, was demonstrated by Citibank's abject apology to the Japanese authorities, after Japan's Financial Services Agency withdrew Citibank's private banking license in late 2004. This dramatic and humiliating step followed the discovery that the Japanese authorities were investigating alleged breaches by Citibank of Japanese banking law. The local Citibank officer admitted the bank had engaged in "inappropriate dealings with customers." Citibank said the management of its private bank had "failed to establish a culture that ensured on-going compliance with laws and regulations."

Wolfsberg has been well received, but it will not stop banks from accepting corrupt money, unless those in responsible positions change their spots. The cynic will say that asking a banker to repress his instincts for a rich man's cash is like asking a cat to forgo killing the bird that sits in front of him. Dictators and their hangers-on are not missing out on banking services just yet. The financiers of cruel regimes are not short of clients or their illegally acquired wealth.

While American banks are supposed to be clean and well regulated, no one in the U.S. Drug Enforcement Administration was surprised when they discovered Mexican banks had some very evasive clients and sources of funds. But when they mounted a sting operation, they were amazed how far up the political tree the poison had spread, as the next chapter demonstrates.

Chapter 10

The Casablanca Sting

Sting operations have vast ramifications in terms of cost, political risk and law enforcers' prestige. Casablanca was the biggest sting of them all, and it sent shockwaves to the top of the U.S. Government.

THE TWELVE MEXICAN BANKERS had come to a casino in the middle of the Nevada desert on a Saturday night in May 1998 to discuss a major money-laundering proposition over dinner before a night out on the town in Las Vegas. Spirits were high as they discussed one of the biggest money-laundering ventures to come their way involving a large $1.15 billion consignment of cash rumored to belong to a Mexican general—and that was not all.

The bankers had been promised an increasing cut of the dirty money that flows from the United States southwards to the drug-producing countries of Latin America. For Mexican bankers with the right connections, business was still booming despite a crisis in the Mexican banking sector so deep that it threatened to engulf even the country's largest banks.

After dinner, the bankers gathered in the foyer of the recently opened Casablanca Casino Resort, a hotel designed to look like the set of the classic Bogart film. As they chatted, not one could have suspected they were enjoying their last hours of freedom. The only ones still celebrating in a little over an hour would be the undercover U.S. Customs agents that had tracked these bankers for the past two-and-a-half years in an undercover operation code-named Casablanca.

After leaving the casino, the Mexican bankers were chauffeured away in their limousines for the evening's festivities. They had been told that their first stop would be a well-known desert brothel; instead the limousines sped them straight into the hands of the police.

The seeds of what eventually grew into the largest-ever undercover drug sting and the arrest of 167 people were sown in 1993 when William

Gately, a Los Angeles Customs Service agent, received a tip-off that drugs money laundering by Colombian cartels was rife among Mexican bankers.

Gately was a battle-hardened cop, who pursued Operation Casablanca with a determination bordering on moral fervor. This doggedness would later land him in hot water with his masters in the U.S. Department of Justice in Washington. He had joined the U.S. Customs Service in 1978, having served eight years with Washington's Metropolitan Police Department and three years as a U.S. marine. In the book he co-authored in 1994 called *Dead Ringer*, Gately portrays himself as a lonely crusader fighting drug crime and bureaucratic red tape. *Dead Ringer* tells the story of an investigation led by Gately into the links between the Italian Mafia and the Colombian drug cartels. Gately demonstrates his supreme confidence in his mission in the book's prologue: "It is the story of one man who refused to succumb to corruption . . . who believed in his oath and mission, and in the consequences he paid for believing in what he was doing."

In the early 1990s, another informant of Gately's had noticed that Mexican and Colombian drug traffickers were depositing large sums of dirty money with corrupt Mexican bankers. The money was then sent back to the traffickers in the almost untraceable form of cashier's checks. The U.S. government had become alarmed at the rising number of bank drafts issued by Mexican banks entering the U.S. banking system. A U.S. State Department report published in 1998 estimated that 500,000 Mexican bank drafts were entering the United States each year, ranging in value from $65,000 to $400,000, an annual total of $3.5 billion.

Bank drafts traded as highly negotiable instruments that could be converted into cash in most Latin American countries. Unlike checks drawn on checking accounts, they identified neither the accounts nor the account holders from which they were originally drawn. As bearer-like instruments they required no identification to cash or deposit at a bank. The checks had only to change hands once to obliterate the audit trail that led to the funds' illegal drug source.

Mexican banks were not scrutinizing the sources of money at this time, as they were desperate for cash. The banks were reeling from the effect of a devaluation of the peso during this period and the system was on the brink of collapse. The banks had only been in private hands since 1991 after a decade of government control, and few had developed adequate anti-money-laundering controls. They were prime targets for

Mexico's drug cartels which had gained power and influence as the authority of government institutions had waned. Years of economic insecurity had bred a culture of poor regulation and corruption, which this investigation would unearth. Financial fragility and lawlessness, as we have seen in earlier countries like Russia (See Chapters 1 through 3), are frequent bedfellows.

Gately, the L.A. Customs agent, was invited to devise a strategy to entrap the Mexican banks. He advised his superiors to use an informant to help his undercover agents infiltrate the system and gather evidence against both the traffickers and their bankers. He planned to create a money-laundering operation using government money instead of drug money. So long as the bankers believed that the money had come from drug sales, the undercover agents could prove charges of money laundering against the bankers in the U.S. courts. The following account is based on interviews with U.S. government officials who conducted the investigation and from the legal documents they presented in court following the arrests.

Gately hired two informants: one was a dubious hoodlum, about whom little is known, and the other was a former emerald trader, born in Colombia, with links to the drug world. He was known then as "Fred Mendoza." Mendoza's current identity is a secret, closely guarded under the terms of a U.S. government witness protection program. But it is possible he is living the high life somewhere on the globe. For in July 1995, the entrepreneurial Mendoza struck a deal with Customs whereby he would receive a commission of up to 10 percent plus expenses for every drugs dollar he helped to launder. Informants who participate in sting operations take enormous risk with their lives and are allowed, under U.S. law, to receive a cut of the profits for their pains.

Mendoza used the false name of Javier Ramirez and agreed to put the word out with his drug contacts that he could launder large volumes of drug profits through his emerald business. He would pick up drug cash for a fee and return it to the traffickers in whatever form they chose. Mendoza secured a meeting with a player who had high-level connections with the Colombian drug cartels, and the sting was launched. His partner among the criminal fraternity was Oscar Armando Saavedra, aka "El Gordo," a money broker based in Cali, Colombia. Saavedra worked for several local drug barons, laundering their profits generated in the United States and other countries. The Colombian cartel's U.S. cocaine money went, in large part, through his hands, and he helped them repatriate their profits without detection.

Saavedra agreed to subcontract out to Ramirez and his undercover associates bulk cash pickups in the United States, Canada, Puerto Rico, and even Italy. He also introduced Ramirez to other members of the cartel interested in laundering drug money through his emerald-trading front company. Ramirez picked up large sums of drug money, deposited it in the banking system, and forwarded it as directed by Saavedra and other cartel operatives.

Ramirez agreed to help Saavedra and his associates, including a money broker identified only as Humberto, to launder drug profits for the Cali cartel. Then the agents were introduced to the powerful Juárez drug cartel and the scale of the operation changed dramatically, as Juárez controlled a large slice of narcotics imports into the United States. The Juárez cartel had long paid massive bribes to corrupt bankers, politicians and army chiefs to secure drug transhipments.

This second front to the Operation gave Casablanca its name. The agents would now repeat the formula they had devised for laundering drugs money for the Cali, when they laundered money for the Juárez. The agents would "play it again," and the name Operation Casablanca was born.

In one of the first deals between Ramirez and Saavedra in the autumn of 1995, the Cali money broker planned to launder drugs cash generated in Chicago that belonged to the Amado Carrillo-Fuentes cartel based in Ciudad Juárez. Saavedra put undercover agents in touch with two key players in the U.S.-Mexican drug trade, José Castellanos Alvarez-Tostado and Victor Alcala Navarro, both closely affiliated with the Juárez cartel.

Saavedra told Ramirez that Navarro and Alvarez had large sums of cash in Chicago that needed to be laundered. Navarro's job was to collect profits from local cocaine wholesalers, launder and repatriate them. He would either be required to wire them to Juárez cartel members in Mexico or to suppliers in Colombia. There were occasions when he would pay off legitimate businesses as part of the laundering process.

The undercover agents' contact with Navarro led to the heart of the U.S.-Latin American drug trade and the bankers who handled their money. Over the next two-and-a-half years, they made regular pickups from several major U.S. cities on behalf of cartel operatives.

The cash collection started in November 1995, when Ramirez flew to Chicago to meet Navarro, aka "the Doctor." Ramirez and another undercover agent met Navarro at a hotel near the outskirts of the city. Court documents refer to a cash pickup of $1.1 million on November 28, 1995, followed by multiple instructions as to where the money should be sent.

The agents did not hear from the Chicago money launderer again for more than six months. Ramirez spoke to Navarro by phone on July 15, 1996 to propose another operation. He visited the undercover informant at his business premises—a front company set up by government agents—in Santa Fe Springs, fifteen miles from downtown Los Angeles. The undercover informant explained that his emerald trading business, Emerald Empire, already provided cover for an extensive money-laundering business.

The empty warehouse, known simply as "the storefront," had been wired for sound and video by U.S. agents. Every conversation, fax, and beeper message was filmed, taped, or logged by agents posing as workers. Meetings outside the Sante Fe storefront took place in hotel rooms furnished with the same clock radio fitted out with a secret recording device. The Doctor's mobile phones had also been wire-tapped, and the agents would later produce around 750 audio and video tapes and more than 8,000 pages of transcripts.

The undercover agents flew most weeks to major U.S. cities to keep up with the constant flow of drug money stuffed into gym bags and suitcases, sometimes millions of dollars at a time. They traveled as far afield as Milan, Caracas, and San Juan, Puerto Rico.

The frequency and size of the pickups grew: in the course of seven days, they are recorded as picking up no less than $2,132,164. The mass haul started on the Thursday, when they collected a bag stuffed with $596,154 from Queens in New York; they took a flight over to Chicago to be there on the following Monday when they were told to be ready to pick up $1,136,030. They had to travel further west, to Los Angeles, for the following Wednesday, when $899,980 was waiting for collection. The amounts of dirty cash got bigger. Documents presented before a grand jury in the Los Angeles courts in the trial of the Mexican bankers show how undercover agents were directed on May 21, 1997 to Chicago, where just short of $3 million in cash was waiting to be collected. Other pickups over the course of the summer of 1997 reached $4 million.

Ramirez transported the cash back to his Santa Fe Springs warehouse to count it after each pickup. Then it was deposited at a number of U.S. banks which, unlike their Mexican counterparts, had been informed that the drug money deposits were in fact part of a massive government sting operation. Bank of America was among those banks which took the drug money, knowing it was protected from prosecution. The transactions were allowed to bypass the required currency transaction report (CTR) filed by U.S. banks on all deposits over $10,000.

Ramirez charged the drug traffickers a fee amounting to "ten points" or 10 percent for picking up the cash, getting it into the banking system, and forwarding it on as directed by the cartel's money managers.

Navarro arranged for Ramirez to meet his boss, José Alvarez-Tostado, in person in Mexico in February 1997. Known to his cohorts simply as "Compadre," Alvarez was the Juárez cartel's chief financial officer at the time. Alvarez oversaw the cartel's cocaine transhipments into the United States and was in constant contact with Navarro, frequently traveling to the United States to negotiate the largest operations, such as the so-called "one-ton (cocaine) deals" and multimillion-dollar money-laundering contracts.

As the agents won the confidence of Navarro and Alvarez, they learned more about the cartel's boss, Amado Carrillo-Fuentes, nicknamed "Lord of the Skies" for his airborne drug shipments. Navarro explained that he worked as a broker between the Mexican and Colombian drug cartels which, although they were competitors, also co-operated on deals. At a meeting in June 1997 in Mexico City, at which Ramirez delivered $1.7 million he had picked up earlier that week in Chicago, Alvarez let Ramirez in on the closely guarded secret that the Juárez cartel paid millions to Mexican officials for protection.

Over the next two years, Navarro became the undercover agents' main link with the high command of the Juárez cartel, revealing more about the secretive organization. Navarro had begun by simply dropping into the conversation that Mexico's Juárez cartel was a big player in the U.S. cocaine trade. But over many meetings and the multimillion-dollar deals that followed, Navarro grew more open about the cartel and the official protection it enjoyed in Mexico.

Navarro was at the top of Mexico's tree of corruption, a crucial money manager for the country's most powerful drug smuggling outfit, which was rumored to bribe senior military and police officials. Within a few months of meeting Navarro, the U.S. agents spoke by phone with the head of the organization. Court records of the conversation reveal that Carrillo-Fuentes told the undercover agent how "pleased" he had been with his work and how he looked forward to "future dealings."

The agents had initially been skeptical about the drug cartels' power and influence, but toward the end of 1997, when they visited Colombia, they were able to develop their partnership with the drug traffickers. The agents headed by Ramirez explained that they were making so many cash pickups that they couldn't find enough corrupt bankers through whom to funnel the money. They asked Dr. Navarro for his help in recruiting more bankers willing to accept drug money. Ramirez asked Navarro to meet him at a heavily guarded villa where he was accompanied by an undercover informant who played the role of Ramirez's boss "Carlos". Carlos explained that their long-standing banking contact who laundered the bulk of their cash had recently died and he asked Navarro whether his Mexican banking contacts who laundered Juárez cartel drug proceeds would also be able to help them launder $500 million of their own money. Alvarez's reply came straight back: "Let me send you my very best people and we will get it done."

Over the next year and a half, Navarro introduced Ramirez to a group of Mexican bankers who were keen to take a piece of the action. The agents paid Navarro a finder's fee for every new banker willing to launder drug money he introduced. Ramirez explained to dozens of bankers recruited in this way that he laundered all the money for the Cali cartel through his organization. The urbane agent explained that he did not deal in drugs, only money, and was looking for bankers willing to help funnel millions of drug dollars through bank accounts in Mexico and the Cayman Islands. Successful meetings were followed by contracts.

As the flow of drug money through Ramirez steadily increased, Navarro brought in his cousin Ernesto De La Torre to help him recruit pliable Mexican bankers. The lead U.S. prosecutor who handled the case, Duane Lyons, said, "No one realized that this operation was going to grow in the way it did on the basis of the relationship with Dr Navarro." One of Navarro's first and most important introductions took place on August 7, 1996, at the branch office of Bancomer, one of Mexico's largest banks, in the Mexican city of Tijuana, just south of the Mexican-U.S. border. Here

Ramirez met Jose Reyes Ortega González, a manager of banking operations in Tepatitlán, and a mid-level Bancomer executive. He would later meet Bancomer managers from Chapala and Tijuana.

Ramirez, flanked by Navarro, explained to these middle-ranking bankers that his people would pay a percentage fee in return for help in shifting millions of dollars of Juárez and Cali cartels' drug profits through accounts at their bank branches. Ramirez was able to establish his money laundering credentials within the Mexican banking community and opened the door to dozens more corrupt bankers.

Toward the end of August 1996, one of the bankers from Navarro's home town of Tepatitlán flew up to Sante Fe Springs to meet the agents. He explained a scheme to Ramirez which involved turning cash deposits into bank drafts and checks. The Bancomer manager, Jose Reyes Ortega González, agreed to open bank accounts at Mercury Bank & Trust Ltd, a Cayman Islands bank owned by his employer, Bancomer. Ramirez was told that deposits in Bancomer's offshore subsidiary had to remain in the account for at least four days before they could be converted into bank drafts or checks. The first deal went through on October 19, 1996, when undercover agents deposited $56,850 in Mercury Bank & Trust, in the name of Sergio Alcala Navarro, another indicted Mexican. Within less than a month, almost $650,000 had been deposited in undercover U.S. bank accounts and then transferred to Mercury Bank & Trust. On November 21, Reyes informed Ramirez that he was preparing eleven bank drafts with a total value of $623,870 that would arrive in two days' time.

The money laundering was successfully completed and Ramirez asked Reyes if he could take another deposit, this time of $1.5 million. Ortega told the undercover agent that deposits up to $2 million would "not cause alarm." Ramirez placed regular deposits in the course of the following months, and Reyes agreed to approach employees at five other Bancomer branches to ask if they would also be willing to launder money. By the end of 1997, the agents' contacts in the Mexican banking sector had grown beyond Bancomer. They opened accounts at regional branches of Mexico's biggest banks in the United States and in the Cayman Islands between 1997 and early 1998, many in the names of phoney businesses,

Mexican banks fell over themselves to grab a chunk of the dirty money. In December 1996, a manager from Banoro, another Mexican bank, agreed to accept deposits of $200,000 every two days and the agents began making deposits into an account in the name of Comercial Textil de Los Altos. Two months later, in February 1997, Confía joined the ranks of banks that received dirty money. This bank was in particular need of the money as it was operating under government supervision, having come close to financial failure. By June, accounts had been set up in Confía's Cayman Islands subsidiary under the agents' direction in order to receive the first wire transfer of $504,875.80. Over the course of the next year, some $11 million passed through Confía. Bital, one of the country's largest banks, was drawn into the scheme in April 1997 and processed $2.7 million between April and May 1998; Banamex, yet another substantial institution, processed $1.85 million between May 1997 and May 1998; and Banpais handled a little more than $2 million between July 1997 and May 1998. These transactions are listed in the U.S. case against Banca Serfin among others. It was heard before the grand jury of the U.S. district court for the central district of California in October 1997. Bital, Banpais, and Banamex were not charged with any wrong doing in relation to Operation Casablanca.

The tentacles of Operation Casablanca reached outside Mexico and into other South American countries. For example, it penetrated Venezuela which had long been regarded by U.S. authorities as a haven for dirty money. Ramirez's Colombian contact, Oscar Saavedra, introduced undercover U.S. agents to high-level contacts and in early 1997, Ramirez met several executives at Venezuelan banks, including Esperanza Matos de Saad, a vice president of Banco Industrial de Venezuela's Miami operations (and also sister of a former Venezuelan cabinet minister). Saavedra also introduced agents to his contact at Banco del Caribe in Caracas and its Netherlands Antilles subsidiary, the Caribbean American bank in Curaçao. The Caribbean American Bank laundered $4.3 million, and Banco Industrial de Venezuela laundered $4.1 million for the U.S. agents. Two other Venezuelan banks were also implicated, and five Venezuelan bankers were eventually arrested and charged with laundering a total of nearly $10 million.

The operation's final big catch was Mexico's long-troubled bank, Banca Serfin, which was on the point of selling a stake to the major British banking institution, HSBC. Navarro introduced Ramirez to Armando Medrano Rayas, an official at Banca Serfin's Tijuana office. Medrano Rayas explained to Ramirez that Serfin's big problem was how to "lift the bank"—in other words, how to increase deposits. He told Ramirez to provide the paperwork for a number of fictitious assembly plant companies, modelled on those companies genuinely financed, that were located along the U.S.-Mexican border. Medrano Rayas told the undercover informant that he had been laundering money for years, that his fee was 2.5 percent of cash that he received, and that he could accept deposits of up to $300,000 per week.

Medrano Rayas, who had boasted of money laundering for a Colombian drug trafficker named Fernando Casas, told Ramirez that his boss at Banca Serfin was pushing for all bank managers to get as much money as possible into their accounts by the end of the year and he did not care about the source. Later on, Medrano Rayas told undercover agents that his boss was "pleased" with the deposits. Medrano Rayas was not the only Serfin employee willing to receive black money to "lift the bank." Manuel Pazzi-Salas, a Serfin manager, later offered to launder money through an offshore account at Serfin's Cayman Islands branch. When Pazzi-Salas was fired for illegal trading activities on the New York Stock Exchange, in a case unconnected with money laundering, he first called Ramirez to warn him that the accounts would be taken over by another employee. Pazzi-Salas explained to Ramirez that he would let his new colleague know about the business and encourage him to retain it.

Court documents allege that Julio Andrade, Pazzi-Salas's colleague, needed little persuading to take over the money laundering activities. Andrade flew to San Diego to discuss the existing arrangements with Ramirez, who had by this stage become an important client. According to a government witness, Andrade was told that the money he would receive would be the property of very dangerous people from the Cali cartel who "get upset" when money transfers are delayed. Andrade remained cool, simply replying that he had no problem shifting $5 million a week. Bankers at Serfin helped the agents launder $7.7 million, with some individual deposits reaching as much as $1.6 million.

By the end of 1997, the U.S. government's undercover informant had confirmed his reputation as a money-laundering kingpin. Both the Cali and Juárez cartels were impressed at the seeming ease with which their money was laundered and were eager to increase the flow of drug dollars. The checks poured into the Emerald Empire's warehouse offices in Santa Fe Springs but the drug traffickers and their bankers did not know that every check was logged by the agents. The undercover task force had now grown to ten undercover agents, 22 surveillance teams of ten members each, two accountants, and three intelligence analysts.

Court documents later listed each of the payments received by the agents to fictitious entities: on one day a check from Confía for $200,675 made out to Pinnacle Courier Service, the next day a check from Banamex for $87,456.01 made out to Global Pictures, four days later a check from Banpais for $86,654.97 made out to DBK Research Associates, the following week a check from Banca Serfin for $33,000 made out to Tri-State Auditor Services. And so it went on, week after week.

During 1997 and the first part of 1998, the undercover Customs agents were criss-crossing the United States and Canada, picking up suitcases stuffed full of drug cash, depositing the drug proceeds into U.S. bank accounts before wiring the money on to contacts in Mexican and Venezuelan banks. The bankers converted the money into untraceable bankers' drafts that were easily tradable on the unofficial foreign exchange market to obscure the funds' origin. Sources close to the Casablanca investigation say that the DEA used money from a variety of sources for its sting operation. One lawyer, who did not want to be named, said: "As the investigation grew, most of the money came from real drug sales. The money was picked up, sent to the bankers, returned by the bankers and then sent on to the real traffickers."

Cartel money brokers told Ramirez where to send the money. In many cases the high-denomination U.S. dollars were traded for Colombian pesos on the black market. The brokers had little problem finding ordinary business people who did not question the source of U.S. dollars available at below market prices. Once the U.S. dollar checks had been traded for pesos, the funds could be safely returned to their drug-producing owners in Colombia (see "Colombia's Half Trillion," Chapter 7).

In just eighteen months, a handful of bankers from the small Mexican city of Tepatitlán handled more than $30 million that they believed to be profits from drug sales in the United States. Most of this—some $19 million—was laundered by just one individual, Jorge Reyes Ortega Gonzalez, through accounts at Bancomer. According to *Time* magazine, the Bancomer employee netted around $200,000, ten times his annual salary.

As the cartel members got more comfortable with their laundering team, they began to let slip more about their businesses. The cartel's principal U.S. money manager, Victor Alcala Navarro, had already revealed the extensive arrangements between the Juárez cartel and Mexican banks. But now he began to hint at another level of official co-operation, this time with high-ranking Mexican government figures.

Navarro confided to agents at a meeting in February 1997 at the Mexican resort of Cancún that the Juárez cartel deployed advanced surveillance technology to monitor cell phone conversations between law enforcement officers. He also revealed that the cartels had a working relationship with General Jesus Guiterrez Rebollo, Mexico's anti-drug chief. Guiterrez Rebollo had been arrested in early 1997, and according to *Euromoney* magazine, this had caused much embarrassment within the U.S. administration since he had been a close contact of the then U.S. drug czar, Barry McCaffrey.

The cartel's alliance with high-level Mexican officials was repeatedly mentioned at meetings with Navarro and his boss, José Alvarez Tostado. But the full extent of the co-operation did not become clear until the traffickers brought along sixteen federal police agents as bodyguards to a meeting in Mexico City on May 16, 1997. A man who identified himself as an official of the Mexican Attorney General's office picked up $1.7 million in cash at a subsequent meeting. This included $415,000 that the undercover agents had brought for the cartel boss himself.

The General's Billion

On March 6, 1998, Operation Casablanca escalated from a fairly routine and successful sting to a major political event. That was the day David Loera, a local businessman, told Ramirez that he knew a Mexican general who had $150 million "to invest." In fact, the general was only the front for the Minister of Defense of Mexico himself, General Enrique Cervantes, according to bankers. And the sums were much greater than at first stated. It is believed that no less than $500 million of these political monies were deposited in New York and another $500 million were waiting in the Netherlands. It now appears that $1.15 billion of drugs money, owned by top members of the Mexican establishment, was offered to the U.S. Customs officials for laundering.

The agents took this information to the CIA, which works closely alongside the Mexican military on drug control issues. But Customs agents received back no more than a terse response that the CIA had no such information about Mexico's Minister of Defense.

Later investigations revealed that several senior generals close to the then defense minister were under investigation by both the Mexican Attorney General's office and a special military intelligence unit. The most extraordinary suggestion to be made to the undercover team was that Cervantes himself might have been no more than a front. Could he have been covering the fact that the money actually belonged to the President of Mexico, himself. This was the implication of some information passed to Navarro from his cousin. The cousin told him that things could be "very dangerous" if the deal got screwed up because the money belonged "to all of them," including the Mexican President. Mexican officials have strongly denied allegations of government involvement. David Najera, a spokesperson for the president, told the New York Times that the claim was "baseless".

Concerns in Washington

When Janet Reno, the U.S. Attorney General, was informed of the new direction the investigation was taking and in particular of the extraordinary revelations opening up before the agents' eyes, Washington started to get alarmed. Tensions ran high as the U.S. Department of Justice called for the Treasury (which oversees the U.S. Customs Service) to wind up the undercover investigation. There was talk of concern about the use of massive amounts of drugs money, but in reality, the issue was one of *realpolitik* at the highest level. Reno wanted Casablanca closed down as soon as possible, foreseeing a massive breakdown in relations with Mexico.

William Gately, the U.S. Customs agent in charge, saw his whole project falling apart, without winning the biggest catch of all, the top brass of another country. He flew to Washington to brief senior officials on the investigation and plead for more time. But his mission was to no avail. His boss, Raymond W. Kelly, the former New York City police chief who was at the time the Treasury Under Secretary responsible for the U.S. Customs Service, was adamant that Casablanca had to be closed down as allegations against Mexican government officials were "vague" and "not verified" by any hard evidence. Kelly suggested that claims concerning the Mexican general, Guiterrez Rebollo, could have been made to exaggerate the launderers' importance.

Gately took his case even higher up the tree. He went to Kelly's boss, no lesser man than Treasury Secretary Robert Rubin. Rubin, the former

Goldman Sachs senior partner and a hard-nosed banker, backed Gately. He said that the undercover agents should continue to investigate the new and alarming allegations. Rubin and Gately's gung-ho attitude was not matched elsewhere in the U.S. Government. Former U.S. prosecutor Duane Lyons says there was concern about the agents' safety as they penetrated the higher reaches of the Mexican establishment. "The question was, how do you balance the personal safety of the undercover agents—whose lives are at risk—against the promise of more information?" Some U.S. officials argued that the agents' cover might have already been compromised by a leak to the media. Others were worried about the possibility of putting a case together given the sheer volume of material that had been collected. Lyons said: "The case was growing so fast, it had become a 600 pound gorilla." He remembers telling the undercover agents "we can't handle any new bankers in this case." Lyons said: "The operation could have gone on for years and years. But the government was having to pay out a massive amount to launder large volumes of drug money in order to infiltrate the money-laundering system. So the real question became, how much drug money can you launder before it is no longer advantageous to run this kind of operation?"

This argument prevailed and it was decided to close the investigation. The undercover agents had then to plot how to bring as many of the bankers as they could north of the border to arrest them on U.S. territory. It was decided to invite the bankers to a party to celebrate the opening of the Casablanca hotel and casino in Nevada. Ramirez told them that he had bought the hotel with his profits from his money-laundering operations. Other bankers were lured to San Diego on the pretext that they were attending a banking conference.

A dozen bankers flew into Las Vegas's McCarran International airport and ten more arrived in San Diego on the weekend of May 16, 1998. The agents had planned to make the arrests as soon as the bankers arrived on U.S. territory. Once out of the airport, highway patrol officers would pull over the limousines, arrest the bankers, and take them to the nearby air force base. But the plans were changed at the last minute as agent Gately decided that the last supper would go ahead before the bankers were delivered into the hands of the authorities. After the meal, the executives were told that they would be taken to a nearby brothel. Instead, they were taken into police custody.

No less than 22 bankers were arrested that Saturday night and Sunday morning and further arrests were planned for the next week. U.S. Attorney General Janet Reno and Secretary of the Treasury Robert Rubin held a press conference the following Monday, before the case was completed and agents were nervous that this might prejudice further arrests. But some bankers and brokers seemed oblivious to the bad news from the U.S. and a number were arrested in Colombia and on the Caribbean island of Aruba. Cali money broker Oscar Armando Saavedra and several associates from Venezuela, including leading attorney Carmen Yrigoyen, were rounded up in Miami and Los Angeles.

Five bankers were also arrested by officials in Mexico after Customs officials flew to Mexico City on May 18, 1998. It was reported that one of those arrested was Enrique Mendez Urena, the personal banker to the former Juárez Cartel boss, Amado Carrillo-Fuentes. State police said he died of extensive head injuries soon after his arrest. The police claimed he had been acting strangely in his cell and had hurt himself.

A total of 167 bankers and cartel members were arrested as a result of Operation Casablanca. Although Navarro was arrested, his boss, José Alvarez Tostado, remains on the U.S. government's most wanted list. He is believed to be in Bogota, Colombia.

The Mexican government at first praised the operation's success, but when it became clear that much of the United States investigation had been conducted on Mexican soil without their permission, their applause changed to anger. They protested that their country's sovereignty had been breached and the Mexican President Ernesto Zedillo complained publicly to the United States that no cause "can justify the violation of our sovereignty nor of our laws." The Mexican justice minister threatened to prosecute the United States agents for conducting the investigation illegally on Mexican soil.

The Mexican administration strongly denied any wrongdoing by General Cervantes, the Minister of Defense, pointing out that the U.S. government had also described the allegations as "unsubstantiated and speculative." Neither has Cervantes been the focus of U.S. suspicion and he remained a partner with the U.S. in its war on drugs in the wake of Operation Casablanca. At the same time, officials, among them U.S. Treasury Under Secretary James Johnson, appeared to become jittery about the key figures targeted by Casablanca and told agents not to mention Cervantes' name unless they had positive proof of his involvement.

Gately later denied that the Mexicans had been kept in the dark about Casablanca, saying that he had informed them of the operation during the early planning stages in 1994. He says he flew to Mexico City to discuss the operation with the Mexican government but met a wall of silence which he interpreted as at best hostility and at worst an indication of complicity.

The political ramifications of Casablanca went to the very top of the American administration. In an angry letter dated May 22, 1998, from the U.S. Secretary of State Madeleine Albright to Treasury Secretary Robert Rubin, Albright berated her junior colleague for causing "deep resentment" within the Mexican government and for not warning either the Mexican government, or herself, about the investigation. Secretary Albright also noted her own "deep concern" at the "negative tone this development introduces into the relationship" with the Mexican government. President Bill Clinton was drawn into the political dispute with Mexico, and was forced to eat humble pie. He expressed his "regret" to the Mexican president that United States officials had not consulted with their Mexican counterparts. The Mexican President, who could not deny that his country's bankers had been found to be deeply immersed in money laundering, offered his commitment to co-operate on fighting drug crimes and the rift between the two countries began to heal.

As the Clinton administration mollified Mexico's politicians, another storm began to brew at home. Some top United States law enforcement officials, notably Gately himself, were privately admitting their astonishment to the media that hardly any effort had been made to pressure indicted suspects to testify against more senior players in the drug cartels and the Mexican government. The public dispute between Gately and the U.S. government deepened as one of the indicted suspects, Ernesto Martin, was questioned by U.S. law enforcement officials. In the last months of the undercover investigation, Martin had been sent by the undercover agents to Mexico City to discuss a deal with Mexicans claiming to represent the Secretary of Defense. Gately said on the CBS News program *60 Minutes* that U.S. officials had cut a deal with Martin. In return for his testimony against a couple of bankers, Gately claims Martin was not asked about his dealings with representatives of the Mexican general in Mexico City.

Following the closure of Operation Casablanca, Gately clashed with his immediate superior, then Customs Special Agent in Charge, John Hensley. Gately spoke out against the U.S. government's handling of the investigation in a *60 Minutes* interview, alleging that when his team tried to test the value of evidence that could have implicated Mexico's Secretary of Defense, his superiors stopped the investigation in order to avoid an international incident. He has since repeatedly claimed that the operation was suspended due to political pressure.

Gately argued that, had the allegations been proven, the U.S. government might have been able to catch one of the largest players in Mexico's drug trade. But the U.S. government did not follow up the claims, made by a money launderer, and secretly filmed on video, that the Mexican Secretary of Defense was connected to a $1 billion money-laundering deal.

Gately also took his allegations to the House of Representatives Subcommittee on Criminal Justice, Drug Policy and Human Resources. In a statement before the House Subcommittee, he claimed that the undercover investigations had found evidence that both the Mexican Defense Minister and senior members of the Mexican President's office were in the market to launder money. Gately said, "It is indisputable that the Secretary of Defense of Mexico was identified as one of the owners of the money on several occasions." He explained that Cervantes was identified as the owner of $150 million, while two other drug traffickers each owned $500 million.

Gately also told the subcommittee that his boss, John Hensley, had leaked information about the operation to a network news executive at a law enforcement conference in Tampa, Florida. Gately also claims that Hensley "torpedoed" a parallel operation targeted at the Felix-Arellano drug cartel. Gately said that when he realized that the U.S. authorities were not going to investigate the case further, he resigned from the U.S. Customs Service. Hensley fought back, accusing Gately of stealing money but the allegations were dropped after an official investigation. Hensley now refuses to comment about the case. Gately went on to receive a $20,000 Presidential award for his work. Both Gately and Hensley have denied the charges and counter charges.

Later investigations have failed to prove whether claims against Mexican officials had any basis in fact, and the U.S. government has consistently argued that the allegations were not substantiated. Many U.S. government figures have gone on record to deny that the investigation was cut short to avoid upsetting the Mexican establishment. Duane Lyons said: "There are references on tape to a general and attempts were made to verify that, but the people who were making the statements really couldn't qualify the information." The Department of Justice has sought to paint Gately as an unreliable witness, saying he is a zealot, who had lost his sense of realism. Stefan Cassella, Assistant Chief of the Asset Forfeiture and Money Laundering section at the U.S. Department of Justice, said: "There is always an agent who thinks that eventually he will get to a Mexican minister. This operation was not cut off to protect the Mexican minister; it was cut off because we had been going two and a half years and we could not go on any longer. So we took it down."

The Department of Justice was greatly relieved when the operation was stopped as they were worried about the drug millions being used to fund Operation Casablanca. Agents are thought to have handled between $150 million and $180 million of drug money, but no more than $35 million was seized as a result of information they provided. At a press briefing on May 18, 1998, Kelly (then Under Secretary for Enforcement) stated that the government hoped to seize a further $122 million in the United States and abroad but officials have since suggested that the amount finally recovered from the banks was substantially lower. A U.S. Treasury release at the time reported that the U.S. authorities had seized $52 million by Wednesday, May 20, 1998.

The low level of recoveries can be explained in a number of ways. First, the undercover agents were almost too successful. They had used the same tools as the cartel launderers themselves, to disguise the sources of the money. But once the money had been disguised, it would not be recovered and confirmed as belonging to the agents. This was because the audit trail of the laundered money had been obliterated in the informal black market for U.S. currency. Many of the cashier's checks received by the U.S. agents had been sold on to bona fide Colombian importers who had bought the U.S. dollar checks for Colombian pesos via black market money brokers. During the 1990s, the Black Market Peso Exchange scam had become a defining feature in laundering Colombian cocaine profits. At this time, officials estimated that up to $12 billion dollars were being laundered each year via black market currency transactions. For further information on the Black Market Peso Exchange, see Chapter 8, "Smoking Guns".

In a related point, it later appeared that the banking schemes devised for the undercover operation were too clever for Government accountants.

More than 100 bank accounts in some 28 different countries posed considerable difficulties for Government lawyers and accountants. Finally the U.S. government faced legal problems in showing that genuine businesses accepted money knowing that it came from the illegal source, namely drugs.

The tortuous routes taken by criminal money is demonstrated by one example, where money laundered by the U.S. government agents ended up in bank accounts in Italy via a money broker. Legitimate Colombian importers had asked the money broker to transfer $100,000 (bought from the money broker for around 90 cents to the dollar) to Italian export companies in order to pay off legitimate business debts. Following a bulk delivery of drug cash in Chicago, the U.S. undercover agents had deposited $100,000 into the Italian bank accounts. "This type of transaction goes on every single day and it is a very difficult system to try to penetrate," said Stefan Cassella.

From the point of view of the two Italian companies to which the undercover agents sent drug proceeds—a jeweler's and a sports shoe business—payments into the companies' bank accounts via cashier's checks would have been indistinguishable from the tens of thousands of other dollars flowing into the business accounts each week as the result of genuine export sales. The only thing that might have made the Italian businesses suspicious was the fact that they were being paid not by the Colombian company invoiced but by a third party based in San Francisco. The U.S. government requested that the Italian companies' accounts be frozen. However, the Italian courts eventually ruled that the deposits had been the result of genuine export deals, and since the companies had been the unwitting beneficiaries of drug money, the funds were released back into their accounts.

Among the proceeds netted from Casablanca were recoveries from Mexican banks, prosecuted by the U.S. authorities. But these were also comparatively small. Mexico's second- and third-largest financial institutions at that time, Bancomer and Banca Serfin, both pleaded guilty in a Los Angeles court to criminal charges of money laundering. Bancomer agreed to forfeit $9.4 million and Banca Serfin agreed to forfeit $4.2 million. They also agreed to pay criminal fines of $500,000 each. Although criminal charges against a third bank, Confía, which had by this time been purchased by Citicorp, were dismissed, Confía agreed in a civil action to forfeit $12.2 million in drug proceeds. Nine other Mexican banks and three Venezuelan banks were also identified as offering money-laundering services but escaped indictment.

A total of 26 Mexican and five Venezuelan bankers were indicted although many were lower-level executives. Much to the embarrassment of the international banking community, some of the Mexican banks had significant foreign ownership. Bancomer, Banca Serfin, and Banca Confía were part owned by Bank of Montreal, HSBC, and Citibank respectively at the time of the indictments. The revelations that Raul Salinas, the brother of former Mexican president Carlos Salinas, had siphoned more than $100 million out of the country via Citibank (see Chapter 9), added to that bank's woes.

Even Banorte, one of Mexico's biggest banks, was implicated alongside its smaller partners and had some of its assets confiscated. It later had them returned, but much damage had been done, says Robert Chandler, the former General Director of Banorte: "Over the next two days [following asset seizures on Banorte's U.S. accounts] our market capitalization fell by 12.3% or $93 million. So real events turned out to be worse than our worst case scenario." The charges against Banorte were dismissed in July 1999 and the bank recovered the full amount seized—some $15 million—plus interest due. Shaken by the investigation, Banorte closed more than 120 accounts deemed "highly vulnerable" to money laundering in the wake of Operation Casablanca.

Operation Casablanca is the largest sting operation undertaken by U.S. law enforcement. It had lasted 31 months and employed no fewer than 200 U.S. Customs Service agents and 35 DEA agents. It involved more than 110 banks in 18 different countries. In the course of the operation, undercover agents had shown their ability to penetrate the chains of command in the Cali and Juárez drug cartels. Casablanca would be analysed by the U.S. Government for quite some time to understand its outcome and implications. A strategy report released by the Bureau for International Narcotics and Law Enforcement in 1998 reported that seizures resulting from Casablanca amounted to $100 million, four tons of marijuana, and two tons of cocaine. It also led to the arrests of 167 people, including 28 bankers from twelve of Mexico's nineteen largest banks. The U.S. government secured more than 40 convictions.

Of course the political fall-out in Washington was anything but rosy and the then U.S. Secretary of State Madeleine Albright was forced into the embarrassing position of signing a formal undertaking that the United States would never again mount an undercover operation in Mexico without first telling the Mexican government. While Mexico would long argue that Casablanca should never have been started, agents inside the U.S. government who put years of their lives into the operation, would complain it should never have been finished. They point to dark political forces among the U.S. political establishment, who lobbied against the operation, in case it upset relations with the Mexican Government which had wedded itself to the North American Free Trade Agreement (NAFTA).

And what of the man at the center of the operation, the undercover agent Fred Mendoza, aka Javier Ramirez himself? He put his neck on the line on countless occasions. He is now a U.S. citizen and has been moved under the witness protection scheme but must still be subject to heavy security protection. No one knows how much of the estimated $10 million payoff he collected, but he certainly made several million dollars out of the undercover operation. Court documents suggest that he had collected at least $2 million paid by the U.S. government for information, expenses, and commissions during the three-year operation, even before he claimed his 10 percent fee of all the drugs and money seized as a result of the sting.

His "handler" and the brainchild of the operation, Bill Gately, is likely to be in a much less favourable position. Having left the U.S. Customs, he remains bitter about the outcome of Casablanca. But regrettably he defied all the author's many attempts to contact him.

Chapter 11

Laundering Footmen

Hawala is a means of moving money across borders almost as old as the financial system itself. It relies on the trust that exists between members of the same ethnic group to fulfill financial obligations. Some of the time transactions are honest. But much of the time, hawala is abused by money launderers, and at worst, by terrorists.

Hawala

HAWALA IS THE HINDI WORD FOR TRUST. The financial system that bears this name is used by Indian and Pakistani communities that want to send money to remote spots in India or Pakistan that are poorly served by banks. It is the Asian subcontinent variation on a principle developed by Chinese merchants in the tenth century to facilitate the movement of money. These ingenious operators created bills of exchange called *fei-ch'ien,* or *flying money.* Mario Possamai, an academic expert on money laundering, described flying money like this: "[Chinese] tea merchants wished to transfer profits realized from the sale of tea in north China back to the tea-producing south, but found the shipment of cash both cumbersome and perilous . . . the transfer problem was solved by the institution of "flying money" whereby merchants deposited cash with . . . "memorial-presenting courts" in return for vouchers guaranteeing reimbursement in designated provinces. Thereby a double transfer of cash was realized without an actual physical transfer."

The Emperors filled their coffers using taxation on money declared to the "memorial-presenting courts." According to Possamai, "The ancient precursors of today's underground banks were created to meet a commercial need during the Chinese T'ang dynasty."

The Canadian academic R. T. Naylor, a respected but cynical observer, suggests that the Chinese informal banking system grew out of "a context of mistrust of formal banks, political turmoil, and persecution of Chinese minorities." The more efficient a banking method, the more likely it will be abused. So *fei-ch'ien*, like *hawala*, has been used to cheat the banking system, says Rod Samler, the former Chairman of the United Nations (UN) Task Force on Money Laundering: "The Chinese underground system was one of the earliest forms of money laundering."

The Asian form of flying money—hawala—is an equally double-edged system. Used properly, it is a simple and above-board method of serving the banking needs of poor people. When it is abused, it becomes a secret and untraceable route for transmitting around the world fraudulent money and terrorist finance.

Hawala works like this. If an Indian worker in London wants to send £5,000 to a family member back home in Delhi, he goes to a hawaladar (the hawala broker who is sometimes called *thakedar*) and gives him the money in cash. He may also put it into a specified local bank account. The hawaladar then calls his counterparty hawaladar in Delhi and asks him to make a payment of the rupee equivalent of £5,000 to the family relative. For security, both the family relative and the Delhi-based hawaladar are given a code number independently, which they can match when the pickup takes place. The hawaladar in Delhi is responsible for bringing the money to the relative's house or arranging a pickup. The London-based hawaladar is responsible for repaying the Indian agent, or providing a service that remits the value of the first transaction.

The great unbanked of the developing world benefit from hawala. Others will use it for more obscure purposes like avoiding the costs and inefficiencies of the formal banking system. The hawaladars for their part receive commissions, although these will be a lot less than the amounts their customers would have to pay their own banks for similar international arrangements, especially when customers are in remote spots. Again, this is a perfectly proper purpose for hawala, and one that all users of the West's expensive banking systems understand.

The hawaladar is drawn from the same community as his customers. Intangible elements like ethnic background, family knowledge, and relationships establish the trust on which the contract is established between the customer and the agent or hawaladar. The hawaladar is not required to provide formal educational criteria, diplomas, verification, and so on. The supposedly objective tests of ability and reliability that govern the relationship between a conventional Western bank customer and his banker or insurance broker do not apply. If one party abuses the trust on which the system is based, the community applies the sanction, not the state. The result is a closed network, resistant to the external controls or supervision that provide the guarantee required by government that their financial system is sound, and used by honest people.

Hawala systems require minimal infrastructure or expense—no more than a telephone and a fax machine or a computer sitting on a desk. This means that hawaladars can move around with ease, slipping through the net of law enforcement when one is found to have handled dirty money or be linked to a crime.

Systems like hawala and flying money do not transfer cash, but do transfer "value." The money does not move, but instead a financial debt instrument or relationship is set up. In the example stated above, the UK-based hawaladar is "in the money" (as the futures and options market would describe it), while the Indian hawaladar has paid out the money and is therefore "out of the money." To use financial markets terminology again, the Indian broker has an option worth £5,000 that he can exercise from the London broker.

The two brokers have many ways of balancing their books or clearing their futures and options. One of these is simply to perform a mirror image of the transaction, for example, when an Indian in Delhi wants to pay a relative in London. In this way the money is reimbursed. But hawaladars can also be used to finance imports and exports. So let us say that the hawaladar in Delhi has been contacted by an Indian-based company that wants to import a number of computers (that have a value of £5,000) from the United Kingdom. In this case, the hawaladar in Delhi would ask the London hawaladar to make a £5,000 payment to the computer dealer. The two symmetrical £5,000 payments would then balance the books for both hawaladars, who would charge their customers a small percentage commission for handling the transaction.

Larger-scale hawala transactions are likely to go through an intermediary, most often found in Dubai—the hub of the international hawala network. Hawaladars boost their profits by speculating or arbitraging currency as part of the transaction. To avoid extended periods of imbalance, a cash transfer may be made by the party "in the money."

The Hawala system is also used by businessmen moving money out of countries where governments impose controls on rates on foreign exchange markets to discourage foreign currency leaving the country. For example, Indian hawaladars, in places where there are large expatriate communities, such as Dubai, will make markets in Indian rupees and Dubai dirhams, for example, giving much more favorable rates than those available in Delhi. The Delhi business person contacts his or her local hawaladar, who in turn contacts a foreign exchange agent or hawaladar in Dubai, where the rupee/Dubai dirham rate can be as much as a third higher than that obtainable in Delhi. The hawala system has a conspiratorial context, as it undermines foreign exchange controls imposed by governments in the Indian subcontinent. But this does not appear to bother Sultan Bin Nasser al Suwaidi, the Governor of the Central Bank of the United Arab Emirates. He told the author in 2004, "Currency control systems have been discredited by the IMF [International Monetary Fund] and the World Bank because they destroy economies."

Hawala is regarded as faster, more efficient, and normally cheaper than other money remitting services, especially those offered by conventional banks. It also allows money to be delivered to remote areas where the local bank branch is far removed. The facets of hawala that make it efficient also facilitate abuse. Use of the hawala is open to any member of the community that it serves who has the trust of the hawaladar. Hawaladars are not regulated, and they do not perform any formal checks on the identity of a hawala user beyond ensuring that the user is known within the community. Those with dishonest intentions can break into the hawala system in three ways. First, they can deceive a genuine hawaladar, exploiting his or her international network and putting genuine brokers at risk. Second, he can seek collusion with the hawaladar, offering incentives to close his eyes to unusual transactions. Third, he can set up his own hawala system, solely to transfer illegal money or funds. Typical abusers of the hawala system include migrant workers on expired visas, evaders of tax or import duties, money launderers, and, most seriously, terrorists.

Islamic terrorists have been found to abuse hawala systems, bringing hawala into disrepute. There are no systems in place to preclude such arrangements, and investigations by law enforcement from outside the community are likely to face obstructions. The beauty of hawala, for the abuser, is that it leaves no paper trail and hawaladars do not keep detailed formal records of their transactions. Indeed, police report that the book-keeping practices are typically extremely rudimentary.

Hawala and Bureaux de Change in the UK

Informal systems of money transfer grew rapidly in Britain during the late 1980s and 1990s as regulators slept. The biggest example of their failure was their reluctance to clamp down on the BCCI scandal. But smaller crooked operations were springing up unhindered all over the United Kingdom. These tiny institutions were supported by larger banks, which at the very least turned a blind eye to their activities.

The country was awash with black money operators, who were assisting the European drug trade. They were using the United Kingdom as a stopping point for the transfer of cash to the Middle East. The United Kingdom had become a home for terrorist money that would play a key role in the terrorist attacks on the World Trade Center on September 11.

The process of laundering money, like Caesar's Gaul, is sometimes divided into three stages. The first stage, *placement,* entails the introduction of dirty cash into the system. The second, *layering,* involves the commingling of clean with dirty money to disguise it; the third, *integration,* involves the investment of semi-laundered cash or financial instruments into objects or bank accounts that make it indistinguishable from white cash.

Placement is the riskiest stage since the individuals must deal with the physical evidence of the laundering, namely the cash itself. The bureau de change manager who is found with massive amounts of money will have to explain its origin and his purpose in moving it. He may well have encountered organized crime operators or drug traders in the process of acquiring the cash, further incriminating him. The money may also have come off the street and have high levels of drugs smeared on it, so-called street money, in which case he will have to be yet more persuasive. Technology to test drugs on cash is becoming more sophisticated, and its results better accepted by courts.

The motley crew of bureaux de change proprietors, managers, couriers, and bag carriers described below, service the needs of organized criminals many stages up the organizational tree. Some of these may have "integrated" such large sums of money that they have been able to acquire respectability as financiers, running apparently clean companies. Others still lurk in the shadows waiting for the day when they can cut free from their roots. The foot soldiers, on the other hand, are locked into the hazardous process of place-ment, and they exhibit many of the characteristics of the small entrepreneur, who must be flexible and lean. They also tend to restrict their physical opera-tions to a single neighborhood and their staff to close family or friends, often from their own ethnic group.

Laundering entrepreneurs at this primary part of the process typically have their roots embedded in ethnic communities. Indeed, hawala banking is sometimes described as "underground" banking. This contrasts with conven-tional, above-ground banking, which is rooted in the establishment and substantially white and middle class. One perhaps naïve view of this divide is that the ethnic groups are left to deal with the money when it is illegal and dangerous while the establishment handles the same money only when it is cleaned, integrated and ready for conversion into financial instruments. Those supporting the established banking system might argue that the last thing upright bankers would suspect is that the funds underpinning their high street or main street operations came through a back street bureau whose customers had taken it off the street after a drug trade. Another, more cynical view, is that the established bankers know that the money is black and, because they are so dependent on its massive flows, turn a blind eye.

Financial institutions have sought to enter that grey territory between basement and establishment at their peril. The most recent acknowledged instance was the now dismantled Bank of Credit and Commerce International (BCCI). BCCI was closed down in 1991 because it claimed to be a bank with a presence on high streets and in financial markets. At the same time it had been found guilty in the United States of handling the drug cash generated by Panama's General Noriega, among others. The fine line between bureaux and banks is maintained by a financial enforcement estab-lishment arguably more interested in protecting its name than in the integrity of its underlying funds.

The amount of cash that these foot soldiers handle is vast. Bureaux and transmitters in the United Kingdom handled some half a billion pounds of dirty cash between 1998 and 2001. British police and Customs and Excise officials woke up to the scale of activities performed by the sector in the late 1990s and began a number of full-scale investigations of cash handlers. They found that that sector was not merely transmitting cash from the British drug market across the world, but was so leaky that drug cash from abroad was imported into the United Kingdom in crates for processing through the British transmitting and banking systems. Much of it was then sent on to Dubai, the destination for a massive amount of drug money, where it was processed for dispatch to other parts of the Middle East, Pakistan, and elsewhere in Asia.

Terrorist outrages and a renewed concern about financial crime have belatedly provided law enforcement with a new enthusiasm for going after the sources of funds. One UK Customs and Excise officer said: "We believe that attacking the money is as important as, if not more important than, attacking the drugs coming into the country. You do more harm by taking the money than you do by taking the drugs when they arrive. Drugs can be replaced but money is much more difficult to get back."

Money seizures hold the prospect of cutting the drug trade off at the roots. Without the money to fund the grower, the drugs do not come out of the ground, let alone make the journey to the United States. The desperation with which the drug trade guards its money is based on the massive leverage that the initial investment provides. A simple comparison of the wholesale and retail prices of heroin shows the inflation of a relatively small amount of seed capital. An overseas wholesaler will sell a kilo of heroin for around £10,000, which can then be sold on the streets of the United Kingdom for around £60,000 to £70,000. If that £60,000 to £70,000 is confiscated before it leaves Britain, then payments for the next six or seven kilos are effectively blocked, theoretically preventing that heroin from reaching the street.

Financiers in Dubai and elsewhere who go nowhere near the street money itself let alone the drugs have set up the systems for bureaux to handle and remit their cash abroad. The experience of Mohinder Singh Basra demonstrates the value to organized crime of a mole in the global financial system. Basra burrowed into his local banks using the pretext that he offered an informal banking system of Hawala before channeling in at least £66 million of dirty money around the world, without a word uttered or red flag raised. The ease with which the global financial network can be accessed by a back street bureau proprietor with a plausible tale and a well-packaged bundle of cash is remarkable.

Basra ran a mobile phone shop cum travel agency in Darlington Street, Wolverhampton, close to the town's financial center. But behind his shop front was an operation that was working much harder than anything the public saw at the front. This soft-spoken but affable man was in reality a hawaladar, or hawala agent. In due course, Basra applied the system developed for hawala to the sinister purpose of changing drug money and transmitting it around the world.

Basra, who was born in 1953, had moved to the United Kingdom from India in the 1970s. He started out in Britain by running a shoe stall in the local market. In due course he bought a shop in the town, selling first phones and then travel services. But the business of selling legitimate air tickets and mobile phones never made much money, and sometimes ran at a loss. So when an Indian friend asked him to make a payment on his behalf in the United Kingdom in return for a commission, he saw a way to add a further money-making string to his bow. That deal went smoothly, and he began to offer hawala services to other members of the local Indian and Pakistani community, many of whom wanted to send money back home to relatives on the Indian subcontinent. Now he not only sold travel agency services and mobile phones, but also primitive banking services for the Asian community, of which he was a part.

He operated out of a small room behind his retail shop front that the police later called his "counting room." His two bookkeepers endured a room without windows lit only by gloomy fluorescent lighting. The room opened onto a driveway that led to the road, an obscure enough location to discourage interest in the property. The room had two working surfaces; the counting machine sat on one, money laid out ready for bagging and onward dispatch sat on the other.

Basra wore two masks. Wearing one mask, he was a provider of genuine financial services to his local community. Wearing the other, he serviced the drug-dealing community, transmitting their illegal money around the world.

In the course of eighteen months, between early 2000 and the middle of 2001, Basra's hawala business may have accounted for as much as £13.5 million, deposited perfectly legally by members of his local community, with needs to transfer small amounts of cash overseas. This figure was later used by the police to assess Basra's genuine business, as distinct from his corrupt activity, and it may well be an over-estimate. One policeman who studied Basra's hawala documents indicated that Basra's shop was little more than a mom-and-pop store with modest clients, and a small turnover. He said: "We have recovered from the shop documents where you can clearly see "£5,000, Miss Singh, £5,000 to Miss Singh senior who lives behind the post office in a village in an area of Pakistan." This has been written down and recorded, and it is proper hawala. The person in this country has paid the money into Basra's bank account and Basra has given them an order number."

While hawala is quite legal if the money is, the integrity of Mohinder Singh Basra's business changed forever when he crossed the fine line between solely providing hawala banking and money laundering in 1999. That was the year when, according to police sources, he met for the first time Javid Actar Chaudhary. Chaudhary came from a quite different background to Basra. He was a wealthy Pakistani with homes in Holland, Paris, Dubai, and Pakistan and two passports, one Dutch, one Pakistani. A qualified lawyer and barrister in Pakistan with service in the Pakistani air force, he also owned companies in Dubai and in the United States. Chaudhary's companies were allegedly involved with the international movement of large amounts of money. The wire transfer documents and documents setting up the bank accounts used by Basra to make international transfers allegedly carry Chaudhary's name as well as Basra's.

The scale and, of course, quality of Basra's business changed very quickly. While Basra's agency was purely acting as a hawala broker, its turnover was measured at the most in the hundreds of thousands. But when, in approximately January 2000, it began to take in dirty money, turnover rose steeply to £2 million. But that was only the start. In February 2001, a bureau was closed down by the Customs and Excise in neighboring Birmingham after a money-laundering investigation, and Basra in Wolverhampton benefited from the cash released onto the market. Basra gave the stray black money a home, and his throughput rose meteorically, first to £6 million and then to £11.5 million in a single month. The total deposits oscillated around £6 million for a few months before the closure of Basra's operation in June 2001. It is likely that some of this money was imported in crates into the United Kingdom from Europe, to take advantage of the lax money transfer and bureau de change regulations that existed in the United Kingdom.

The black money was delivered to Basra by drug dealers and their bag carriers in a manner that was as carefully planned as it was sleazy. Meetings took place in anonymous supermarket parking lots and small side streets where bags of cash were transferred from one car trunk to another quickly and secretively. Both depositor and Basra wanted to disappear into the night as quickly as possible, and barely a word was spoken between them during the handover. Given the amount of cash in transit and the risk of compromise if the two men were caught together, these operations were planned with almost military precision. Basra would be called beforehand and given precise details of his parking location, the rendezvous time, and the car bringing the money. One policeman commented, "They would just shake hands, say, 'how are you,' and then, bang! The money went into the boot, and off they went. That was the way money was collected."

The rendezvous were scattered around England, in locations as far apart as London and Yorkshire. On a single day, Basra had a rendezvous in a side street in London's East Ham district before making the long journey over to Wembley in North West London where he went to the Asda supermarket parking lot for another collection. An Iranian operator provided him with a bag containing half a million pounds worth of cash. This had come from Money Link International, another bureau-type transmitter suspected by UK Customs of money laundering. This Iranian was in turn connected to a group of convicted drug dealers.

Police and Customs pursuing Basra had to go to great lengths to show that he was handling the proceeds of drugs and not merely legally gotten money that anyone can handle with impunity. So it was quite a triumph when they discovered that the bag full of cash given by the drug dealers to the Iranian appeared to be the same bag that the Iranian passed to Basra. They also claim that Basra had a rendezvous in Rotherham (a town in the north of England) with a man who subsequently went on trial for importing £5 million worth of Ecstasy. Three of the men that Basra met were found to be part of a gang who were subsequently given a total of 30 years in jail. Basra had embarked on a business at the very riskiest end of the money transmission spectrum. His business partners were actively under investigation by the police.

The frequency and anonymity of these meetings indicated a pattern of behavior later cited as suspicious by police investigating the case. One asked, "Would a reasonable person drive 140 miles from Wolverhampton to London to meet someone in a car park in London at 9 o'clock at night, that he didn't know, to collect a bag containing £150,000? A normal individual would think that was suspicious."

The best explanation that was given by one participant in this dubious trade was that he was "collecting bags full of clothes for the poor of the Indian community." As Basra drove back to Wolverhampton along the motorway from his strange meetings, he must surely have wondered what kind of person would trust a stranger like him with hundreds of thousand of pounds in cash. The deviation from the "trust banking" that had started his career as a money handler was stark and in the end devastating.

Back at his Darlington Street shop, Basra counted the money, and bagged it, before depositing it in one of his numerous bank accounts. The UK bank that received the majority of the dirty money was National Westminster Bank. With the money safely handed over to the bank, Basra went back to his shop and faxed a wire transfer to the bank detailing a series of immediate funds transfers to deposit the money abroad. Invariably large sums were "smurfed"—broken down into smaller chunks—to make each transfer less conspicuous. Each transfer involved a transit point in an American bank, and an end destination, which was usually in Dubai. Police sources say the primary four recipients of the money in Dubai were bureaux called Sajwani, World-Link, Multi-Link and The Federal Exchange. Investigators later reported that the red flag that alerted the bank was the speed with which Basra wanted the money moved out of his accounts.

Dubai has long been the Middle East's unregulated trading center where Arab business operates freely. This is hardly surprising. Its financial sector has sprung up topsy-turvy to service the Gulf's oil and construction boom. The large numbers of expatriate Asian workers, primarily from Pakistan, India, and Sri Lanka, who need to send money home, uses its hawala and bureau operations. Until recently, this sector was almost completely undisciplined. In recent years it has passed money-laundering laws and regulations requiring it to assist with requests from international police forces. The implementation of these laws will require trained and competent staff, traditionally largely missing from this region.

While the channel between Western drug markets, Dubai, and the Indian subcontinent was freely used by drug traffickers who needed to fund the Afghanistan, Nepalese, and Pakistani drug-growing combines, it is widely suspected that terrorists also used it, in conjunction with the drug dealers. Money that flowed through the channel would be used to disguise the terrorist money, whose end goal was to fund either Islamic operations or arms purchases. Indeed, sophisticated bureaux in Dubai and Saudi Arabia have been pinpointed by Jean-Francois Seznec, a banker who formerly worked for JP Morgan Chase in the Persian Gulf, as primary conduits for terrorist money. Seznec says bureaux and money transmitters are ingrained in the culture of the Gulf: "Moneychangers have existed in the Gulf since the time of Abraham, literally. They were the moneychangers to the *hajj*, the pilgrimage, and the pilgrimage existed before Mohammad. These people have been very much appreciated because they provide very cheap, decent quality service." But Seznec also accepts that the system has been abused. "Some drug people, the mules, get five or ten thousand dollars from the merchants in Jeddah and then they send that money to various places. The poorly regulated state of the Dubai financial system means that these people will be able to transfer more sizeable amounts." Moneychangers in the United Arab Emirates and Yemen, where regulation is very weak, may also be used by terrorist financiers.

Dubai-based bureaux were the primary recipients of the Chaudhary money, but there were some other recipients. For example, money was sent to companies in the diamond industry in Hong Kong and Uganda. Several million pounds was also paid to an apparently respectable Finnish tobacco company for cigarette shipments thought to be routed around Cadiz, Spain and Angola, but whose ultimate destination was the illegal UK market.

Money transmission of black cash from the United Kingdom to international banks and bureaux using the banking system was Basra's principle activity. But his travel agency provided another service to the black market money handlers. This was money changing in a manner identical to that provided by the master of this black art, Ussama El-Kurd (see below). Black-money handlers came to Basra to change street money—that is, money from drugs trading—into guilders for onward dispatch to Holland. Basra used the services of local banks, where, of course, he was a regular and well-known customer, to change the street money for large guilder notes. These were then allegedly taken to Holland by a man called Mahmoodi who was an associate of Chaudhary.

Mahmoodi was no stranger to the world of black cash delivery and receipt. He not only owned his own money exchange company in Dubai called M International but seemed to do much of the delivery himself, saving the cost and risk of hiring third parties, no doubt. The stamps in his passport showed that he traveled almost constantly—a telltale sign, in this world of secret cash and subterfuge, of a global courier with a lot of dirty money to dispense. He was so close to Chaudhary that the latter, police sources say, arranged and paid for his travel and hotels when he was delivering his black cash, although Mahmoodi later ordered Basra to pay Chaudhary back. A sum of £50,000 was found to have gone from Basra to a Chaudhary bank account.

When Mahmoodi was caught in February 2001, he was wearing the strange uniform of the experienced drug money courier. This unmistakable giveaway involves a specially constructed set of underpants designed like boxer shorts but with large pouches at the front attached to shoulder straps to prevent them falling down. These ensure that wads of cash stuffed into the pouches do not fall down in mid-journey, embarrassing the carrier at best and revealing his hidden wares at worst. Mahmoodi and his female associate claimed the strange clothing was a precaution against being robbed. Mahmoodi was convicted of money laundering and sentenced to five years in prison.

As Basra's illegal business thrived, the mysterious Chaudhary spent less time in the shop and more time in Dubai where, police sources assume, he was organizing the reception of the money, and perhaps even spending it. The fact that Chaudhary was out of the country when Basra was closed down was no surprise to the authorities.

The whistle was blown on Basra by one of the banks where he regularly deposited the money after a counter clerk noticed how average individual deposits of £5,000 (the receipts from simple hawala) had skyrocketed to over £100,000. A suspicious transaction report (STR) was sent to the National Criminal Intelligence Service and an investigation begun.

The police obtained a court order that allowed them to watch in secret the movement of money through Basra's accounts, and they were staggered by the amounts. On some days, around £500,000 cash would be deposited, and in the month of April 2001, no less than £11,689,956 went through the JM Exchange account. Basra was placed under surveillance and was soon being trailed daily up and down the country.

Between January 2000 and June 2001, police watched £66 million move through the accounts of the shabby JM Exchange. They made their move to stop the operation and bring Basra in on June 4, 2001. Basra was followed to the parking lot of a Happy Eater restaurant (a popular chain of eateries) on the edge of Manchester, where he was observed taking a large bag from someone who quickly sped away. The police pulled Basra over on his way back to Wolverhampton and found that the bag contained £180,000 in cash. A subsequent raid on the JM Exchange offices yielded a further £220,000 cash. When you add in the £200,000 he deposited in the bank before going on his collection round to the Happy Eater, the amount handled that day came to over £600,000.

The police raid on Basra's house, which followed the bust, sent his family into trauma. "When we kicked in the front door," the officer recalled, "one of the daughters was revising for her exams." Basra told police that he had no idea that the money was dirty. Police said later tests on the banknotes recovered from the raid showed abnormally high traces of heroin, although this evidence was not submitted at his trial. By way of a wry aside, police also noted that whoever owned the money had shown no interest in trying to recover it after it had been impounded.

The proceeds were simply those of hawala banking, said Basra when interrogated. His case was weakened by his inability to show evidence of how the money was made or indeed proper records of its source. He appears an altogether incongruous criminal; his paperwork was so slapdash and unprofessional that some of his records for the year 2000 were written haphazardly on the pages of a 1997 diary, while there was no evidence of someone who had made a large amount of money and spent it lavishly. He lived with his wife and three children in a modest house, and drove an old BMW. Friends in the local community were astounded that this pillar of their community could be so involved in crime, and a number offered to stand the million pound bail required by the courts.

Police estimated that over £60 million of black money had gone through the Basra accounts, yet when the case came to court, they accepted that much of the money he handled was legitimate hawala deposits and Basra was only charged with laundering £25 million of dirty money.

He pleaded guilty in December 2002 and was given an eight-year prison sentence. The difficulty in distinguishing clean money using Basra's hawala service and black money using his laundering service plagued the police investigation. It was impossible, for example, to decide whether twelve payments of £500 each into a Basra account, made at a cash machine just before the bank opened in the morning, were legitimate hawala transactions, or "smurfing" to disguise a £6,000 deposit of black cash.

While investigations of the British accounts were difficult, researches in the United States were immensely time consuming and the British police took eight months to get evidence of the American accounts from U.S. banks. Retrieving material from Dubai took longer still. However, in October 2004, UK police tracked Chaudhary to Holland where he was arrested. He was subsequently extradited to the UK and charged with money laundering offences. Chaudhary pleaded not guilty. He has yet to face trial.

If Basra engineered the entry of black cash into the financial system, another British practitioner of the cash-handling art persuaded banks to part with clean money in exchange for his dirty street notes. Ussama El-Kurd, dubbed by those in the trade of black money as simply "Sammy," was a bureau de change proprietor who gained some additional legal acclaim as the first person to be convicted of drug money laundering without a conviction for the underlying offense of drug trafficking. El-Kurd's bureau in central London did nothing more than change "street money" into clean notes in currencies that suited the drug dealers and drug suppliers. Nevertheless, the cartels for which he worked considered his role so valuable that they poured no less than £70 million through his system, making him rich in the process. The wealth was very temporary, as British Customs and Excise caught him and put him through the British courts, which quite quickly prosecuted, fined, and imprisoned him.

Ussama El-Kurd

While Britain's National Crime Squad were investigating Basra, their colleagues in the Customs and Excise were tracking the activities of a Palestinian Arab who was accepting large amounts of black money into a central London bureau. This was Ussama El-Kurd, who was born in Jerusalem in 1948. He moved to London in the 1970s and gained British citizenship soon afterwards, settling in a modest semi-detached house in the outer West London suburb of Greenford.

British police first noticed him in 1988 when he was convicted of gold smuggling in Athens. El-Kurd had imported gold into Greece without paying appropriate duties, and then charged the taxes to his customers. The financial trickster absconded from Greece before serving his sentence and appears to have avoided extradition.

El-Kurd came to the United Kingdom, setting up one retail venture after another. First he established a shop selling newspapers and other low-value goods in London's Edgware Road, a street popular with the capital's Middle Eastern community. Then he set up a car rental agency. After that he went into the video rental business, operating out of premises at 22 Notting Hill Gate, a prestigious address. Finally El-Kurd added a six foot by six foot cubicle to his video outlet and set up a bureau de change, called The Notting Hill Exchange. This bureau may have started as a service for the area's many tourists and foreign visitors. But by 1994, it had become known as the favored cash converter for some of the country's top drug smugglers, criminals, and professional money launderers.

One of these was Peter McGuinness, an unemployed Liverpudlian, who must have thought he was on the road to riches when local drug barons paid him handsomely for transporting large amounts of cash to the London bureau. Those in the local mafia called him their "bagman," and McGuinness served them diligently. McGuinness passed the time drinking at a local public house, while El-Kurd counted the money.

The link between El-Kurd's operation and McGuinness's Northern English drug gang is significant for the way it shows the changing cultural mix of organized crime. The cultural homogeneity that typified American gangs as a way both of guaranteeing security and facilitating communication between people of a similar background has been abandoned. Gangs now operate across social and cultural barriers, sometimes taking advantage of one community's particular skills. Taking this one step further, organized crime groups are by definition extraordinarily hardheaded, driven by opportunities to make money rather than by patriotic or other emotional criteria. So there is ample evidence of groups belonging to one nationality trading arms or other illegal commodities with those belonging to a nationality whose country is at war with them. So Croatian arms traders dealt with Serbians while the two countries were in a state of war. Extraordinarily, one dealer who was involved in the BCCI fraud sold weapons both to Christians and Muslims during the civil war in Lebanon.

McGuinness left his modest council house in Liverpool each week and took the train to London to drop off the bag of money at the Notting Hill Exchange. He kept the process as simple as possible. When he had no more than £250,000 to bring down to London, McGuinness stuffed it into a bag that he slung over his shoulder. When his clients had had a good week and he needed to bring down £500,000 for conversion, he put it into a suitcase and carried it by hand.

El-Kurd invariably counted the money as soon as McGuinness arrived, to exclude any possibility of error or misunderstanding; then he stacked the notes into neat piles and wrapped elastic bands around them to keep them trim. Finally, he put them into bags to allow the money to be deposited with minimum complication into bureaux de change and banks in central London. McGuinness was said to have been connected with an enterprise set up by the notorious British gang leader Cocky Warren, who had holed up in Holland, where he bought drugs for supply to the north-west of England. Cocky needed the sterling proceeds converted into guilders. This was where El-Kurd and his team were so useful.

El-Kurd's role as a central London-based bureau proprietor enabled him to claim to banks and respectable travel agencies like Thomas Cook that he acted as a conduit for the cash of many London bureaux. "He had gained the confidence of the banks and the major money brokers because he was able to describe the type of business he was running," observed a detective involved in the case. So when his minions brought in very large amounts of cash and asked for guilders or other European currencies and dollars, high street banks or main street banks, like Barclays, who were hungry for his business, even if they suspected it was dubious, accepted his word. Barclays had taken in no less than £30 million worth of El-Kurd cash before it at last became suspicious and alerted the National Criminal Intelligence Service (NCIS).

El-Kurd's staff hawked their dirty wares around London banks and Thomas Cook outlets unimpeded for some two years. They traveled between the branches on London buses carrying hundreds of thousands of pounds, and one can only wonder how their fellow passengers would have reacted had they known what was in their plastic bags. This austere form of travel was less an attempt to mingle and disguise the cash carriers with London crowds than a means to save the expense of taxis. El-Kurd was obsessive about expenses and completely ruthless with anyone who wasted money or carelessly risked security, putting his well-oiled operation in jeopardy. A tyrannical boss, driven by greed, he threatened his staff with the most ferocious penalties if they let him down. The members of his team dutifully brought the guilders or other foreign notes back from the bank to the bureau, where El-Kurd handed them over to McGuinness. He arranged for couriers to move them to Amsterdam. As one commentator put it succinctly, "El-Kurd was just a man in a shop who took money in and delivered money back."

The sums El-Kurd's team brought to the banks were so large that the cashiers might have suspected a deception. Another suspicious element was the fact that El-Kurd's staff insisted on changing their sterling street cash for 1,000 guilder notes, the largest Dutch denomination, worth some £330 at the time. Notes as large as this were relatively scarce in London, and on many occasions he exhausted a bank's supply. But El-Kurd needed them to reduce the physical bulk of the cash he was holding. A sports bag holding £250,000 in £5, £10 and £20 notes would become just a few large parcels once they had been converted into 1,000 guilder notes. This greatly simplified the courier's task of hiding his money as he smuggled it out of England across the English Channel en route to Holland.

Police brought the El-Kurd laundry to a halt at the end of October 1996. When they banged on the bureau door and broke into the basement counting house, they found McGuinness laying out over £200,000 worth of dirty bank notes on the counting table. Customs stopped two El-Kurd couriers at Dover at the same time, and removed hundreds of thousands of pounds worth of guilder from their persons. The money was stuffed down their underpants. One source reported, "Dover Customs men found the equivalent of £250,000 in 401,000 guilders, 190,000 Deutschmarks and 4,000 Swiss francs."

When these discoveries were made, El-Kurd was arrested but allowed out on police bail. He could not resist one more fling before his trial, and a month later, while he was under close police surveillance, supplied the cash that enabled more couriers to make their way over to the Netherlands. One courier was caught at a port with £100,000 worth of guilders stuffed down his pants. More allegations were tacked onto El-Kurd's charge-sheet that would be used to powerful effect by his prosecutors over the next two years as they built up their case.

The investigation unearthed a string of crooks and bagmen who visited his bureau to fuel El-Kurd's insatiable appetite for dirty cash. This was later described by police investigator Dave Thompson: "By mid-1994, El-Kurd was changing cash for criminals across the country. . . . Almost every day couriers from there would show up with bags crammed full with cash and leave with their pockets lined with foreign notes . . . having purchased foreign notes, McGuinness would usually hand over the small bundles to the couriers who would take them abroad. One member of the gang was described as the airline KLM's best customer, having made 143 trips to Holland, often going every day. Sometimes he didn't leave Schipol Airport, simply handing over his cash to another in the chain of couriers and returning to Heathrow on the next flight."

Police estimated that over two-and-a-half years, no less than over £70 million belonging to British criminals had passed through El-Kurd's hands. His share was around 5 percent of the takings, or £3.5 million. Investigators found £250,000 at El-Kurd's house in Greenford, a modest suburban area of West London, and some £800,000 worth of jewelry and cash stashed in two safe-deposit boxes. Some £1.2 million had been deposited in 52 bank accounts in the United Kingdom, the Channel Islands, and Switzerland. A portfolio in shares and property made up the balance of his earnings. The passion for holding cash proved much greater than for spending it, as El-Kurd lavished nothing on his family or himself, staying in the same house in Greenford that he had bought when he was a simple newspaper vendor.

The case came to court in 1999 and lasted over five months, subsequently going to appeal. The issue of El-Kurd's knowledge of the source of the money he changed proved pivotal. His defense claimed that El-Kurd could not have known that the money was the proceeds of drug trafficking or other criminal conduct. But the prosecution argued that in money-laundering cases it is impossible to prove that the money came from a particular drug importation or crime, as it would have passed through several people's hands before it reached El-Kurd. They relied on circumstantial evidence to show that El-Kurd must have known that the money came from an unlawful source, in particular the drug industry. According to a Customs officer connected with the case, "Such was the volume and the openness of El-Kurd's trade that he neither cared nor made any attempt to find out where this money was coming from. The denomination of the notes concerned, and the types of monies that he was exchanging were such that it had to be clear that he was getting involved in criminal activity. That was why this is a landmark case."

El-Kurd was the exception, as he was not convicted of any offense that produced the money. He was, in fact, charged with drug trafficking, but acquitted. Nevertheless, the prosecution proved that he must have known the money was dirty, even though they did not prove his involvement in the drug dealing that the prosecution said gave rise to the dirty funds in the first place.

El-Kurd was found guilty and given the maximum sentence allowed at the time for laundering—a hefty fourteen years (reduced to twelve years on appeal). He was also fined £1 million. McGuinness—arguably the launderer who was much closer to the drug dealers than El-Kurd—skipped bail as the trial was about to start. He was sentenced in absentia to ten years' imprisonment, but has still to begin his sentence.

Luis Eduardo Hurtado

While El-Kurd's bureau appears to have serviced the needs of a range of British gangs, the World Exchange bureau de change controlled by Luis Eduardo Hurtado and his confederates serviced only the financial needs of Colombians. The efficiency of this group of launderers matched that of the financial management at any multinational corporation, commented a policeman close to their activities. He said, "Colombians, when they are dealing with drugs, have got a real end-to-end system. They organize the drugs all the way here and they organize the money from the sale of the drugs all the way back again. It is not put down as sale to a wholesaler and then sale to a semi-wholesaler and then on into the dealers. They will control the sale through to 'Wholesale UK' and know who they sold to and be expecting a set amount of money back from it. They will launder the proceeds of those sales and arrange for that laundered money to be either smuggled back out primarily in dollars, or have it telegraphically sent out."

Hurtado came into the country when he was 28 and, by 1997, was a familiar face around London's bureaux de change. He had worked in a bureau called Giro Express before founding World Exchange and was known as a canny operator who took great care to keep his operation as low profile as possible. Over the years, Hurtado had built up a network of Colombian runners to collect street cash from drug dealers and bring it to the bureau.

Once the money was counted, it was packed up in ordinary-looking plastic carrier bags and sports bags and then given to couriers who took it off to a series of bureaux run by operators who were part of the gang. Their role was to change the money into large-denomination dollar bills so that couriers could export it more easily and safely—an operation very similar to that controlled by Ussama El-Kurd. The most significant of Hurtado's network of bureaux was the 7 Day Change. This was no more than a small glass cubicle in a sweet shop in Bayswater, West London, just a few hundred yards from El-Kurd's establishment, and run by Chantana Platt. Platt, who was 50 when the scam was at its most active, was born in Thailand but had acquired British citizenship. She owned a Thai restaurant, which served both as an additional laundering outlet and as an anonymous point to collect and pick up consignments of dirty cash. Hurtado brought her street cash for exchange into clean, large-denomination notes. On one occasion, ironically just after Customs had warned her of her money-laundering reporting obligations, she was forced to purchase $785,000 from a legitimate wholesaler to have the clean money in her bureau to meet a money launderer's need for clean money. Platt laundered $28 million through her bureau.

Hurtado embodied Colombian efficiency and toughness. He ensured all his runners were "clean skins," that is, they did not have criminal records. He also made them travel in the same manner as El-Kurd's team, by public transport to avoid arousing suspicion. Bureaux scattered around London participated in the operation by accepting Hurtado's dirty money in exchange for clean. These included Latin Linkup (owned by Hurtado's partner, Juan Manuel Salgado) at Camden Town; and Rishtan (owned by Suresh Chopra) in Victoria. Colombian gangs are famously clannish and fourteen of Hurtado's sixteen-strong gang were Colombian. While Platt and Chopra added to the range of bureaux Hurtado could tap for clean cash, neither was admitted to the gang's planning process.

Much of the gang's courier work was undertaken by Yolanda Roa-Jiminez, an air stewardess for Avianca, Colombia's national airline. Police tracked her movements closely and obtained the damning evidence of a connection with Hurtado's gang when she was seen accepting bags of cash from Hurtado and his business partner, Mario Giraldo Lopez, in her room at the very smart Royal Garden Hotel in Kensington. She was stopped by UK Customs officers the following day at Heathrow Airport and found to be in possession of $132,000 in cash hidden on her body and concealed in her luggage. She was jailed at the ensuing trial.

This gang's sophistication is underlined by a number of laundering transactions involving financial techniques far removed from physical couriering. For example, they maintained a series of bank accounts that were used to disguise large transfers of black money to Colombia. Hurtado's team paid money into a sterling account that he held in the United Kingdom. Then it was transferred into a dollar account at the same bank and sent telegraphically through a maze of different accounts in Miami, New York, Bogota, and the Isle of Man to a cartel-owned account in Colombia.

In another money-laundering scheme, one of Hurtado's associates paid top-up or replenishing premiums amounting to $835,000 into four financial instruments, called "Long Term International Investment Policies" taken out at offshore institutions. Premiums of this kind are paid as lump sums into insurance policies, which can be used as instruments to save money. About six months later, the policies will be surrendered, and although the policyholder incurs a financial penalty because the policy has not yet matured, the transaction is worthwhile because it generates a "clean" check for the policyholder. Sophisticated launderers have made good use of the lax systems employed by reinsurance agents, often working in unregulated regimes in the Caribbean or Far East. According to insurance expert Stanley Rose, black money in any denomination and in any dubious juris-diction introduced to the system at the lowest end of the reinsurance pyramid can be moved around within the pyramid, enabling the launderer to gain a dollar check drawn on a reputable insurance company in a regulated jurisdiction when it is withdrawn.

Hurtado's operation was brought to a sudden halt in April 2000. He had just left the 7 Day Change in Bayswater with a bag containing $382,000 when a 100-strong team of policemen made simultaneous swoops on the gang. A counting house at the North London home of John Serna Munera, a gang member, was of particular interest.

There police found fourteen large bundles of dollars and a sports bag holding thirteen bundles of dollars and mixed sterling totaling over £2 million. A panel under the bath was used as a hiding place. "An extraordinary number of empty holdalls," two body belts, and suitcases with the lining ripped out of the top and the bottom to reveal a secret compartment for holding cash were key elements in this launderer's armory. An electronic cash counter and a telephone bug detection device were among the gang's other paraphernalia. Forensic work on computers showed emails directing Hurtado to expect deliveries of sterling, while other emails told him to send money to specific accounts in Colombia.

The gang had succeeded in remitting around $70 million of street cash to the Colombian cartels—money that had been generated by the sale of around 2,500 kilos of cocaine on British streets. Hurtado was sentenced in 2002 to eight-and-a-half years in jail, while twelve of his associates were sentenced to a total of 47 years between them.

The tightening of UK regulations concerning bureaux de change since 2001 has no doubt made life harder for launderers. But it is extremely difficult for a government to devise legislation that distinguishes between those activities that are helpful to launderers and the perfectly legitimate and valuable services that the bureaux offer. The sheer number of bureaux, and their obscure locations in tiny booths tucked away in the corner of high street shops, also complicates the law enforcers' monitoring role. Indeed it is that very informality and obscurity that make them so attractive to launderers, and it seems likely that many of them continue to be used for illegal purposes. The ethnic basis of the Colombian criminal bureaux in particular also impedes their infiltration by law enforcement. Bureaux de change and hawala-type networks are best investigated by police working undercover, but there are very few Colombians working for European police forces that could pass muster inside a Colombian gang.

The amount of money that passed through the operations of El-Kurd, Hurtado, and Basra is vast; in a matter of just a few years, these three men handled well over £200 million of street cash, most of which almost certainly came from drug dealing. These cases no more than hint at the scale of street cash laundering in the United Kingdom. Many more schemes like theirs and others yet more ingenious are undoubtedly still operating across the country, processing the billions of pounds that the British drug trade produces. But the United Kingdom is not exceptional in its consumption of illegal drugs. Its situation is replicated across Western Europe and beyond, and it is dwarfed by the size of the drug business in the United States. Indeed, the amount spent annually in the United States by users of illegal drugs has been put at half a trillion dollars, a number that completely overshadows the European industry.

The risk that hawala and bureaux de change systems may be abused by organized criminals, in partnership with terrorists, to effect the international movement of illegal money, raises the pressure on the authorities to introduce some global standards of regulation. While this would be a mammoth (and in some quarters, deeply unpopular) task, the security of the wider financial and civil system make it imperative.

SECTION V

What the World's Doing

Chapter 12:

America's Clampdown on Terrorist Financing

The United States largely turned a blind eye to money laundering and financial abuse prior to September 11. A culture of complacency and corruption was allowed to prevail in the U.S. financial system, unchallenged by regulation. The terrorist outrage prompted the Patriot Act.

THE PATRIOT ACT'S VERY NAME indicates the political thrust of today's current campaign against money laundering. The United States P.A.T.R.I.O.T. Act, which has the rubric of "Uniting and Strengthening America," is a pithy acronym for Providing Appropriate Tools Required to Intercept and Obstruct Terrorism Act. Congress passed the Act on September 25, 2001, just two weeks after the terrorist outrage.

The Patriot Act was the result of a long campaign by American law enforcement agencies to have the American money laundering rules beefed up, indeed brought in line with international norms. They had been resisted by a host of special interests including the financial community, pressure groups working on behalf of offshore centers, by banking organizations, and most importantly by those pursuing the libertarian philosophy of George W. Bush and earlier administrations. The critics said such a law would slow down business, be expensive and put the United States at a competitive disadvantage. That argument had won the day, and the need for controls had slithered down the political agenda. Indeed, as late as 1998, the U.S. Congress had thrown out the fundamental principle that banks should "know their customer," on the grounds that it breached the customer's right to privacy. That would later be the keystone of new controls and a new culture.

Then came terrorism on U.S. soil, and all arguments fell apart. Carol Sergeant, the former managing director, regulatory processes and risk directorate, at the United Kingdom's Financial Services Authority, later commented that, with terrorism, "The United States suddenly caught religion. Prior to Patriot they didn't have terribly good powers and they were almost doing their anti-money laundering work via stealth because there wasn't the legislation that they now have. There wasn't anything like the appetite for going after money laundering that they now have in the U.S."

The Patriot Act's goal is to bring banks around the world in line with America's security interests. It has sent a shiver through the world's financial markets. It has also sent a shiver down American spines, arguably drawing regulators' attention to the weak state of controls at some of America's largest corporations, in particular Enron and World Com. These companies went bust in the wake of September 11, and although the cause was fraud, in the case of Enron money laundering was also involved. The Sarbanes-Oxley legislation, which strengthens the governance of companies, arose out of a similar sense of panic as the Patriot Act.

In its desire to present a single American front against terrorism, the Patriot Act seeks to control foreign banks dealing with U.S. institutions, and that means virtually every bank on the planet. Any bank that deals in dollars must have a relationship, however slight, with an American institution. The result has been a flurry of anti-money laundering activity inside banks not seen since the first laundering laws were passed two decades ago. The Patriot Act has a "long-arm" provision. That means that if the foreign bank has had dealings with the blacklisted person or country anywhere in the world, the bank is barred from dealing with a U.S. banker anywhere in the world.

The Patriot Act dramatically extends powers taken by the U.S. authorities to boycott Cuba. David Baron of the Washington law firm, McDermott, Will and Emery, showed how the law will affect terrorist access to the U.S. banking system, "If you have any contacts with the United States and part of your transaction takes place in the U.S., if you ever touch New York City, if you ever touch Miami, we have jurisdiction over it! It is a terrific and empowering stature. Section 326, customer identification, basically boils down to no more terrorists opening bank accounts in the U.S. with false social security numbers. You have to identify and verify the identity of not only naturalized persons, but also corporate persons. It involves very detailed documentation and all U.S. regulators have agreed with it."

Regulators and bankers may not be so enthusiastic as this lawyer claims, although they are struggling desperately to comply, says R.T. Naylor, an academic at McGill University in Canada and author of *Hot Money*. "Everybody's struggling like crazy to build systems that will somehow meet the approval of the American agenda. The U.S. is trying to force this model on everybody else and Canadian law enforcement doesn't like it. They constantly feel they are being sandbagged by the U.S. police. The same is true of Revenue authorities in most places."

The September 11 outrage fired the enthusiasm in some quarters for more surveillance of every crevice of the financial system. The federal government obtained the right to trace, pursue, and require information and disclosure, when its agencies suspected malpractice. The Patriot Act also greatly extends police powers to conduct surveillance and wire intercepts. These provisions are bitterly resented by the American civil rights lobby that regard such provisions as unconstitutional.

That said, the legislation will make it harder for the sneaky financier to feather his or her nest in a dark corner, out of reach of the bright light of government. More questions will be asked about the provenance of his or her money and history.

The panic that gripped the U.S. enforcement agencies on September 11, 2001 changed a hands-off government, into a probing, interventionist band of big brothers. The suddenness of this about-turn was itself ominous, says Adam Bates, a partner at the accounting firm, KPMG, "The U.S. changed its laws very quickly. The Patriot Act was a combination of many ideas. Some people said it is not the greatest law but it was done with haste. Other countries have spent time thinking about it and have been more deliberate in their thinking."

Republican politicians had fought long and hard against the statutory imposition of Know Your Customer (KYC) rules. They had also resisted attempts to ban the setting up of banking systems in offshore havens where they did not have to declare a beneficial owner. Timon Molloy, the editor of the UK publication, *Money Laundering Bulletin*, commented, "One year before 9/11, America didn't give a damn about Know Your Customer. They were positively opposed to Know Your Customer rules and they said this is a gross intrusion and we will not permit it." The theme is taken up by Mike Adlem, head of the UK office of fraud and money laundering consultants, Protiviti, who conveys the strength of international skepticism of the Patriot Act. "Prior to September 11, 2001, terrorism was not a problem that greatly interested the U.S.A. That is why its anti-money laundering legislation was weak and ineffective. It did little or nothing about the Northern Irish Aid Committee (NORIAD), long suspected by the UK security services and police of providing funding for weapons and bombs to the PIRA—a claim that NORIAD has denied. When the UK unsuccessfully tried to extradite PIRA prison escapees and suspected bombers from the U.S.A. they were deemed to be 'freedom fighters' and not terrorists. It is therefore not surprising that countries that have been dealing with the 'terrorist' problem for many years get fed up of being told by the U.S.A. what they should be doing to combat terrorism . . . or perhaps we should refer to it as freedom fighting!" NORAID is a U.S.-based organization that raises money for republican causes.

The Patriot Act emphasizes the KYC principle, but remarkably the legislation exempts U.S. lawyers from KYC obligations on the grounds that it undermines the client relationship. This puts U.S. lawyers in a privileged position to their European counterparts as European lawyers and accountants, as well as other groups in Europe who handle large sums of money, are caught up in legislation that requires due diligence of clients and reporting of suspicion to law enforcement authorities.

The emotion of the moment completely defused the opposition to the Patriot Act. Professor Naylor says he has talked to many bankers who told him, "Look, I know it's stupid and pointless, but we don't have any choice. We cannot say publicly that we are opposed to this because we will be accused of being soft on crime! Bankers are quite scared of the police and they are scared of the public backlash that the police can create for them. That has not been true in the past; the police view bankers as strange creatures. When the bank has to know about the client's business and whom the client does business with, the bank becomes basically a private detective agency. That is ludicrous."

Xenophobia is another feature of the Patriot Act, comments Rowan Bosworth-Davies, a British money-laundering consultant. "The primary focus of Patriot legislation is not about internal banks, it's about dubious foreign banks. It's all aimed outside, at nasty foreigners." Senator John Kerry, the unsuccessful Democratic candidate in the 2004 Presidential election justifies the national self-interest that lies behind some of the requirements of the Patriot Act. He said in 2001, "We are imposing [anti-money laundering] controls on our own banks and it is going to put them at a competitive disadvantage as foreign banks can rush in and grab our business! So what we have to do is ensure that all foreign banks have the same administrative over-heads that we do and the same infringements on autonomy and secrecy."

The Patriot Act regime works on the binary principle that nation-states are either good or bad, and players in the financial system—both institu-tions and people—are either exemplary or evil. So states in the 'axis of evil' are "baddies," while a so called "white list" proposed by the Patriot Act, includes multilaterals like the World Bank, Western governments, charities, and non-governmental organizations.

Other institutions which the list seeks to outlaw are banks and compa-nies with opaque ownership structures. Foreign political figures connected with a bank or an account will also face scrutiny. Curiously, the legislation does not require American Politically Exposed Persons (PEPs) to be inves-tigated. PEPs is a catchall phrase (first devised by the Wolfsberg group of banks) for people active in public life who might have received bribes. It includes politicians and their families, those involved in administration and the military or in state industries. Publicly quoted banks are already required to disclose their ownership and many have adopted tough poli-cies against handling the funds of PEPs. Private institutions will face a tougher time on both counts.

The offshore world gets particular attention. Much odium had been heaped on U.S. companies especially those that sought tax shelters in offshore jurisdictions prior to September 11. So the Patriot Act bars United States and foreign institutions from setting up a U.S. bank account to shift funds between onshore accounts and offshore "nameplate" banks, that is, those who do not have a physical presence.

Opposition to the Patriot Act has started to surface from within the banking community. For example, banks from outside the United States seeking correspondent relationships with U.S. banks have argued that they do not fall under the U.S. regulatory umbrella and should not be brought within the Patriot Act's jurisdiction. But here John Kerry's principle of reci-procity applies. One U.S. attorney said: "U.S. institutions are currently required to disclose the identity of their regulator, their owners and their agent for service of process, so the same must apply to foreign banks. No excuse will be acceptable to the U.S. authorities.

"When the Attorney General says, 'I want documents from you,' even if they are located somewhere in the middle of Asia in a bunker, you have to agree. Here's my agent for service of process, and I will produce those documents as a condition of being allowed to move money in and around the U.S."

The Patriot Act's tightening up of banking relationships with correspondent banks has its origins in a Senate Sub-Committee report, which slammed correspondent banking as "A Gateway for Money-Laundering." For further details of this report, see Chapter 9, 'Cover-up! Bankers and Their Corrupt Clients.' The report describes the difficulty that banks have had controlling chains of correspondents on whom they rely for due diligence of money re-deposited in the onshore bank. According to the report, many high-risk foreign banks, denied their own correspondent relationship with U.S. banks, access the U.S. financial system by becoming involved with another foreign bank that has its separate correspondent relationship in the United States.

This so-called "nested correspondency" can be used to launder funds from loosely regulated regimes to mainstream centers. The report said "U.S. correspondent banking provides a significant gateway for rogue foreign banks and other criminal clients to carry on money laundering and other criminal activities in the U.S. and to benefit from the protections afforded by the safety and soundness of the U.S. banking system. Shell banks, offshore banks, and banks in jurisdictions with weak anti-money laundering controls carry a high risk of money laundering. Because of these high risks, foreign banks typically have limited resources."

The situation is particularly hazardous when staff operate in an international arena outside their licensing jurisdiction. According to one observer, "U.S. banks have routinely established correspondent relationships with foreign banks that carry high money laundering risks. Most U.S. banks do not have adequate money laundering safeguards in place to screen and monitor such banks. U.S. banks have particularly inadequate anti-money laundering safeguards when a correspondent relationship does not involve a credit-related service. So therefore, if it's straight-through processing, rather than the bank offering them a credit line, the level of due diligence undertaken is lower and not sufficient."

Sanctions for non-compliance with the Patriot Act are severe. Non-U.S. financial institutions face a loss of access to all financial markets that deal in dollars. One observer noted, "Countries that do not use U.S. style transaction-reporting systems could be excluded from use of the U.S. central banking clearance system, which would of course destroy their banking systems."

While much of the Patriot Act is directed at money laundering by criminals, some of it is particularly relevant to transfers of terrorist money. The Act introduces the concept of "reverse money laundering" where the (usually terrorist) crime is committed after the money is withdrawn from the system not, as in the conventional definition, before it is introduced to the banking system. Reverse money laundering does not relate to the "predicate" crimes of theft, fraud, or counterfeiting—which is the standard test for money laundering—but to the criminal purpose to which the money is put when it leaves the bank, namely the purchasing of explosives, the funding of flying lessons for terrorists, or the payments of living expenses to latent terrorists.

Funders of terrorists may be charitable institutions or wealthy, untainted individuals who have been tricked or corrupted into acting as shields for the money transfers. Hence the absence of a predicate offense. These names will only trigger alarm bells in banks or regulators if they originate from a suspect location or engage in unusual financial activity.

But Stefan Cassella, the deputy chief, in the asset forfeiture and money laundering section of the United States Department of Justice, argues that the same techniques used to launder money are also used to reverse launder it. Cassella said, "They use the same professional money network, they use the same convoluted transactions to hide the location of the money or where it's going. They can use the same clandestine shipments of cash to avoid paper trails. They can engage in the same international shell games as they move money from this account to that, from one country to another as the money is disguised as legitimate funds for some lawful purpose when it really is to finance new crimes and new criminal enterprises . . . . The source of the money doesn't matter, it is what deadly purpose the money was intended to fund that matters."

Cassella goes on to argue that the standard anti-money laundering tools of asset confiscation, bank regulation and prosecution that apply to money laundering, apply equally to reverse money laundering. One practical measure introduced in the Patriot Act was the strengthening of controls against those carrying cash above $10,000 across borders that do not first notify the authorities.

The Patriot Act's provisions are far-reaching, but there is far from universal acceptance of its success. One money laundering reporting officer who wished to remain anonymous argued that implementation had been patchy. "The systems and procedures dictated by the Patriot Act have either not been implemented, or their implementation has been delayed and watered down to the point where they are ineffective," he said.

The Patriot Act may look, with the benefit of history, like an exercise in moral supremacy designed to stamp the authority of national regulators on the world community at a time when the United States is wounded and vulnerable. For the moment, banks must take it seriously and impose the controls it requires or face painful and expensive examination. Whatever its effectiveness or message, the Patriot Act's tone provides the backdrop for the panic that grips the enforcers of anti-money laundering legislation. The next chapter asks whether the Patriot Act can be sustained in the face of international reservations about its tone and demands.

Chapter 13

Enforcement in a Frenzy

The push against money laundering was given a new impetus post September 11. Yet doubts grow about the sustainability of this level of enforcement and international cooperation.

COOPERATION BETWEEN LAW ENFORCEMENT OFFICERS across borders and across departments is the linchpin to the success of the fight against money laundering. But cooperation is restrained by legal nicety and constitutional argument.

On September 11, those restraints were removed. Politicians saw how slow and cumbersome the system of cooperation between forces around the globe had become, and they loosened the constraints on attempts to hunt the terrorist money. This was the response to a political crisis, calling for exceptional measures.

Police officers the world over rejoiced at their new-found freedom. For once information flowed more freely and police, intelligence officials, bankers, and regulators engaged with their counterparts to share sensitive information. Intelligence services as well as police felt the confidence to demand more money to deal with the perceived threat from terrorist financing. So British intelligence groups, MI5, MI6, and the GCHQ tracking center reputedly won a 20 percent increase in their government funding between 2003 and 2005, bringing the total expenditure on United Kingdom government spending on intelligence to a massive £2.4 billion.

The international banking community responded to the sense of crisis and threat to society and implemented greater controls. Powerful laws were passed in an atmosphere of frenzy and fear.

In the wake of the terrorist outrage, banks came under unprecedented pressure to yield to information requests from the law enforcement community. "Banks were terrified of being found handling terrorist money purely out of selfishness" said an investigator at the Interpol law enforcement agency in Lyon, France. "The damage to their reputation would be immense." The potential risks to an institution were seen as so grave that money laundering concerns became strategic issues for companies. They spent heavily on anti-money laundering systems and consultants.

The reaction to September 11 was instinctive and demonstrative. But did it go below the surface and deal with structural issues involving the making and hiding of dirty money? Here there is much more doubt. Within a year of the outrage, law enforcement officers began asking whether the blocks to liaison and information exchange that formerly inhibited co-operation, would be re-established. The obstacles are formidable. In addition to resentment of the Patriot Act, cultures, languages, political creeds, local histories, and traditions are already re-asserting their divisive tendencies. The old prejudices that used to prevent American police from working with Chinese police or Sunni Iranian police from working with Shi'ite police in another country have surfaced.

One Federal Bureau of Investigation official speaking at the Cambridge Conference on Economic Crime in 2002, asked, "How long will this cooperation go on? And how deep will this cooperation be? Has the prosecutor's world really changed so fundamentally from all the things that we've learned over the years, or is this one very tragic special case?

"The next time one of our agents talks to someone on the trail of the proceeds of a people-trafficking ring or Russian organized crime, will he really get quick cooperation? Or will he simply be told, as often happens in both directions, you need to submit the formal paperwork before we can even talk to you and no one is going to be here until next month! International cooperation is a hell of a lot of work. My office can only handle a few such international cases and then we are stretched."

The FBI official cited above also spoke about the need for greater cooperation. He said, "Cooperation goes against the grain of law enforcement. It goes against almost all the lessons that agents and prosecutors have learned over the years. To take a phrase of John Lennon and turn it upside down, law enforcement thinks locally and it also acts locally! It can be a huge problem just getting two states to share information on a common target, let alone trying to get prosecutors from an American city to share sensitive information with a minister in Beijing. There is a lot of mistrust and suspicion between any two investigators from the very start, but you also have to add the very real problems of different languages and incompatible legal systems. We continue to talk about the value of international cooperation, but precious little changes!"

One optimistic straw in the money laundering wind is the tightening up of Switzerland's secretive banking regime. The country's confidence was badly dented by the very overt discovery that its banks had hidden the proceeds of Abacha's, Marcos', and Mbutu's criminal activity. It was subjected to great political pressure from the U.S. and other governments that carried the banner of transparency. Further pressure came from American investors who threatened to boycott Switzerland if the country failed to open up the accounts of Jews who had deposited funds in Swiss banks during the Second World War and not lived to reclaim them. Switzerland's vulnerable position on the margin of the European Union and the Euro-zone adds to its susceptibility to be influenced by international agencies. This pressure has paid off with the introduction of a more co-operative banking and taxation system.

But issues continue to concern the international community. The international banking agencies want the country to rescind the provision in its law for banking secrecy. The country also looks benignly on tax exiles or economic tax migrants. The Swiss Revenue office regards a foreigner's tax affairs as a concern for his home country not his newly adopted Swiss home. Similar laxity is shown by Austria and Liechtenstein, and some observers argue that as Switzerland closes its doors to the criminal fraternity and their money, those countries are opening theirs.

Those eager to see the implementation of money laundering statutes take comfort from the growing confidence of the Financial Action Task Force (FATF) and the International Monetary Fund (IMF). Based in Paris and operating under the auspices of the Organization for Economic Development and Cooperation, the FATF matches countries' money laundering legislation against international standards.

Until recently, the FATF had the power to blacklist countries, and this draconian authority persuaded many legislatures to pass model anti-money laundering laws set out by the international agencies. But blacklisting has been opposed by the IMF on the grounds that it freezes a country's economy and excludes it from the forces for change available within the world's economic system. The IMF won the argument with the FATF and its blacklist was itself frozen in 2002. The chairman of the FATF wrote to the IMF in 2004 saying that the FATF would not make further additions to its blacklist. In the meantime, the IMF and the World Bank have adopted a more low-key approach with their Reports on Observance of Standards and Codes (ROSCs).

Countries that have refused to comply with FATF requirements, like the South Pacific island of Nauru, which had built a considerable financial center with minimal anti-money laundering laws (AML), face a grim fate. Nauru has been banished into the economic wilderness; institutions or individuals handling U.S. dollars know that once they land in Nauru, they will be unacceptable outside.

Black money and flight capital—the money that leaves economic and political hot spots and whizzes around the world searching for safer havens—served to inflate Nauru's economy. For example, much criminal money that passed through the Benex and BECS system that operated under the umbrella of Bank of New York (see Chapter 2, 'BoNYgate') was directed to a Nauru-based company called Sinex.

When the Nauru bubble burst the country's economy slumped. Its population has barely any other economic means of subsistence. Black or grey money moves quickly to take advantage of a new loophole or particularly slack government regulator. When international agencies move quickly to close down the least regulated of these "centers," they move off the criminal map.

Eastern European countries like Hungary and Russia have complied with FATF rules and passed the laws, but few believe they have been implemented. Their governments have put minimal investment into police and regulatory agencies to make those rules effective. One observer in Hungary was impressed that the country had passed the full anti-money laundering rulebook into law. But the small staff policing the rulebook means that the chances of a money launderer being apprehended there are slim. Money launderers appreciate this and continue to enjoy a favorable climate in Central and Eastern Europe.

Countries aspiring to expand their commercial links with the world community are under the greatest pressure to pass anti-money laundering legislation. But where economies are moribund, and arguably where corruption is greatest, such legislation is neglected. So with the exception of South Africa, it is a shocking observation that no country on the African continent has anti-money laundering legislation.

Laws without implementation have led to widespread skepticism about much anti-money laundering rhetoric. David Marchant, editor of the anti-money laundering publication *Offshore Alert,* paints a bleak picture saying: "Many financial institutions and financial service companies either know they are laundering money but don't care or don't want to know so they don't carry out any credible background checks into clients. There are 700,000 daily electronic money transfers involving $2 trillion. With this magnitude of transaction, trying to find criminal money by asking customers personal questions may be like looking for a needle in a haystack. In any event, the U.S. Treasury has estimated that 99.9 percent of the criminal money coming into the U.S. is successfully laundered. Dirty money is not unique to low-tax nations and it is not necessarily associated with financial privacy. Indeed, as the UN reports, money laundering can proceed very easily without bank secrecy. In fact it may well be that launderers avoid it because it is a red flag."

Emerging countries that have agreed to introduce anti-money laundering legislation, at the behest of the United States and the FATF, may still prove unwilling to sign up to United States requests and treaties to share tax information. Low levels of disclosure and minimal tax regimes make offshore havens attractive to investors. The havens bolster their argument for their reluctance to disclose information by pointing to some double standards in the U.S. position towards tax disclosure and evasion. Rowan Bosworth-Davies, a British money-laundering consultant, commented in 2003, "The Americans are levering open the offshore sectors' accounts using the terrorism argument. But if the information they get has anything to do with a European citizen, they're unlikely to share that information. The Americans don't want to undermine the value of the U.S. as the biggest recipient of international capital flight. They're quite happy to welcome everybody else's tax evaders coming to them, but they don't want their tax evaders taking their money elsewhere and hiding them in the offshore sector as certificates of deposits or Treasury Bills. If you are a tax evader from Germany and you've got a dollar or Eurodollar account in a bank in Frankfurt, you can invest in dollar-denominated instruments, U.S. Treasury bonds for example, and the U.S. economy benefits very greatly."

United Kingdom tax authorities are equally alert to the possibility of chasing revenue from tax evaders who have made disclosures to the police. Critics of the system argue that this breaches a fundamental principle, namely that information given to the Revenue is privileged and should not be disclosed. But the United Kingdom's Inland Revenue has discovered an important channel for catching black money and two of its officers are attached to the Financial Intelligence Unit of the National Criminal Intelligence Service to catch the evaders traced by Suspicious Activity Reports made by banks.

UK enforcement of tax and laundering crimes has been beset by an ambiguity that permeates thinking in both government and the City of London, about the UK's status as a haven for the rich. The UK exchequer wants both the tax rake-off and the reputation for flexible, non-bureaucratic regulation that so appeals to roving companies and executives. The next chapter examines how the UK seeks to look both ways at the same time, and it shows how that sometimes means it misses the scandal staring it straight in the face.

Chapter 14

London: Offshore, Onshore

The City of London has been beset by financial scandals. The collapse of the Bank of Credit and Commerce International, which funded drugs and terror groups through London, was especially devastating and had a global impact. London reacted by passing laws and shuffling around its institutions. But its massive $4 trillion financial sector still looks vulnerable to invasion by launderers.

London increasingly looks like an offshore center serving many dubious financiers while at the same time claiming to have regulation that puts it among the world's top onshore jurisdictions. Its offshore status is underlined by the large number of banks and branches of foreign banks located in the City. More are based there than anywhere in the world. Its onshore claim rests on a long-held reputation for respectability—who would ever cast an aspersion on the Bank of England—buttressed by a mass of anti-money laundering and anti-fraud regulation that is as severe as any in the world. But as each new scandal breaks, London's status looks increasingly ambiguous.

London's vulnerability to launderers is not in its laws but in their implementation. Government has failed to invest in sufficient skilled law enforcement officers or regulators to curb its sprawling financial system. But this is no accident. The UK's economy cannot afford to curb its income from the "invisible" financial sector while its industrial sector becomes anorexic. As the United Kingdom feeds its addiction to finance and hot money, its regulators bluster ever less convincingly about the security of its financial system and its antipathy to money launderers.

Anti-money laundering legislation has mushroomed in the United Kingdom to keep this offshore haven in line with international standards.

Most recently there has been the Financial Services and Markets Act of 2000 (FSMA) which provides the legal basis for the Financial Services Authority (FSA). The FSA acquired its money laundering powers on December 1, 2001. Regulation of the UK's financial industry was dispersed around numerous small agencies prior to 2000. Most significantly, banking regulation was undertaken by the Bank of England. This department was held responsible for the United Kingdom's failure to police the Bank of Credit and Commerce International. The new Labor Government of 1997 took an immediate initiative, driven by the Chancellor of the Exchequer Gordon Brown and his associate Ed Balls, to remove banking regulation from the Bank of England and to put it into a separate and independent entity. This triggered the creation of the FSA, which serves as an umbrella organization for the regulation of the entire UK financial sector. The FSA was billed as London's equivalent of the Securities and Exchange Commission, with its toughness in dealing with errant bankers.

The second piece of UK legislation on money laundering was the Proceeds of Crime Act of 2002 (POCA) which took effect on February 2003.

London, like every other jurisdiction, had let the implementation of its money laundering controls lapse prior to the attack on the World Trade Center on September 11. Its regulators would smirk that the United Kingdom was ahead of the United States in terms of banking regulation (note the comments of the FSA managing director Carol Sergeant quoted in Chapter 12) but City operatives saw the laws and regulations grossly neglected. One money laundering reporting officer (MLRO) noted, "Prior to 2001, no one did a damned thing! People just weren't interested. It was another 'tick in the box' exercise. You had a compliance department, you probably had an old bombed out compliance officer who was the money laundering reporting officer, who had no resources and no respect. The guidance notes were generally geared to the retail sector and badly written. But it didn't really matter because no one really worried about them. The banks saw no risks to themselves, no one was going to fine them and no one was going to give them any grief. They were never going to get caught by the law."

The Financial Services and Markets Act has instilled a sense of fear and foreboding into UK banking. This law allows for banks to receive surprise dawn visits from regulators to check that their procedures correspond with the bank's perceived risk as well as with the regulator's own principles and regulations. Bank training in money laundering procedures has mush-roomed, creating a demand for jobs for consultants and trainers.

The minutiae of the law and regulation are closely watched by the regulator, says one former FSA officer, but more complex problems of vulnerability to fraud or abuse are overlooked. Bureaucratic competence is valued by the organization which answers to Her Majesty's Treasury, but lateral thinking into a bank's deeper weaknesses in knowing client affairs is harder to obtain.

Understandably, banks are less than enthusiastic about the powers avail-able to the FSA, so some sour grapes, or resentment is inevitable among the anti-money laundering community. One MLRO of a foreign bank based in London said caustically, "The people that have been fined so far have made pretty glaring errors in terms of basic identification of clients. The FSA would probably not feel capable of fining people who had the right docu-ments on file, ticked in the right boxes, but would fail to make the conceptual leap to understanding the client and the client's business."

The MLRO continued, "The FSA prefers to keep people back in the office, doing what it likes to call desk-based reviews of firms. It is less likely to find wrongdoing in its patch; it has far too many firms to look after for its complement. More staff would increase the cost to the industry, and that in turn would increase the pressure on government." Mike Adlem, the London-based managing director of the consultants, Protiviti, commented, "Have we lost the plot? The whole point about AML legislation was to go after criminal money, freeze it and take it out of circulation. But we have now got to the point where it is only a compliance issue. The vast majority of the effort is now focused on ticking boxes and making sure that the FSA are happy. What about the money? The sums recovered are negligible and totally out of proportion with the amount that is being spent on compliance."

Banks that are caught not complying with the rules face a two-fold sanction: they are fined and their name and a general description of their errors are disclosed. The FSA regards each fine as a public warning to the banking industry on its money laundering preparedness.

The fines are progressively steeper. The Royal Bank of Scotland was the first to feel its wrath, when it was fined £750,000, (a fine of £1m less £250,000 for good cooperation.) The Northern Bank, (a small, Northern

Irish bank) was later fined £1.25 million, (£1.5 million less £250,000 for good behavior). Other institutions fined included: Abbey National, Halifax, Bank of Scotland, Raiffeisen, and Bank of Ireland. The higher the impending fine, the greater the pressure to tighten up a bank's money laundering controls.

Once a bank has been investigated and found wanting, the pain suffered in placating the regulator's wrath is much greater than the pain of the fine, public humiliation, and criticism from colleagues and customers. The cost of working with the regulatory audit, the time required to cooperate with regulators crawling over the bank's systems, and the payment of the fine make the process particularly painful. Said one money laundering reporting officer, "Goldman Sachs was one of the banks named and shamed in the Abacha scandal. Has it affected their profitability? Not in the least. The reason banks are fighting money laundering is to fend off the regulators."

Some cynical observers argue that the government now treats banks and financial institutions as its anti-money laundering agents. They are required to monitor their clients' affairs, and make secret reports to police where they have a suspicion. These reports are called Suspicious Activity Reports (SAR) and are sent to a police agency called the National Criminal Intelligence Service (NCIS).

Practitioners have two particular problems with the system. The first is that police require them to wait seven days for consent to continue with a transaction that appears suspicious. The person making the report to NCIS must stall his or her client without tipping the client off in the hope that the transaction can proceed. The second has been the subject of a number of law cases. It involves what the bank must do with money held in a bank account when the authorities have required the bank to freeze the account, because it is under suspicion. Some lawyers claim that a "constructive trust" exists between the client and the bank, and the money must be returned, however dubious its source. One consultant described the problem in the following terms: "It's a Catch 22 situation. If the banks become aware that money in their possession is in dispute then they have a legal duty to not release it. If they do release it and it can be proved that they knew it was in dispute, then they can be sued. On the other hand, once they freeze the account the account holder can sue them to release the money. The banks can't win."

Bankers have received many mixed messages about the purpose of the SAR. Many appear to be under the impression that the police would use the information they provide in their report to follow-up the facts with a view to apprehending the miscreants and no doubt retrieving money for the bank's eventual benefit. But this demonstrates rather a naïve understanding of how the police work. According to Rowan Bosworth-Davies, a former policeman and now money laundering consultant, interviewed in 2003, no more than 4 percent of all SARs produced by the financial sector resulted in a money laundering prosecution. Tristram Hicks, detective chief inspector with the Metropolitan Police in London, told the author that SARs rarely prompted an investigation. They were more often used to provide a trail once a crime has been reported and an investigation has been launched.

Low numbers of prosecutions for money laundering have led to disillusionment among bankers. Said one MLRO, "We are being pressured by the government and regulators to make lots of reports but we know that nothing is going to happen to the vast majority, even those that go to the intelligence agencies, because there are not the resources to cope with the load."

UK banks have spent heavily on software to find exceptional transactions that indicate money laundering. They have also trained MLROs and staff. Martyn Bridges of United Kingdom consultancy, Bridges and Partners, estimated that the UK regulated sector will spend over £1 billion on money laundering-related investment. Bridges said, "There is no upside for banks. It is all cost and no benefit."

Banks had at least expected a high level of consultation with the authorities to confirm that their investment was bearing fruit. That has not been forthcoming. Bankers have not seen the money launderers detailed in their reports coming to court and going to prison.

The September 11 outrage sent the number of SARs rocketing in a desperate bid to protect banks from the slightest taint of terrorism. How else does one explain the jump in reports between 1999 and 2004? In 1999 reports totaled 14,500; in 2000 the number was 18,400; in 2001 it had grown to 31,250; in 2002 it was 64,000; and in 2003 it was 94,000. It reached a massive 135,368 in 2004. The police interpreted the rise in reports as an exercise in "back-covering." Fear ruled in Threadneedle Street, the headquarters of the Bank of England. Bank chairmen were hassled by the government, by the regulator, and by their American counterparts.

The bulk of the new reports was called "defensive"—that is to say that the banks made the reports, not because they thought laundering was necessarily in progress and they wanted it investigated by the police, but because they wanted to minimize future risk of their own incrimination. This could occur if they failed to make a report on a transaction where their suspicion should have been alerted. But defensive or offensive, the reports piled in, and piled up at the Pimlico, London, headquarters of NCIS. Nothing was heard of most of them, although the police said they were stored for use as retrospective evidence once a case had happened rather than as proactive leads for crimes that might yet happen.

U.S. bankers were foremost in pumping out large numbers of reports following September 11, due in part to pressures from their New York headquarters and in part to a culture of reporting at the least cause. U.S. bankers file a report to FinCEN (the Financial Crimes Enforcement Network, part of the U.S. Treasury) following each transaction of $10,000. The reports are stored, and seen largely as forming part of a retrospective trail to a crime, rather than evidence for a current investigation. The equivalent reporting figure for Europe is €15,000.

The surge of suspicious reports in the United Kingdom caused as much suspicion as they solved, in particular among Muslim groups who suspected they were being targeted in the wake of the rising "Islamophobia" that followed September 11. The system is seen by some as an intrusion into the confidential relationship between customer and banker, although Jack Blum, the distinguished U.S. lawyer who aided the U.S. Senate's investigation of BCCI, seeks to allay fears about the system's effectiveness.

He says FinCen is one of the "great blue smoking mirror operations of the world. There's no one there. You think they're spying on you? Relax. The lights are on, that's about it. Do you understand how big and complicated it is to track financial transactions? If everyone singled you out for investigation and all the agencies of the government bore down on you, you're screwed. OK. But that's going to happen with money laundering controls or without them.

"J. Edgar Hoover figured out how to do that in the 1930s when the banks weren't reporting anything. He used it for political purposes, he used it to blackmail people. That stuff is ugly, it goes on all the time. Merrill Lynch has 20 million customers globally and they report the bad apples on 250,000 transactions a day. They have a computer system that scans them and tosses up 2,000 of those quarter million transations a day; the computer system now is going to turn over 2,000 reports to the Federal government and that will mesh with the 2,000 from Citibank and the 6,000 from Bear Stearns, and the twelve guys in money laundering in Justice will do what? So what are you worried about?"

Police and NCIS admitted that there was a huge backlog of SARs in 2003, and bankers and regulators said they thought the police were either incompetent or overloaded. The situation had become so heated that the dispute flared in public. John Goodfellow, the chairman of the UK's Building Societies Association, said in May 2003, "Although we are filing more and more notices, it seems they are disappearing into a black hole. We have no idea if the cases we report are even being investigated, let alone if criminals are being caught and prosecuted. What effect our efforts are having in reducing money laundering crime remains a mystery."

Carol Sergeant, the FSA's former managing director for markets and risk (she left the position in 2004), said, "The information that the banks are providing may not actually meet the needs of law enforcement, but they are not getting any feedback or guidance on what law enforcement people want. One of the main areas that has been successful has been terrorist finance because it has been much clearer as to what the authorities want."

Government responded to these complaints by hiring the accountancy firm, KPMG, to complete a £500,000 consultancy exercise to examine the suspicious reporting system. KPMG has called for a total overhaul of the SAR system and a move to create efficiencies to cut the backlogs of suspicious reports. In the meantime, the commercial sector reels under the pressure of a system that risks disrupting much commercial activity.

Police say they are overloaded but seek to shift the blame to others for their lack of performance. They argue that government fails to support the financial policing service with investment and manpower. Britain has no more than 800 policemen dealing with financial crime. This is a small percentage of the total number of police investigators of general crimes, although some three quarters of all crime is said to be "acquisitive" rather than violent or physical.

The FSA's low complement may explain its hands-off style. In an analysis of the FSA's strength relative to some other jurisdictions, Deloitte and

Touche shows that many advanced economies have at least twice as many staff per billion dollars of assets in the market compared with the United Kingdom. Australia, for example, has 1,800 staff to oversee a market whose asset value is $556 billion. Canada has 1,655 staff to oversee a market with assets of $873 billion. The United States has 30,000 regulators for assets of $16 trillion, The Republic of Ireland has 320 staff for a market of $320 billion. The United Kingdom has a mere 2,971 staff for a UK market with assets worth over $4 trillion.

Michael Foot, the FSA managing director with responsibility for deposit takers confirmed in May 2003 that the United Kingdom had a considerable problem in maintaining and enforcing anti-money laundering procedures. He said, "operation of procedures to combat the laundering of the proceeds of drugs and other crimes through banks and building societies is not satisfactory. There is a great deal of money laundering going on throughout the UK."

Paradoxically, London's attractiveness to money launderers is enhanced by the very fact of its good reputation. According to Sean Holohan, an executive at Protiviti, the management consultancy, "Money launderers target specific financial advisors to add credibility and assurance to their schemes. Lawyers and accountants, known as 'gatekeepers,' are selected because they are in financial difficulty or because their integrity is known to be suspect. Crooks are likely to assist and not ask too many questions. These financial advisors get hooked by a fat fee and then are compelled into continuing to put a legitimate face to a crooked scam. Money launderers would consider a giant financial center like London as the holy grail. You need only ask yourself, 'which would you prefer, to invest in a scheme based out of London or one based out of the British Virgin Islands?' This is why foreign criminals so often bring their funds to, or at least through, London."

The creation of a Serious Fraud Office, whose job is to handle large frauds of at least £1 million in value, has done something to raise the morale and performance of police engaged in routine but substantial fraud. But there is a suspicion that the SFO was created in 1990 to deal with politically sensitive cases rather than particularly 'complex' cases. Which fraud cases are not complex? The loss of a number of high profile cases has stirred up incipient police and public concern that the authorities do not have the clout to handle the very large cases.

The growing ranks of dissenters in the anti-money laundering community were joined in 2003 by long-standing bank customers. Under new anti-money laundering legislation, banks (but not the rest of the financial sector) were required to carry out a Current Customer Review (CCR) which involved due diligence of the entire client base. Banks started to demand evidence of identification and address from customers with accounts opened before anti-money laundering regulations were introduced in 1993, coming into effect on April 1, 1994. These customers put their feet down, and protested to banks and Members of Parliament. The regulator yielded to bank concern and withdrew the order. Some banks persisted in the hope that it would buy them future favors from regulators.

While regulators look for a delicate balance between restraint and bureaucracy on the one hand and freedom for individual flair on the other, banks and the police are in a disagreement over their commitment to attack money laundering and their ability to police the system. The importance of subscribing to anti-money laundering principles is not disputed in public. But privately there is massive skepticism about the scale of the problem and the efficacy of the solutions.

The United Kingdom must be seen to do its American master's bidding, but privately UK banks query its value and go their own way.

Confiscation

Law enforcement must look at every way of attacking organized crime. The most obvious route is to prosecute the criminals who perform and direct it, as they are they brains of the organizations. The other route is to hit them in the pocket and show them and others that crime does not pay. That way at least they cannot enjoy so many of the fruits of their crimes, even if they can enjoy their liberty. It is second best, but possibly also the more realistic approach. Incidentally, it is one that governments favor as they seek to boost their national budgets with an extra source of revenue. Seizures of the proceeds of crime may be regarded as a form of taxation on criminals, replacing formal taxation which most purveyors of criminal money evade.

The system risks being mixed with self-interest, and so falling into disrepute, in countries or states where police agencies can use the proceeds of confiscation to boost their own budgets. This is particularly the case in the United States where seizures of cash are used to fund law enforcement activities. U.S. police forces have acquired considerable purchasing power in the market for helicopters, telecommunications equipment, and vehicles as a result of the pursuit of organized criminal bosses.

Seizing the money does not merely deprive Mr. Big of his next villa or large car; it will also hurt his organization. The Drug Enforcement Administration (DEA) says this is particularly valuable. "Our mission is to disrupt and dismantle criminal organizations, the highest criminal organizations that are dealing in drugs. If we take out every retail distributor, every wholesale distributor, even if we arrest the head of the drug cartel, we still leave behind the financial infrastructure that services that organization. There is always a second lieutenant to replace the head and then continue the process. If you take away the profitability, who is going to sell the drugs and risk going to jail for ten- to fifteen-year jail sentences."

A number of financial consequences for organized crime flow from a cash seizure. First, cash is the product of a long process of investment, laundering, and deception. The goods have had to be made or grown, transferred along a production and development chain (not unlike that of above-board industrial goods), then sold. The proceeds of the sale are gathered together into a large lump of cash, or several smaller lumps for "smurfing purposes." The cash is likely to have been earmarked to pay off costs and expenses incurred, not least the profits for the criminal operatives. Economic damage impairs the fabric of a criminal organization, the DEA's precise goal. According to one lawyer, "It is only by removing that profitability that you end up dismantling an organization. Enron would continue to be an empty shell today were it not for the fact that their financial black hole brought the scandal to light. If you take away the drug organization's ability to hire confidants, to induce and prevent witnesses from cooperating again, the chances of its collapse are much greater."

The prospect of future criminal activity is also marred by a seizure of cash, if that money has been earmarked for future purchases of raw material or production machinery. The cash may also have been leveraged, that is used as collateral for future borrowings or purchases. Enron's skilful use of energy derivatives, devised by its investment banks, JP Morgan Chase and Citibank Salomon Smith Barney, secretly leveraged its future earnings using offshore havens. The result was a huge but undisclosed gap in its accounting numbers. One DEA officer asked, "How can they continue to buy all the raw materials, the glassware, the retail distributors, the smugglers that move the ultimate drugs, the chemicals that work it, and the chemicals that are needed for the chemical process to manufacture the drugs, if you take away the money? Only by attacking the financial infrastructure can you do this."

Cash seizures have a third importance. The authorities may choose to allow the seized funds to flow through the banking system, and watch who handles them, and who picks them up. In other words, seized money may trap other criminals..

Wealth that is accumulated by crime enables the leaders of organized gangs not merely to pay for complex systems of "cut-outs" to elude the dirty fingerprints on their bank notes, but also to afford the best accountants, and lawyers, and even "jury-nobblers" to keep justice and detection at bay. Jurisdictions that allow those charged with financial offenses to use the proceeds of an alleged crime to pay lawyers hired to act for them in their case may pay a heavy price. One lawyer says, "If you seize and tie up all their assets, there is less money available to try to extort, or to pay off, or to coerce witnesses against them. You limit that opportunity; they can't make bail, which they would simply use to evade prosecution and to continue their activity in another jurisdiction."

Capturing the proceeds of crime may be a second best solution to implementing justice. The best is surely the public trial and conviction by a jury of a major criminal. But it is a recognition of reality, says Felix McKenna, the chief bureau officer of the Dublin-based Criminal Assets Bureau, that the instigation of criminal prosecutions against gang lords is often cumbersome and unreliable as the wealthy gang leader is likely to be nearly untouchable. He said, "You're not getting the big boys or the principals of the crime organizations. You won't get the godfathers or the man who's controlling everything. You won't get him into a criminal court and have him convicted of his crimes, and he will still be able to enjoy the benefits and profits that he has generated through his group or gang of the criminal activities they've been involved in. You'll catch his runners and his people lower down the gang.

"The big guy can avoid prosecution through the threat of intimidation, fear, and the reluctance of people to give evidence against him within his own organization. They have no inhibition about hiring a contract killer to kill a witness and intimidate witnesses and intimidate their families. They intimidate juries. They go to, not extreme lengths, but they're just the normal run of what organized crime does, this fear factor that they instill in people."

Pinpointing and seizure of criminal funds is no less straightforward than hitting the criminals' beneficiaries. Due legal process must be observed by agencies charged with confiscation. The pressure to facilitate asset confiscation in the United Kingdom has resulted in an important and controversial legal innovation. Civil recovery, the process of seizure using a civil burden of proof, was introduced with the Proceeds of Crime Act and has proved highly controversial.

The seizure of assets from a criminal in the United Kingdom can take place at three points in the legal process. The first point is before or during a criminal investigation when police can persuade a court that it needs a court order to freeze assets that might otherwise be spent or secreted. The assets may be returned if the defendant is not convicted.

However, at that point the police can go to the High Court and claim that the defendant has a "criminal lifestyle," that they have enough evidence that he lives on the proceeds of crime and has no visible means of income. In this case, the burden of proof is reversed and, rather than the Crown having to prove his guilt, the defendant has to prove the genuine provenance of his wealth.

The defendants who argue that the proceeds were obtained from legitimate business are likely to be told to hand their papers over to the taxation authorities who can levy a charge that is so heavy that the man is put out of business. According to Sara Dayman, a partner at accountants BDO Stoy Hayward restraint and confiscation unit, "It looks like double jeopardy. I can't see that it can be right. It is very difficult to see how you can go after someone civilly without having an attempt at prosecution! If the proceeds are the proceeds of crime, they must have been criminally obtained, and if they have been criminally obtained then that should be shown in a court. This is a very dangerous territory and it is very new."

The UK's Asset Recovery Agency (ARA) is not unique and its powers and processes are far from exceptional. The model for this form of organization is the Irish Criminal Assets Bureau (CAB) which was founded in the wake of the murder of the journalist Veronica Guerin. Guerin had been investigating drug dealing by Irish organized criminals when she was murdered. Ireland had developed a considerable armory of weapons to deal with terrorists, but the nation was stunned that commercial gangs used terror methods. Its response was quick and decisive.

The CAB was at the forefront of Ireland's largest money laundering investigation, when it played a pivotal, cross-border role in the search for the £26.5 million stolen from Northern Bank.

The CAB has a mix of legal and fiscal remedies to confiscate criminal assets. The key to its powers is its capacity to freeze suspected criminal assets for no less than seven years using civil standards of proof before a single judge. The criminal deprived of his assets for so long is likely to be put out of business or imprisoned. If the alleged criminal can prove the assets are legitimate, he can, of course, persuade the court to require the government to release them. If he fails, the government keeps the assets, taking a tidy bonus into the exchequer. Felix McKenna says the agency has taken on a hundred cases under the Irish Proceeds of Crime legislation, and around half the defendants have walked away from their assets without a contest. The rest engaged lawyers to contest the order and most ended up doing a deal with CAB. This may involve handing over their assets in return for a lighter sentence where a criminal prosecution follows.

McKenna said, "Some people might say the CAB is taking the easy option by using civil remedies. In fact the CAB is set up to target people that mainstream policing cannot do anything with. We've gone in to hit the top layer of the crime bosses and we're using civil remedies to take away their profits, and we owe no apologies for that at all. People that we investigate must be suspected of some type of criminality otherwise we don't touch them. If we find evidence to substantiate a criminal charge we call in the units that are involved and pass the evidence to them."

Threats to the lives of the civilians within the CAB suggest the organization is hurting many of the right people. McKenna said, "To allow the civilian staff at the Bureau to work in a hostile environment populated by organized and dangerous criminals, there are very important and significant anonymity provisions protecting their anonymity and prohibiting the publication of their identity and their families. Tax officials, customs officials, social welfare officials, and anyone working inside the CAB who is not a police officer are all protected."

The use of civil powers to hit gang leaders has been attacked on both grounds of efficiency and fairness. R.T. Naylor, at McGill University in Canada, argues: "It is more effective to go after assets with tax law than all the convoluted anti-money laundering legislation. The police are duplicating expertise that has already built up over hundreds of years by the fiscal authorities. The whole criminal justice system is twisted in favor of the police, making the job of the fiscal authorities more difficult.

"Under civil forfeiture, they say they are seizing your money because it came from cocaine. They have made you a cocaine dealer in the eyes of the public and you have not had a criminal trial. So they have undercut the distinction between civil and criminal codes, totally destroyed it, leaving you smeared as a criminal without the chance to prove the contrary. That is a moral abomination." The power of this argument, albeit not its validity, appears to have been recognized by Jane Earl, the director of the Asset Recovery Agency. Earl has said she expects to face severe challenges to establish a legal precedent.

Confiscation by civil means has struggled to win acceptance in the United Kingdom. The Crown's ability to prove a "criminal lifestyle" is particularly doubtful.

The Irish CAB regards the tax route as merely another string to its bow. McKenna says the CAB has raised tax assessments against 150 subjects and collected around 45 million Euros. One of the Irish revenue's most notorious cases was brought against Jerry Hutch, dubbed the "Monk." McKenna said in this instance: "Our counsel decided we were a little bit weak going after this man's assets using Proceeds of Crime legislation because he had owned them for so long. He recommended that we go down the Revenue route. That meant looking at his assets and also looking at the Guarda or security information that he robbed a particular security van in a particular year. We raised a tax assessment against what we determined was his cut from that security robbery. We determined that he was the leader of the gang and his cut was a certain percentage.

"Following an investigation in 1996, we raised a taxation assessment for one particular year. We were involved in a lengthy litigation in the High Court. He saw that we were about to get a judgement against his private house and any other assets that he owned. He struck a deal with us that he would pay us £1.5 million. We said he must give us a statement of affairs in relation to tax. Part of his settlement was to sell four properties under the public glare. There was a public auction, and the money came straight to us." This was accomplished despite the fact that Monk was never convicted of any criminal act.

The system of confiscation has administrative benefits for law enforcers, who have encountered legal obstacles in catching the gang leaders. There have been cases where the CAB has placed a freezing order on suspected criminal funds before the funds have reached their banking destination. McKenna said in this case, "My investigators would know people in the compliance offices very well, first name terms, same as the Financial Intelligence Unit (FIU) along the way. They know that when we serve orders we want results fairly promptly. If they see large amounts of money going out of the bank, they will make a disclosure to money laundering. Depending on how well they know the people in here they will ring here as well. We have a very unusual movement of money, we're making a disclosure on it."

High technology and greater training power the confiscation regime. But the proceeds of crime need to be checked before they enter the banking system. As the following chapter shows, the backroom technological researchers have been drawn into the hunt for dirty money and the launderers that introduce it to the system.

Chapter 15

Cyber Launderers, Cyber Detectives

The Internet and cyberspace cannot be ignored. They have evolved from a technical playground for academics to an environment for doing business. Launderers go where tekkies once trod. Now the tekkies are being used to tackle the menace.

HACKERS AND FRAUDSTERS were the first to exploit the criminal opportunities presented by cyberspace and they have since been joined by cyber launderers eager to wash the proceeds of both virtual and real-world crimes.

The Internet has the same level of security as that shown by the business owner who goes home at night, carefully locking the front door of his premises while leaving the back door wide open. The Confederation of British Industry's 2001 Cyber Crime Survey showed that two-thirds of respondents had suffered a "serious incident" relating to e-business risks such as fraud, hacking, and virus contamination, with B2C (business-to-customer) e-business viewed as a higher risk than B2B (business-to-business).

Cyber-based economic crime has escalated in the United States according to the Federal Bureau of Investigation who have said that cybercrime increased by 43 percent between 1997 and 1998. The FBI opened 419 new computer crime cases during that period but only 83 charges were filed as a result. The FBI said in 2003, "For an issue that the federal government is making such a major deal out of, trying to stop computer crime and information warfare, there are remarkably few prosecutions."

International money transfers via online banking channels cause the greatest concern. Cooperation between law enforcement officers globally has never been more critical or harder to implement. "There are serious evidentiary questions and jurisdictional questions in these cases," said Mark Rasch, a former computer crime prosecutor, now working as a computer security consultant for Global Integrity, based in Virginia. "Law enforcement may present you with a perfectly good case, against a defendant in Kuala Lumpur. But how quickly can we get to know Malaysian law on the Internet and how well will it mesh with our law?" asked Rasch.

While the range of jurisdictions poses problems for all prosecuting authorities, the speed of change in Internet law and the global reach of the Internet make investigation and prosecution particularly problematic. For example, web services such as online casino banking, online auctioneering, consumer Web sites, and credit trade have all attracted the criminal fraternity.

The Financial Action Task Force (FATF), the global body for compliance standards in money laundering, has stated that criminals are exploiting online commodities for their money laundering purposes. Regulators and financiers happily mouth the key phrases "Due Diligence" and "Know Your Customer," but no one can truly know with whom one is dealing when their business client is slumped in front of a computer monitor 4,000 miles away. "A potential risk exists at any stage of the contact between a new customer and a financial institution," says a report from the FATF.

The Web's structure also makes tracing funds and following audit trails particularly complex. The Internet differs from non-cyber-based money laundering in a number of ways. "Any business that deals in large amounts of cash could be a vehicle for money laundering," said Nevada gaming attorney, Anthony Cabot, in 2004. "But if it's properly regulated, then the prospects for money laundering on the Web decrease significantly and could effectively be eliminated."

The Internet can be exploited for money laundering and financial crime in numerous ways. The following are some of the areas where abuse has been tackled. But in this fast-growing area of technology the golden rule applies, namely that the criminal fraternity are ahead of the enforcement game, offering schemes for get-rich-quick suckers that regulators and police will not have heard of. They will only track them down when the damage has been done and the loss sustained.

E-cash

E-cash is a term used to describe Internet-related funds and value transfers. While the Internet is a complex and bewildering sphere for financial transactions, banks argue that the funds involved in online transactions are ultimately real and not something that only exists in the electronic realm of cyberspace. According to one banker, "All the transactions are actually pretty transparent. All transactions go through banking systems—credit cards, wire transfers, or checks." Ultimately, the Internet is a conduit for any fiscal deal that takes place between the consumer and the relevant e-commerce business. The consumer uses the online capability to transfer value payment from one business to another, and in most cases the Web sites are seen only as the facilitator of these transactions.

The speed with which the Internet and its many functions is growing has caused serious concerns among law enforcement bodies the world over. Launderers use e-cash by opening Internet banking accounts. Dirty money is fed into bank accounts by "smurfs" in smaller amounts sufficient to bypass currency transaction reports (CTRs) and suspicious transaction reports (STRs). Once the money is placed in the various accounts its value is converted into e-cash. This e-cash can then easily be transferred to offshore Internet accounts through Telnet, the basic Internet command containing the protocol that enables one computer to connect to another. By using Telnet, launderers are free to transfer money via the Internet from one juris-diction to another at lightning speed. This process is similar to the system of moving money by wire transfer. However, the Internet can provide additional anonymity. Money launderers target jurisdictions that have the least strin-gent anti-money laundering legislation. The lack of transparency regarding audit trails is the prime function of Internet money transfers.

The emergence of smart card and stored value technology is quickly becoming another thorn in the side of the regulators. Laundering illicit money is facilitated by using smart cards (otherwise called stored value cards) because the cards hold the actual cash value stored digitally within them. Therefore, merchants do not need to dial bank or credit card companies to gain the necessary approval before any transaction can take place. Users can add cash value to these cards at machines. The number of smart cards a person may possess is unlimited.

The use of smart cards is growing steadily in Europe and Asia, while their popularity within the United States is marginal. Financial value may be added to these cards from an individual's account through Internet cyber bank transfers, through wire transfers from ordinary accounts, or via

ATM/self-serve kiosks where cash can be digitally converted to smart card value.

In 2002, the U.S. Drug Enforcement Agency (DEA) released a document entitled *DEA Headquarters Financial Operations Section DOF—Cyber Threat*. Within this document the DEA outlined its prime concerns regarding the emergence of smart card technology. These were:

- Anonymity: Many of the cards currently available do not retain transaction records. The anonymity afforded by smart cards is similar to the privacy normally afforded by cash transactions. It is useful to launderers and traffickers who wish to hide the paper trail.

- Bulk Shipments: Pre-loaded smart cards may be transported or smuggled anywhere in the world. Unlike bulk shipments of black money, the smart cards are small, lightweight, and very easy to conceal.

Online Auctioneering

At the end of 2002, worldwide law enforcement agencies stated that Internet auction fraud was by far the largest form of cybercrime being reported. Online auction houses such as eBay attract consumers and launderers because they are accessible and inexpensive.

Criminals manipulate these sites by first purchasing an antique item and then putting the object up for grabs. The launderer, in the guise of an antique dealer, then employs two or more of his acquaintances, or "smurfs" to bid against one another with dirty money, often bidding over-the-top amounts for the item. Once it has been sold, the launderer is issued a check for the amount paid by the overriding bidder. The resulting auction house check may then be paid into one of the launderer's accounts, apparently clean and legitimate—a process that makes the placement stage of money laundering easier as it is sufficient to bypass the STR checks that bank cashiers are required to carry out.

One recent case involved a gang of three Americans: Scott Beach of Lakewood, Colorado; Kenneth A. Walton; and Kenneth Fetterman of Placerville, California. These fraudsters manipulated the online auction site, Ebay, with style and cunning. The perpetrators made hundreds of "shill" bids using more than 40 false user names. Shill bidding is a term meaning false bids. These false proposals included bidding exorbitant amounts for a forged Richard Diebenkorn painting during May 2000. The closing bid was no less than $135,801. The auction process provided the cover for numerous exchanges of dirty money that over time would be exchanged with clean money.

Fetterman was indicted in March 2001 on counts of fraud and using the Internet to launder money, but the moment he realized the whistle had been blown he fled the state. On April 17, 2001, Kenneth A. Walton pled guilty to three counts of wire fraud and four counts of mail fraud, while Scott Beach, pled guilty to one count of wire fraud and three counts of mail fraud for making the false bids. Walton and Beach actually admitted they had created more than 40 user identities on eBay by providing false registration information. This allowed them to make numerous false bids and so inflate the prices of the hundreds of paintings they auctioned. The total value of these bids exceeded $450,000.

Online Casinos

The World Wide Web is now suffused with gaming sites, from blackjack to roulette, from fruit machines to online betting. Setting up an online casino is straightforward. The person intending to launder money must first apply for a gaming license. He is then free to employ an offshore site operator to devise and set up the online casino business. Under the guise of tax avoidance the launderer then needs only organize offshore accounts for the gaming site before business can commence. These offshore accounts often use large respectable overseas correspondent banks in turn. The U.S. Senate Permanent Sub-Committee on Investigations reported in 2001 that correspondent banks including Bank of America and JP Morgan Chase moved millions of dollars in Internet gambling proceeds.

So how do the criminals use this ever-growing medium to their own ends? Firstly, online gambling is useful as it has very erratic cash flows. Mobsters use their laundering counterparts, often known as "smurfs" to disguise the origins of their cash. The "smurfs," who might be based anywhere in the world, gamble on the site using illicit profits via credit cards and debit card technology, often known as e-cash, and feed large and sporadic amounts into the casino's accounts. If criminals wish to keep their gaming sites hidden, there is no need to advertise or to register with search engines such as Google and Yahoo.

Dirty money can also be washed by simply placing a deposit on the gaming Web site. A small amount of this money is then gambled. The launderer, regardless of whether he wins or not, then asks for the return of the remainder of the deposit, which would be sent back in the form of a refund check, clean and adequately disguised.

Regulators and licensed online gambling hosts dispute the degree to which online gambling is vulnerable to money laundering. A spokesman for the online industry stated, "In the cashless world of Net betting, many punters are tied to an account number, making it hard to hide."

Bankruptcy Fraud

Several forms of Internet fraud have emerged in recent years, the most common of which are bankruptcy schemes using petition mills, equity skimming, and credit repair operations.

Petition mill fraud schemes have mushroomed in large U.S. cities with poor or immigrant populations. The crook advertises a service on the Internet that will help a tenant keep his home if faced with eviction. The service charges the individual an exorbitant fee for secretly filing a bankruptcy on his behalf. The scam is technically termed a "multiple filing fraud scheme" and it is operated in two ways.

The first method involves the crooked service filing for bankruptcy in different states, using true personal identifiers. The second method involves using false names and/or Social Security Account Numbers (SSAN) to file in the same or different states. When a debtor files several bankruptcies in two or more states, he lists nearly identical assets and liabilities in each filing. The debtor becomes discharged from the debts and, in the process, makes off with several of the assets omitted from a particular petition.

The fraud perpetrators instruct their victims to pay their rent or mortgage payments through their Web site. This transaction is based on the fact that the fraudsters promise that the Web company will deal with the victim's creditors to resolve any threatened foreclosure or eviction dealings. The perpetrator files a bankruptcy case in the victim's name in order to take advantage of the automatic stay. In a short while the collection efforts cease, leading the victim to believe that his or her financial woes are being dealt with. The victim continues to make the payments to the fraudsters, not realizing exactly where the money's true destination lies.

Telemarketing Fraud

Financial fraud using the Internet has grown as the system has increased in popularity. Law enforcement agencies say vast numbers of Internet-related scams involving get-rich-quick schemes are particularly prevalent. These Web sites usually encourage their unsuspecting public to call toll-free numbers often linked to telemarketers, eager to pitch their wares and persuade the consumer to send money via e-cash, plastic cards, or hard cash. The goods arrive only after a very long wait, or not at all.

During the summer of 2002, David Sussman of Westmoreland County, Pennsylvania, was arrested and tried for telemarketing and wire fraud. Sussman had telemarketed photo packages to students, youth clubs, and graduates. Sussman used companies that were owned by him to sell the service, but it later emerged that these companies were fictitious. Sussman's victims paid for the services before they arrived, and when they realized that nothing was forthcoming, they demanded their money back. Sussman sent them false computer generated checks, containing account numbers of non-existent bank accounts.

Sussman also defrauded eBay users by putting nonexistent items up for auction, including gemstones, expensive watches, and jewelry. Sussman gave eBay patrons false checks to pay for items he had bid for. He was sentenced in 2002 to 41 months in prison for wire fraud, mail fraud, and bank fraud, with five years supervised release.

Operation Cyber Sweep

Authorities in the United States have been swift in their response to cyber-crime. In 2003 the United States Department of Justice launched Operation Cyber Sweep to tackle the alarming rise in cyber-related crime, in particular money laundering, fraud, software piracy, and fencing stolen goods. Cyber Sweep involved the coordination of several government authorities including The U.S. Secret Service, The Postal Inspection Service, 34 U.S. Attorney Offices, the Federal Trade Commission, the Bureau of Immigration and Customs Enforcement, as well as numerous state, local, and foreign law enforcement agencies.

The U.S. authorities used Cyber Sweep to infiltrate this new mysterious world and alert cyber criminals to the authorities' long electronic arm. "Online criminals assume that they can conduct their schemes with impunity," said the then-Attorney General John Ashcroft. "Operation Cyber Sweep is proving them wrong, by piercing the criminals' cloak of anonymity and prosecuting them to the fullest extent of the law."

More than 125 investigations, with 130,000 victims who had collectively lost upwards of $100 million, were targeted by Cyber Sweep. Over 90 search and seizure warrants were executed and 125 launderers and cyber crooks were arrested and convicted. Cyber Sweep revealed a huge range of computer crime, from spamming offenses (sending illegal junk advertising email) to electronic hackers and wire fraud scams.

One interesting case involved a 21-year-old hacker named K.C. Smith. Smith promoted a fraudulent scheme promising investors handsome returns on "international tax-free" investments in the Maryland Investment Club, which he advertised through the use of bulk, unsolicited email. His victims did not know that the Maryland Investment Club was fictitious. Smith laundered the proceeds in business accounts set up for a bogus company. He pleaded guilty to charges of securities fraud and money laundering and was sentenced to fourteen months in prison.

Operation Cyber Sweep has shown how regional and multistate authorities can cooperate when need arises. But the threat of global cyber crime and cyber laundering remains largely untackled. The use of the Internet by global terrorists is law enforcement's new frontier.

Cyber Terrorism

Determined hacking by dedicated amateurs can prove extremely irritating and costly to corporations whose sites are penetrated. But the Internet also risks being used as a vehicle by terrorists in their bid to cause economic destruction and instability. This is an area where governments and law enforcement need to become involved as the determined zealot will be bent on causing as much damage and destruction as he can before firewalls and investigators intercept his efforts.

John Thompson, chairman of Symantec Corporation, an online security consultancy, says, "Every business, small or large, and every individual who owns a PC and is connected to the Internet, could be unwitting participants in malicious cyber acts simply by not being protected against attacks. Everyone has the opportunity and responsibility to secure his or her portion of the global virtual border."

Vast economic losses have been caused by viruses attached to elicit "spam" emails. Singapore's Senior Minister of State for Law and Home Affairs, Ho Peng Ke, says, "Instead of a backpack of explosives, a terrorist can create just as much devastation by sending a carefully engineered packet of data into the computer systems which control the network for essential services, for example, the power stations."

Terrorist groups have long exploited the anonymity of Internet chat rooms as secure communication platforms. Internet finance transactions are also useful due to the fogging of audit trails. For instance, the perpetrators of the September 11 destruction of the World Trade Center used email and wire transfer technology. An FBI spokesman has said, "Terrorists use IT facilities to formulate plans, recruit, and raise funds." According to the FBI, terrorists using hackers and cyber tools can secretly infiltrate national infrastructures such as electricity grids, transportation networks, nuclear facilities, and hospitals. Once inside, they can shut them, steal information or maliciously divert their systems.

A series of widespread cyber intrusions hit the U.S. Department of Defense computer system in February 1999 and FBI officials feared terrorists might be involved. The FBI's Cyber Crime Division found that the hackers were in fact nothing more sinister than two young men living in Northern California engaged in a prank. Stephen Cummings, director of the National Infrastructure Security Coordination Center, said the incident highlighted the potential for future terrorist-based attacks. "Terrorists are aware of the potential, Al-Qaida would be interested in developing the capability."

Authorities worldwide have released a list of potential targets for terrorist cyber-criminals. It includes:

- Food processing plants
- Pharmaceutical processing plants
- Electric and natural gas utilities
- Train crossings and traffic control systems
- Next generation air traffic control systems
- Virtually all modern military equipment
- Military and public safety communications
- Civilian communication systems
- Hospital facilities

Industry observers argue that more action is needed from law enforcement authorities if private sector users of computer systems are not to be victims of terrorist as well as commercial criminal attack. Improved sets of guidelines and more carefully calibrated systems and firewall controls must be developed to stay ahead of the criminal fraternity, which is on the look out for weak spots in the world's cyber system.

Online Banking

Italian police have uncovered extensive use of the Internet for laundering by members of the Sicilian Mafia between 1998 and 1999. Over $330 million was moved between a U.S. company incorporated in New Zealand and banks in the Cayman Islands, Spain, and Israel. The money was then deposited in Switzerland and smuggled by hand to banks in Romania, Croatia, China, Russia, and Liberia. A large amount of black cash was traded over the Internet in currencies, shares, commodities, and securities. "The Internet is a powerful weapon," said Professor Mario Centorrino of Sicily's Messina University. "It eliminates the middleman. There's no need to find corrupt bankers." The system applies the same principles as the hawala system used by the Asian community, where agents, in this case Internet service providers, are used to cut out bankers who take a fee on each movement of money.

Internet banking is plagued by sloppy security. The NatWest bank was a victim of "phishing," a classic email scam. It was even forced to shutdown its online bank after a fake Web site was discovered purporting to be a NatWest site. The perpetrators sent vast amounts of emails to NatWest customers instructing them to visit the site and fill in confidential account details online. Although the site was quickly uncovered, it highlighted online banking's vulnerabilities. Customer confidentiality is one of the main risk areas for Internet facilities. "The Internet is a tool, which unfortunately seems to facilitate fraudsters. It's something all financial institutions need to be aware of," said Conor Leeson of Euroclear, the European transaction clearing system.

Nigerian 419 letters, sometimes called Nigerian "Love Letters" (See Chapter 9 concerning Citibank and President Abacha and Nigeria), are major users of the Internet. The typical email requests the recipient to give access to a bank account to deposit a large sum of money in return for a 10 to 30 percent commission payable to the account holder. As soon as the victim's transit codes are revealed, the fraudster drains the bank account, leaving the victim with no recourse. This form of scam illustrates the basic rule of unwanted emails—if it sounds too good to be true, it almost certainly is! A spokesman for the United Kingdom National Criminal Intelligence Service said in 2003, "In online business there is the problem of whether you know who you are transacting with. When somebody is opening an account, you have to be particularly careful." A multi-jurisdictional scam ring designed to defraud cyberspace users mimicking the official sites of Euroclear France has demonstrated how the Internet aids criminal conspiracy.

Commercial banks have invested heavily in creating secure platforms for their Internet patrons. During January 2003, Barclays Bank made an unprecedented effort at tightening its online banking security systems by releasing information to clients, earnestly encouraging them to ignore emails requesting customers' security information. This plea appears to have fallen on deaf ears as the bank continues to be plagued by hackers using its name.

Iraqi Internet Scam

In July 2003, someone posing as a "former Iraqi minister" connected with Saddam Hussein, the toppled dictator, contacted prospective victims via a chat room and politely informed them of large amounts of money, formerly belonging to the regime, that needed to be laundered overseas. Victims lured into the fraud through an email correspondence were instructed to email their personal online banking information to the "Iraqi minister." The victims were also asked to send blank invoices, official stationery, and bank statements. As soon as the con artist had acquired the relevant account details he raided the victim's accounts. Bruce Gale of Hill and Associates, the political risk consultancy, said "The scam played on religious sentiments as the appeal was made from one Muslim brother to another."

Banking Detectives and Technology

Regulatory authorities have increased the pressure on banks to upgrade their existing money laundering compliance procedures and systems in the light of growing cyber crime. Frank Yu, an analyst at Ion Global in Hong Kong, said, "Banks do not have the due diligence procedures to find who they are accepting money from and who they are giving money to."

Cyber payment systems are most vulnerable to attack as they often leave a black hole in place of audit trails. The problem is accentuated when business transactions take place between two or more jurisdictions. Rick McDonnell of the Sydney-based Asia/Pacific Group on Money Laundering Secretariat, a body affiliated to the Financial Action Task Force (FATF), said, "The Internet is harder to regulate, the laws are a little behind the play in terms of technology, and audit trails are far less, so that's going to be a big problem in the not too distant future."

The FATF has looked into cyber laundering with much tenacity. Its 2002 annual report highlights various "vulnerabilities that the Internet might offer for money laundering," particularly the expansion of online banking. An FATF spokesman in Paris commented in 2004, "There are vulnerabilities that the Internet might offer for money laundering." He pinpointed:

- the ease of access to accounts through the Internet

- the absence of face-to-face transactions between the online bank, and the customer and the immediacy of electronic transactions

The FATF outlined several steps countries should take to combat cyber laundering. These include:

- requiring internet service providers to maintain accurate and thorough subscriber information;

- requiring the establishment of log files, showing access and telephone number identity;

- ensuring that information is made available internationally.

Regulatory pressure on banks to upgrade their existing compliance systems has been stepped up since September 11, 2001. The U.S. Patriot Act (See Chapter 12), the United Kingdom Proceeds of Crime Act (See Chapter 14), and the European Union anti-money laundering directive urge banks to deploy high technology countermeasures against the cyber launderers.

The Banks' Response

At the core of a policy to tackle cyber laundering is the well-accepted principle, of "Knowing Your Customer" (KYC). This is done through training front office staff to check the identity of customers opening new accounts and looking out for suspicious deposits or withdrawals. Identity checks are open to manipulation and abuse by the determined criminal. Banks sift through financial transactions that flow in and out of the bank to counter identity fraud and spot money laundering. High-tech computing has been harnessed to the task of transforming a highly manual and paper-intensive activity into something more effective.

Enter the Computerized Sherlock Holmes

Banks have used artificial intelligence as fraud detectives since the mid-1980s when credit card fraud losses started to escalate. Computerized fraud detection systems take in huge volumes of transaction data and look for tell-tale patterns to identify possible cases of fraud.

The system is far from fool-proof and computer scientists are struggling to develop technology that delves deeper into transactions to separate out the more suspicious cases. The latest advance involves developing high tech "transaction sniffing systems" that make use of a body of rules that define the way that money launderers typically carry out their activities. These rules are founded on the "three Vs" of profiling—the volume, value, and velocity (timing) of transactions. If the rules are triggered, then the activity can be deemed "suspicious" and worthy of further investigation. Suspicious transactions include:

- a customer uses an account for no more than a single large transaction or only for a short period of time

- a dormant account is suddenly reactivated for no apparent reason

- funds are withdrawn very shortly after their deposit

- an account receives large sums of money out of its normal transaction range or use

- any deviation from the historical profile that an account normally exhibits

Where do the rules governing the system come from? The first stage of any system is to apply the laundering methodologies and standards set by the FSA and the British Bankers' Association in the UK as well as the 40 recommendations of the Financial Action Task Force.

This approach targets the least sophisticated money launderer. So scientists are seeking to apply more exotic forms of artificial intelligence that simulate the human brain's ability to spot patterns. David Porter, director for risk at the Detica consultancy, says: "They work in the same way that we pick out constellations in a starry sky. These technologies sift through a huge amount of data to work out for themselves what is suspicious without having to refer to a checklist of rules."

The detection system is activated at the end of each business day, looking at that day's transactions and detecting signs of potentially suspicious behavior. Many banks are now considering moving from this "end of day" analysis to "real time" analysis.

Problems and Pitfalls

As banks faced growing pressure to increase the power of their anti-money laundering systems after the September 11 outrage, the technological issues came to the fore. Early efforts to upgrade products produced huge volumes of suspicious cases, most of which turned out to be benign. Poor input data was partly responsible for this, confirming the classic computing saying "garbage in, garbage out." But even more of it was due to inadequate tuning of the detection rules by analysts who underestimated the time and effort required to fine-tune these systems. The same problem of excessive reporting also plagues the National Criminal Intelligence Service (see Chapter 14).

Banks also failed to prioritize their suspicious cases using "to do" lists to oversee the pursuit of each case either to the point where it should be disclosed to a law enforcement authority, or where it should be stored in a "no further action" archive. One project manager commented, "Routing the output of the detection systems to the right people and managing the investigation process turned out to be another can of worms."

Future Trends: Consolidation and Cooperation

Risk management activity is being driven by a new raft of international banking regulations. The 2002 U.S. Sarbanes-Oxley Act, a post-Enron measure aimed at stamping out corporate fraud and corruption, and the Basel II Accord which deals with operational risk such as fraud and money laundering, now drive the technology and banks are having to upgrade their data storage, analysis, and reporting systems to comply. One project manager said, "This constant upgrading of our technical infrastructure is a bit like different utility companies coming along and digging up the same piece of road. Consolidating these activities into one coherent program will be the smart way forward."

Banks are developing single systems that monitor transactions for evidence of suspicious behavior including fraud, money laundering, hacking, and corruption. One project manager reported, "Criminals don't recognize these artificial boundaries, so why should we?"

Banks are under pressure to improve links between money laundering compliance officers and those in fraud prevention and credit control. Occasional suspicious transaction reports should be passed to fraud investigation teams while information gathered about individuals for credit assessment purposes should be used to assess suspicious customer behavior.

A common case-management database enables negative case files to produce management reports and subsequent action.

Banks may ultimately need to turn to biometric technology to improve confidence in verifying customer identity. Biometrics are unique, measurable, physical characteristics of a specific individual which, once captured and digitized, can be stored on a smart card or a central database. Biometric technology is no longer confined to secure military installations and Hollywood blockbusters. One forensic technologist commented, "The technology is now robust and affordable. Fingerprint, retinal, or facial biometrics will be featured on the forthcoming United Kingdom identity cards."

The fight against cyber criminals has tended to focus on the hackers, fraudsters, and money launderers who exploit the Internet as a weak spot in a company's defences. But threat from insiders is often understated. For example, 60 percent of all fraud, money laundering, and other financial malpractice involves an organization's employees. This is a systematic, long-term activity perpetrated by people who know the different systems and controls and how to get around them.

As staffing levels in middle management are cut, the opportunity for insiders to commit financial crime is increasing. Flatter organizations and reduced supervision and accountability make corporate structures vulnerable to exploitation by corruptible or criminal elements. Recent well-publicized corporate scandals, such as Enron, Tyco, and WorldCom, plus heightened concerns over global terrorism and organized crime, show that internal malpractice is set to remain very much in the public eye. The U.S. Patriot and Sarbanes-Oxley Acts and the Basel II Accord put organizations under increasing pressure to get internal malpractice under control.

Detection systems monitoring employees will gather together data from the huge number of audit trails that are generated by a company's multiple electronic systems. These include door entry systems, telephones, printers, Internet browsers, and the various logs recorded when employees make use of front and back office computer systems. The systems then look for patterns of behavior indicating that an employee is engaged in unusual or potentially suspicious activities. In time, these systems will be linked with those monitoring unusual customer transactions for deeper analysis.

New compliance regulations require management to monitor, store, and report on employee communications across technologies and data conduits such as email, instant messaging, text messaging, and telephone calls. David Porter says, "This so-called 'unstructured data' is the next frontier in high tech monitoring. The volume of data stored and retrieved from this form of detection system will be huge and new kinds of technology will be needed to detect rogue communications. The artificial intelligence community will seize this opportunity to put some of their most advanced technology to commercial uses, including reading an email or listening to a telephone conversation, and actually understanding its content."

Technology Alone Isn't the Answer

Banks and law enforcement agencies are playing a continual game of catch up with money launderers, fraudsters, and other financial criminals. Both sides harness technology's speed and power. Yet much "cyber laundering" and "cyber fraud" is simply old scams in new guises, traditional crimes supported by the Internet and other forms of high technology. Porter says, "people, not machines, still remain at the heart of all this activity and technology is therefore only part of the solution to cyber laundering. Banks thought that they could install detection software and rely on that alone. They have since realized the hard way that they were wrong." One compliance officer commented, "Technology is only one part of our armory against money laundering—we will still get hammered if we have sloppy procedures and people."

The cyber launderer will be put out of business by skilled employees using well-designed procedures, and advanced technology. The amount of information generated by computers is increasing at an exponential rate and it is clear banks and law enforcers need to deploy technology to analyze this information and derive better intelligence from it. Timothy J. Muris, chairman of the Federal Trade Commission, sounds a warning to the cyber criminal community when he says, "We intend to send a strong message to those who use the Internet to break the law: Cyberspace is not outer space and we will trace you, track you, and stop you."

Conclusion

THE FAILURE OF FINANCIAL REGULATION, political opportunism and the pursuit of free market policies have created a dangerous world where money laundering and the black market have thrived. Diamonds are exchanged for drugs, drugs for arms, arms for cash, and cash for real estate. The real estate will later be sold to acquire the means to re-start the money-go-round with the purchase of some more arms or drugs.

These economics exist in a universe without morals. They put people trafficking into the same profitability equation as arms, drugs or diamonds smuggling.

Western governments and intelligence agencies have looked on as criminal groups have expanded their power bases. Countries in South America, Africa and Asia have collapsed altogether, leaving mafias holding political and economic power. Black economies have expanded and merged together. In due course, this has enabled them to acquire a critical mass to threaten so-called legitimate economies.

Burgeoning underground trade challenges the global economy in a number of ways. The cash economy deprives nations of taxation, from which they fund their necessary social and other services. The trade in black diamonds, and stolen, forged or counterfeit items undermines legitimate producers, who declare their earnings and must abide by standards of employment. A free-for-all in weapons is the West's nightmare. But it has become a reality following the break-up of arsenals that were once under the control of the Former Soviet Union.

Terrorism has thrived amidst this free-for-all. The seeds of terrorism are to be found in the black markets where terrorists trade their wares. The tell-tales signs of a terrorist attack are evident long before the criminal money begins its circuitous route to reach the hit-men or suicide bombers in Jeddah or Baghdad. Security agencies have long experience of financial sting operations to tap into criminal markets. They are doubtless now trying to tap into the criminal arms markets. Intelligence officials and their political masters have not always been trustworthy handlers of state money.

But the challenge of terror now looks too serious to be undermined by turf-watching in different parts of the U.S. administration. It is time to stop the power-plays between governments, that have bedevilled the effectiveness of intelligence agency work in the past.

Banks are equally dubious policemen of the systems of markets and cash transmission. They pursue bottom lines of profit, often teaming up with criminal and corrupt elements in developing countries. It is extraordinary that governments ask these institutions to manage 'anti-money laundering systems' when the movement of money is a key profit center.

So what explains the push in western banks to avert money laundering? Conspiracy theorists argue that government has other unspoken agendas. Some cite government's desire to curb the black economy. Others cite the State's interest in snooping more deeply into individual affairs.

If Western law enforcement is seriously concerned about the menace of organised crime and terrorism, where should it direct its energies? Undoubtedly, the loosely regulated offshore world deserves much greater attention. More pressure must be placed on jurisdictions that create legal and political fictions to allow organised criminal groups to cover up crooked deals.

Large quantities of black cash enter the banking system through tax loopholes and these can be closed. This means closer observation of bureaux de change in Europe, money transmission systems in the Middle East, in particular Dubai, and informal transmission systems or hawalas across the UK, Asia and China. Money is more vulnerable when it is on the move than when it is neatly packaged for deposit into a bank account.

Finally, there is seemingly constant need to control corruption. Corruption does not just create unfairness, resentment and market distortions within a country, but it creates weak links in the global ring fence against criminal cash. Countries with corrupt officials or politicians are not reliable gate keepers when presented with black money. Once the money enters the world's washing machine, it stays there.

Money laundering has entered the global consciousness in the last five years. It has become an icon, part of the Zeitgeist of fear and threat that has been induced by the onset of worldwide terrorism. Every player, from the wealthiest to the poorest, in the global market plays at some level to the money launderer's tune. The quicker the music stops, the quicker the world will reach an honest economic equilibrium.

Glossary

Acronyms

AML   Anti-Money Laundering

BCCI   Bank of Credit and Commerce International

BMPE   Black Market Peso Exchange

BND   German Federal Intelligence Service (Bundes Nachrichten Dienst

CIA   Criminal Intelligence Agency (U.S.)

CTR   Cash Transaction Report

DEA   U.S. Drug Enforcement Administration

DKB   Depositano Klearingovi Bank (Russia)

DRC   Democratic Republic of the Congo

EUC   End User Certificate

FinCEN   Financial Crimes Enforcement Network, part of the U.S. Treasury

FARC   The Revolutionary Armed Forces of Colombia

FATF   Financial Action Task Force

FBI   Federal Bureau of Investigation (U.S.)

FIU   Financial Intelligence Unit

FTATC   Foreign Terrorist Asset Tracking Center

IMB   Inter-Maritime Bank (Geneva)

IMF   International Monetary Fund

IRA   Irish Republican Army

KYC   Know Your Customer, rules for bankers in screening their clients

LTTE   Liberation Tigers of Tamil Eelam

MPLA   Popular Movement for the Liberation of Angola

MLRO   Money Laundering Reporting Officer

NCIS   National Criminal Intelligence Service

NCS   National Crime Squad (UK)

PEP   Politically Exposed Person, an individual holding a position of public trust, who might have received a bribe

PIC   Private Investment Corporation

PIRA   Provisional Irish Republican Army

PKK   Partiya Karkeren Kurdistan

RCD   Rally for Congolese Democracy (the Rwandan-sponsored terrorist army in the DRC)

RIRA   Real Irish Republican Army

ROSC   Report on Observance of Standards and Codes

RUF   Revolutionary United Front (rebels in Sierra Leone)

SAR   Suspicious Activity Report

STR   Suspicious Transaction Report

UNITA   National Union for the Total Independence of Angola

VAT   Value Added Text that appears on product packaging

Terms

airports of convenience   Hubs in which dubious cargos can disappear, commingled in a vast quantity of legitimate goods

Al Qaida   Literally "the base," refers to offices Bin Laden ran in Peshawar, Pakistan, near the Afghan border during the war against the Soviet Union

black money   Money made through money laundering or in the black market

bunk (usually used in the phrase, "do a bunk")   A hurried departure or escape

conflict diamonds   Diamonds used as trade in weapons smuggling

cybercrime   Criminal acts that take place online via the Internet

e-cash   Internet-related funds and value transfers

flying money   Ancient Chinese underground system of money transfer

freilagers   Swiss tax-free zones

garampeiros   Artesian miners operating in the Democratic Republic of Congo

Hawala   A means outside of traditional banking for moving money across borders, used by Indian and Pakistani communities

honey trade   Transportation of drugs and weapons in honey to avoid customs

money laundering   The use of disguises to hide the origins of illegal money

mujaheddin   Islamic guerrilla fighters

Oxfam   A world-wide development, advocacy, and relief agency working toward putting an end to poverty

paper reorganization   Process of constructing extra layers of confusion that investigators will find impenetrable

private banking departments   Separate departments within commercial banks set up for rich and famous customers and staffed by tax experts

prokrutki, **"spinning"**   Whirling millions of dollars of Russian money around the world's financial system so fast nobody could follow the paper trail

pyramid scheme   Scheme in which each fraudulent transaction is dependent on the last, until a brick is knocked out of the construction, and it collapses

shill bidding   False bids used in online auctions

smurfing   Form of money laundering in which large sums are broken up into amounts small enough to be deposited into the banking system without arousing suspicion

Sources

Introduction

The analysis in Sections One and Two of the threat to Western democracies and companies from organized crime groups and mafia was taken from interviews which the author conducted with Interpol officials at Interpol headquarters in Lyon, France, in 2003. These interviews were given with a guarantee of anonymity.

The analysis of the black economy in Section Three uses multiple sources. They include

a.   Documents attached to the report on private banking, published by the Senate Permanent Subcommittee on Investigations.

b.   Public research on the drugs trade from the International Monetary Fund.

Section Four on offshore finance draws on research published in 1994 by Professor R.T. Naylor in *Hot Money and the Politics of Debt* (Black Rose Books, 1994)   It also draws on chapter four, "Treasure Island", in Naylor's book, *Wages of Crime: Black markets, illegal finance and the underworld economy,* (Cornell University Press, 2002).

Other information on offshore finance was gleaned from an author-interview with Charles Raw in 2004. The author also used the 2002 edition of "Tax Havens and their Uses," an Economist Intelligence Unit report, edited by Caroline Doggart. The following works were also consulted in preparation of the Introduction:

The Laundrymen, Inside the world's largest business, by Jeffrey Robinson,
   (Simon and Schuster, 1994)
The Sink: Terror, crime and dirty money in the offshore world, by Jeffrey
   Robinson, (Constable, 2002)
Money on the run: Canada and how the world's dirty profits are laundered, by
   Mario Possamai, (London, Viking, 2002)
Organised Crime and Money Laundering, edited by William B. Z. Vukson
   (G7 report Inc. Toronto. Orca Book Services, 2001

The Money Lenders: Bankers in a dangerous world, by Anthony Sampson,
    (Hodder and Stoughton, 1981)
A Practitioners Guide to International Money Laundering Law and Regulation,
    Consultant editors Andrew Clark and Peter Burrell, (City and Financial
    Publishing, 2003)

The analysis of terrorism and methods of fighting terrorism in Section Five
draws on material from, among other places, "Organised Crime and
Terrorism: Tracking and Attacking the Assets of Economic Crime and
Terrorism." This was the International Chamber of Commerce annual
lecture, given by Professor Barry Rider on 20 June, 2002.

SECTION I
Criminal Oligarchy

CHAPTER 1: Russian Mafia

The section in this chapter on the sociology and history of the Russian
mafia draws on:

Books

Frederico Varese, *The Russian Mafia: Private Protection in a New Market
    Economy* (OUP: 2001)
James Finckenauer and Elin Waring, *Russian Mafia in America: Immigration,
    Culture and Crime* (Northeastern University Press, 1998)
Lionel Kochan, ed., *Jews in the Soviet Union since 1917* (London/New
    York/Toronto: OUP, 1970)
Claire Sterling, *Crime Without Frontiers: The worldwide expansion of organised
    crime and the Pax Mafiosa* (Little, Brown & Co., 1994)
Alan A. Block and Constance Weaver: *All Is Clouded by Desire: Global
    Banking, Money Laundering and International Organized Crime* (Praeger
    ,2004)

Papers

Alan A. Block and Constance Weaver, *All is clouded by desire: Global Banking,
    Money Laundering and International Organized Crime* (Praeger, 2004)
Tom Poole, "Russia: a Criminal Oligarchic State", lecture, 10 May 2001,
    University of Queensland, Australia.

Kurt Schuler and George Selgin, "Replacing Potemkin Capitalism: Russia's Need for a Free-Market Financial System", Cato Institute, Policy Analysis, No. 348, 7 June 1999

B. Kalachev, et al., "The Money laundering Problem in Russia," Vserossiskii Nauchno-Isseldovatelskii Institut Ministerstava Vnutrennih report prepared for the United Nations Office for Drug Control and Prevention, 2000

Lecture Presentations

Viktor Melnikov, deputy chairman of the Bank of Russia, "Questions relating to the implementation of the Russian Federation law on countering the legalisation (laundering) of criminally obtained incomes", presentation at "Russia's fight against capital flight and money laundering", a conference under the auspices of the Royal Institute of International Affairs, London, 30 May 2002

Author Interviews

Dr Mark Galeotti, director, Organised Russian & Eurasian Crime Research Unit, University of Keele, U.K. Galeotti is an expert on Russian organized crime, as well as an adviser to the government.

Professor Leonid Fituni, director, Russian Academy of Sciences, Centre for Strategic and Global Studies. Fituni specialises in Russian sociology and criminology.

Ben Aris, Moscow-based journalist, 2001.

Ian Comisky, partner, Blank Rome Comisky and McCauley LLP, Philadelphia, PennsylvaInia

This chapter also covers specific individuals in some detail. The sources used to provide this material are cited in the context of each individual.

Legal Documents.

Semion Mogilevitch:

Mogilevitch's only brush with the Western legal system occurred when his company, YBM Magnex International collapsed.

Case 1. Before Ontario Court, general division, 18 December 1999:

Roger Mondor and Amit M Karia vs Igor Fisherman, Jacob G Bogatin and others, including Deloitte & Touche. The claim is brought by shareholders of YBM Magnex International Inc. "who suffered a loss" by buying the shares.

Case 2. In the U.S. District Court, for the Eastern District of Pennsylvania. 26 May 1999:

The action was brought by shareholders of YBM Magnex International Inc. against YBM Magnex International Inc., Deloitte & Touche, LLP and others.

Newspaper Articles

Lucy Komisar and Ivan Feranec, "NY Bank Scandal", Pacific News Service,
    6 August 2002
David Leppard et al., "Hunt for the Red Don", *The Sunday Times,* London,
    5 September 1999
Robert I Friedman, "The most dangerous mobster in the world", *The
    Village Voice,* 26 May 1998

CHAPTER 2: BoNYGate

Legal Documents

Lawsuit brought by the depositors of the Russian bank, Inkombank, against the Bank of New York (first amended complaint), 15 November 1999

The people of the State of New York against Harry J. F. Bloomfield QC and Stuart Creggy before the Supreme court of the State of New York, United States, District of New York, Southern District of New York

In re: Bank of New York, derivative litigation, amended verified shareholder derivative complaint on behalf of the shareholders of the Bank of New York:

United States, District of New York, Southern District of New York.

United States of America vs Svetlana Kudryavstev, November 2 1999: United States, District of New York, Southern District of New York.

United States of America vs Peter Berlin, Lucy Edwards, Aleksey Volkov, Benex International, BECS International, Torfinex Corp., 3 November 1999.

Newspaper Articles

Timothy O'Brien of the *New York Times* obtained the fact that the bank was under investigation from an anonymous source, thought to be inside the bank itself, to the chagrin of police investigators both in the U.S. and UK. He subsequently followed it closely and tenaciously. There was enormous coverage at the time. Key articles include:

Raymond Bonner and Timothy O'Brien, "Activity at Bank raises Suspicions of Russian Mob tie", *New York Times,* 19 August 1999

Timothy L. O'Brien, "The Money Movers: Tracking how pair went from Russia to Riches", *New York Times,* 19 October 1999

Timothy L. O'Brien, "Bank of New York Ex-Employee charged in Russian case", *New York Times,* 1 December 1999

Timothy L. O'Brien, "Doubts raised about source in Bank of New York Enquiry", *New York Times,* 17 January 2000

Benjamin Weiser and Lowell Bergman, "U.S. officials say Bank of New York transfers involved money in Russian tax cases", *New York Times,* 15 September, 2000

The Wall Street Journal was something of a follower in this case, but it published at least one key article:

Ann Davis and Paul Beckett, "Natasha Kagalovsky rose fast, fell hard at Bank of New York", *The Wall Street Journal,* 23 November 1999

Papers and Reports

Vito Tanzi, "Money laundering and the international financial system", IMF working paper, 1999

Lectures

Address by Representative Ron Paul to the hearing on "Russian Money laundering" at the House Committee on Banking and Financial Services, 22 September 1999

Internet

Andrew Cave, "Russia Mob Probe hits City", Electronic Telegraph, 20
     August 1999

"Yeltsins deny accepting $1m 'pocket money", Electronic Telegraph 27
     August 1999

Ben Aris, "Yeltsin's daughter linked to £10bn money laundering",
     Electronic Telegraph, 28 August 1999

"Foreign Loans diverted in monster money laundering? The Mafia,
     Oligarchs and Russia's torment", Transition Newsletter (The World
     Bank Group) 16 September 2002

"Money laundering enquiry 'biggest ever'", Electronic Telegraph, 17
     September 1999

Author Interviews

UK National Crime Squad officers, at N.C.S. Pimlico, London H.Q. in
2003

N.C.S. is thought to have uncovered this case, and then worked closely
with U.S. counterparts in New York.

Lawyers at the New York District Attorney's Office, New York

Dr Mark Galeotti (see above under Russian Mafia)

Other individuals and investigations relevant to the BoNY affair are
discussed in this chapter. The sources are described below.

Marc Rich

Books

A. Craig Copetas, *Metal Men: Marc Rich and the 10 billion dollar scam,*
     (Harper & Row, Perennial Library, 1986)

Articles and Reports

P. K. Semler, "Rich linked to money laundering", *The Washington Times*, 21
     June 2002

Alan A. Block, "The serious crime community in oil and banking", *Journal
     of Financial Crime*, vol.4, no. 3

Bruce Rappaport

Paul Beckett and Michael Allen, "Bank of New York Investigation widens to include Swiss Financier Rappaport", *The Wall Street Journal*, 22 February 2000

Operation Spiderweb

The author was assisted in this research by members of the anti-mafia police in Rome and Bologna and by lawyers involved in Loutchanski's case against *The Times* newspaper.

Nick Paton, '$9b money laundering ring broken', *The Guardian*, 16 June 2002

Grigori Loutchanski

Loutchanski sued *The Times* newspaper of London and won costs for an article it published which the UK courts judged to be defamatory. The following court documents were presented in the case:

Witness Statement of Grigori Loutchanski in the case of Grigori Loutchanski and Times Newspapers, in the High Court of Justice, Queen's Bench Division, 11 December 2000

Re-amended defence in the above case, 3 November 2002

S. C. Wynne and Larry Gurwin, "The Russia Connection, Special investigation of Grigori Loutchanski", *Time* magazine, 8 July 1996. This article is not available outside the United States for legal reasons.

CHAPTER 3: 'Merchant of Death'

The research into Victor Bout was conducted largely from published material. Much of this was contributed by the UK-based NGO called Global Witness, which has conducted extensive investigations into Bout and his commercial activities in natural resources in Africa. The key sources are described below.

Articles

Douglas Farah, "Top Associate of V. Bout Arrested and Reveals…", *The Washington Post*, 26 February 2002

Peter Landesman, "Arms and the Man", *New York Times Magazine,* 17 August 2003

David Pallister, "Former Russian Partner Accused of Supplying Arms to African Rebels", *The Guardian,* 5 August 2000

"The Merchant of Death", "Making a Killing" series, part 11, International Consortium of Investigative Journalists, Center for Public Integrity website, 20 November 2002

Reports

UN Final Report of the Monitoring Mechanism on Sanctions Against UNITA, S/2000/1225, 21 December 2000

UN Addendum to the Final Report of the Monitoring Mechanism on Sanctions Against UNITA, S/2001/363, 11 April 2001

UN Supplementary Report of the Monitoring Mechanism on Sanctions Against UNITA, S/2000/966, 12 October 2001

UN Additional Report of the Monitoring Mechanism on Sanctions Against UNITA, S/2002/486, 26 April 2002

UN Additional Report of the Monitoring Mechanism on Sanctions Against UNITA S/2002/1119, 16 October 2002

Executive Summary of the UN Report of the Panel of Experts on Liberia, S/2001/1015, 26 October 2001

Internet

David Omaruso, "Gangsters Incorporated" (http://gangstersinc.tripod.com/VictorBout.html)

Matthew Brunwasser, "The Embargo Buster: Fueling Bloody Civil Wars", Frontline World (Producers of U.S. TV documentary "Gunrunners") website (http://www.pbs.org/frontlineworld/stories/sierraleone/bout.html), May 2002

SECTION II:
Terrorist Finance

CHAPTER 4: Al Qaida

This topic has changed dramatically since the research for this book was begun in late 2001. A combination of new and growing terrorist outrages, provoking more and deeper coverage, together with further thought about the principles and practises of terrorist money-laundering changed the landscape week by week. There is a plethora of material, of which what follows is only a small part.

Academic Lecture

Professor Barry A. K. Rider, Director of the Institute for Advanced Legal Studies, "Organised Crime and Terrorism: Tracking and Attacking the Assets of Economic Crime and Terrorism", ICC Commercial Crime Services Annual Lecture, London, 20 June 2002.

Professor Rider is the director of the Institute of Advanced Legal Studies, University of London, and fellow of Jesus College, Cambridge.

Articles

Dr. Rohan Gunaratna, "Bankrupting the terror business", *Jane's Intelligence Review*, August 2000

"Soupcons de financement de la guerilla tchetchene dans un dossier financier instruit à Paris", *Le Monde*, 28 October 2003

Chris Dishman, U.S. Commission on National Security, "Terrorism, Crime, and Transformation", *Studies in Conflict & Terrorism*, 24:43-58, 2001

Kirstie Hamilton, "Unclaimed $5m share profit raises suspicion—War on Terror—Stock Market", *The Australian*, 1 October 2001

"Terrorism: Bin Laden Network Under the Magnifying Glass", Indigo Publications, France, 2000. This is a substantial document written largely in French.

Books

Dr. Rohan Gunaratna, *Inside Al Qaeda: Global Network of Terror* (Hurst & Company, 2002)

Zacarias Moussaoui with Florence Bouquillat, *The Making of a Terrorist* (Serpent's Tail, 2003)

Loretta Napoleoni, *Modern Jihad: Tracing the Dollars Behind the Terror Networks* (Pluto Press, 2003)

Author Interviews

Rohan Gunaratna, 2002

Lawrence Joffe, 2001, is the author of "Keesings guide to the Middle East Peace Process", 1996. He is a contributor to "Revolutionary and dissident movements of the world", John Harper Publishing, 2003. He was interviewed in London.

Jonathan Winer, 2002. Winer was interviewed in Washington DC, and at the International Symposium on Economic Crime, Cambridge, in 2002

Internet

Zvi Bar'el, "Not every terror attack is Al Qaida", www.haaretzdaily.com, 17 November 2003

Osama Bin Laden, "A Chronology of His Political Life", Frontline, http://pbs.org/frontline, 27 May 2004

Rick Wiles, "Bush's Former Oil Company Linked to Bin Laden Family", American Freedom News.com, 2001

CHAPTER 5: The Many-Headed Hydra—Ireland, Turkey, Sri Lanka

Academic Research

Substantial use is made of important research undertaken by the House of Commons subcommittee on Northern Ireland. This research delves deeper into Irish terrorist-funding than any previous work.

House of Commons, Northern Ireland Affairs Committee, *The Financing of Terrorism in Northern Ireland, Fourth Report of Session 2001-2002,* vols one and two, Minutes of Evidence and Appendices

Articles

Margot Dudkevitch, 'Iran funds Jihad via Damascus', *Jerusalem Post,* 7
January 2004

Books

James Adams, *The Financing of Terror: Behind the PLO, IRA, Red Brigades and
M19 Stand the Paymasters* (NY: Simon & Schuster, 1986)

Author Interviews

Jean Francois Seznec, lecturer, Columbia University, New York, 2001.
Seznec is a banker with connections in the Gulf and Saudi Arabia

Carol Sergeant, 2001,(then) head of Compliance and Risk, Financial
Services Authority

David George, 2002, lecturer, University of Newcastle

William Tupman, 2002, director, Unit for Research and Community Safety,
University of Exeter, UK. Tupman spoke to the author at the International
Symposium for Economic Crime, Cambridge

Paper

Bill [William] Tupman (see above), "The Business of Terrorism", 2001

SECTION III:
Black Markets

CHAPTER 6: Diamonds: A Launderer's Best Friend

The massive research by the United Nations into the diamond industry sets
the standard for all subsequent research into this area. This work provided
a fundamental resource for this chapter.

Articles

Peter Landesman, "Arms and the Man", *New York Times Magazine,* 17
August 2003

"UNITA Adapts its War as Sanctions Bite", *UN Integrated Regional Information Networks,* 8 November 2001

Books

Matthew Hart, *Diamond: The History of A Cold-Blooded Love Affair* (UK: Fourth Estate, 2002)

Reports

UN Interim Report of the Monitoring Mechanism on Sanctions Against UNITA S/2000/1026, 25 October 2000

UN Final Report of the Monitoring Mechanism on Sanctions Against UNITA, S/2000/1225, 21 December 2000

UN Addendum to the Final Report of the Monitoring Mechanism on Sanctions Against UNITA, S/2001/363, 11 April 2001

UN Supplementary Report of the Monitoring Mechanism on Sanctions Against UNITA, S/2000/966, 12 October 2001

UN Additional Report of the Monitoring Mechanism on Sanctions Against UNITA, S/2002/486, 26 April 2002

UN Additional Report of the Monitoring Mechanism on Sanctions Against UNITA, S/2002/1119, 16 October 2002

Author Interviews

Charmian Gooch, Alex Yearsley, Simon Taylor of Global Witness, the UK-based NGO active in investigating conflict diamonds

CHAPTER 7: Colombia's Half Trillion

Newspaper and Academic Research

Alfred McCoy, *The politics of heroin. CIA complicity in the global drug trade'* (Chicago: Lawrence Hill Books, 1991)

Carlos Fazio, *El tercer vinculo. De la teoria del caos a la teoria de la militarizacion* (Joaquin Mortiz, 1996)

Author Interviews

Interviews were conducted with officers of the Federal Bureau of Investigation, the Drugs Enforcement Administration and Interpol who must remain anonymous. Also interviewed were UK National Crime Squad officers who investigated the Karagozlu drugs and money laundering ring, UK Metropolitan police officers investigating Colombians in London, and George Henry Millard, Delegado Seccional de Policia, Secretaria de Seguranca Publica.

Chapter 8: Smoking Guns

This chapter is substantially drawn from a law case between the European Community and R. J. Reynolds. Impressive research by the European Community legal team unearthed fascinating alleged links between a U.S. corporation and organized crime.

Court Document

U.S. District Court Eastern District of New York: The European Community acting on its own behalf and on behalf of the Member States, Plaintiffs *vs* R.J.R. Nabisco, Inc., R. J. Reynolds Tobacco Company, R. J. Reynolds Tobacco International, Inc., R. J. R. Acquisition Corp., f/k/a, Nabisco Group Holdings Corp., R. J. R. Nabisco Holdings Corp., R. J. Reynolds Tobacco Holdings, Inc., Defendants. Lawsuit filed 31 October 2002.

Papers

U.S. Department of Justice, Drug Enforcement Administration, DEA Headquarters Financial Investigations Section, DOF, "Black Market Peso Exchange", 2000

Mohammed El Qorchi, Samuel Munzele Maimbo & John F. Wilson, "Informal Funds Transfer Systems: An Analysis of the Informal Hawala System", A Joint IMF-World Bank Paper, International Monetary Fund, Washington DC, 2003

Internet

Oriana Zill & Lowell Bergman, "The Bell Helicopter Case", www.pbs.org/wgbh/pages/frontline, 9 August 2002

Author Interviews

Gerhard Schmid, 2003, member of the European Parliament, re: E.C. law case against R. J. Reynolds

Bob Fenton, 2003, security liaison manager for Tobacco Manufacturers Association

Reports

House of Commons, Northern Ireland Affairs Committee, *The Financing of Terrorism in Northern Ireland, Fourth Report of Session 2001-2002*, vol. 11, Minutes of Evidence and Appendices

SECTION IV:
Bad Banks

CHAPTER 9: Cover-up! Bankers and Their Corrupt Clients

The permanent committee on investigations of the U.S. Senate opened an extraordinary rich mine of information when it investigated Citibank. This material is relied on here for much of the commentary on private banks' relationships with their corrupt clients. The committee report must be read with some caution, as it relies very heavily on its research into a single bank, Citibank. But as the work in the section on General Abacha, and other sections shows, many other global banks were equally complicit in hiding away their dealings with powerful, rich and corrupt politicians. No-one knows about this in detail as these relationships have simply not been investigated.

Government Reports

"Private banking and money laundering: a case study of opportunities and vulnerabilities", by the U.S. Senate, minority staff of the permanent subcommittee on investigations, 9 and 10 November 1999
"Correspondent banking: a gateway for money laundering" by the U.S. Senate, minority staff of the permanent subcommittee on investigations, 5 February 2001

Newspaper Articles

Nick Kochan, "Banks tighten their scrutiny of 'politically exposed persons'", *The Asian Wall Street Journal*, 25 May 2004

Peter Lee, "Is Citi back from the dead?", *Euromoney* magazine, December 1992

Peter Lee, "Reed reshuffles the pack", Euromoney magazine, April 1996

Internet

Michael C Ruppert, "Vampires in the City: Bloodsuckers in a Castle called Citigroup", talkcity.com/reporters alley/thecatbirdseat 19 July 2002

Author Interviews

Jermyn Brooks, executive director, Transparency International

The sources for this chapter are divided into sections, much as the chapter itself is divided.

President Abacha of Nigeria

"Private banking and money laundering", see report cited above

"Nigeria in political transition" CRS issue brief IB98046, 24 September 1999

"How the grand lootocracy beggared Nigeria's people", *The Observer*, 22 November 1998

"Nigeria seeks help in tracing billions taken by former military leaders", *Financial Times*, 23 July 1999

"Swiss freeze accounts of Nigeria's Abacha", Reuters, 14 October 1999

Author Interviews

Enrico Monfrini, Monfrini, Bottge et associes, Geneva. Monfrini is a lawyer who represents the Government of Nigeria in its efforts to reclaim funds stolen from the country by Abacha.

Bernard Bertossa was the Genevan magistrate who investigated this and other key cases involving financial crime.

Jean Ziegler is an outspoken critic of Swiss money laundering and an academic at the University of Geneva.

President Bongo of Gabon

"Private banking and money laundering" report cited above

"Swiss investigators seize Gabon president's bank account", AFX news, 29 August 1998

Asif Ali Zardari

"Private banking and money laundering" report cited above

Tim McGirk, "Asia: Bhutto's Billions: Is Pakistan playing fair in its relent-
less pursuit of the former prime minister, her husband and their
wealth", *Time International*, 18 May 1998

"Swiss Action puts Bhutto, Zardari in the dock", South Asian Business
Analyst, 22 September 1997

Raul Salinas

"Private banking and money laundering" report, cited above

"Private banking: Raul Salinas, Citibank and alleged money laundering",
30 October 1998, published by United States General Accounting
Office

CHAPTER 10: The Casablanca Sting

This chapter makes extensive use of court documents, together with an
interview with the prosecutor, Duane Lyons, who assisted in compiling it.
Operation Casablanca spawned numerous court actions, of which these are
the most detailed.

Court Documents

United States vs Banca Serfin

United States District Court for the Central District of California

United States of America vs Oscar Armando Saavedra aka El Gordo,
Gustavo Chavarriaga-Gomez,

John Doe #1 aka Humberto, Alvaro Chavarriaga-Gomez, aka Luis Alfonso
Ramirez Guerrero, aka Galo Victor Manuel Alcala-Navarro aka Dr
Navarro, October 1997

Statement by Donnie Marshall, acting administrator, Drug Enforcement Administration, U.S. Department of Justice before the Senate Drug Caucus on International Narcotics Control, 21 March 2000

Luis Astorga, "Drug Trafficking in Mexico: a first general assessment", UNESCO, 10 July 2002

Luis Astorga, "El siglo de las drogas", Mexico Espasa-Calpe, 1996

General Records of the Department of State, Record Group 59

"Threats to U.S.A.-Mexican border security", Roy Godson's testimony to the Committee on the judiciary, subcommittee on immigration and claims, U.S.A. House of Representatives, 23 April 1997

Bruce Michael Bagley (ed.), *Drug Trafficking in the Americas* (North-South Center Press, University of Miami, 1996)

Author Interviews

Duane Lyons, former U.S. prosecutor, 2002

Senior investigators, board of governors, Federal Reserve Banking System

Stefan D. Cassella, deputy chief, asset forfeiture and money laundering section, U.S. Department of Justice. The author spoke to Cassella at the International Symposium on Economic Crime at Cambridge in 2003.

CHAPTER 11: Laundering Footmen

Articles

Passas, Nikos. "Indicators of Hawala Operations and Criminal Abuse." *Journal of Money Laundering Control 8,* no. 2 (2004): 168–72.

Passas, Nikos. "Law Enforcement Challenges in Hawala-Related Investigations." *Journal of Financial Crime 12,* no. 2 (2004): 112–19.

Author Interviews

Police officers of the National Crime Squad in Bristol, UK, 2002

UK Customs and Excise investigators 2002

The section on Hawala draws on the following sources.

Papers and Reports

Abdirashid Duale, "The development of Somali remittance: adaptation and innovation", 2004 (private publication)

Roger Ballard, "Processes of consolidation and settlement in remittance-driven Hawala transactions between the UK and South Asia", Centre for Applied South Asian Studies, University of Manchester, October 2003

Harjit Sandhu,"The Hawala banking system and its role in money laundering", paper given to the Cambridge Conference on Economic Crime, 2003

Professor Nikos Passas, "Informal Value Transfer Systems and Criminal Organizations, a study into so-called underground banking networks", Wetenschappelijk Onderzoek en Documentatiecentrum, Den Haag/The Hague, 1999.

"Parallel Banking", a report published by countermoneylaundering.com in 2003

Christine Howlett, "Investigation and control of money laundering via alternative remittance and underground banking systems", published by Churchill Trust, 2001

SECTION V:
What the World's Doing

CHAPTER 12: America's Clampdown on Terrorist Financing

Books

Phil Williams and Ernesto Savona, *The United Nations and Transnational Organised Crime* (London: Frank Cass, 1996)

Louis R. Mizell, Jr., *Masters of Deception: The Worldwide White-Collar Crime Crisis and Ways to Protect Yourself* (U.S.: John Wiley & Sons, Inc., 1997)

Author Interviews

R T Naylor, lecturer, McGill University, Canada, 2002

Jack Blum is a former special counsel to the Senate Foreign Relations Subcommittee on Terrorism, Narcotics and International Operations.

John Moscow is a partner in Rosner, Moscow and Napierala. He was formerly a lawyer at New York's district attorney's office

Jonathan M Winer, partner, Alston and Bird LLP, Washington DC, 2002

David Baron, partner Mcdermott, Will and Emery. Baron is an expert on the Patriot legislation. He was interviewed in London in 2001.

Journals

Tamara Loomis, "The Rising Costs of Patriot Act Compliance", *New York Law Journal*, 9 May 2003

Papers

Vito Tanzi, "Money Laundering and the International Financial System", IMF Working Paper No. 96/55, Washington; International Monetary Fund, 1996

Daniel Thelesklaf, TvT Compliance Ltd., Switzerland, "The New Challenges to Private Banks, Offshore Institutions and Correspondent Banks": paper presented at Money Laundering in Eastern Europe Conference, Prague, 7 November 2002

Press Release

Financial Services Authority, *Assets frozen in the United States*, FSA/PN/125, 25 September 2001

Statements

John S. Pistole, Deputy Assistant Director, Counter-terrorism Division Federal Bureau of Investigation before the Senate Committee on Governmental Affairs: 'Terrorism Financing: Origination, Organization, and Prevention', 31 July 2003

John C. Varrone, Executive Director, Operations East, U.S. Customs Service before the House Committee on The Judiciary Subcommittee on Crime, 10 February 2000

CHAPTER 13: Enforcement in a Frenzy

Articles

Jimmy Burns, "Intelligence Services in hunt for biggest cash boost since cold war", *Financial Times*, 12 March 2002

John Burton, Shawn Donnan and *FT* Reporters, "PM warns on 'grave threat' of terrorism in SE Asia: Arrests of Islamic militants in the region are seen as serving only to illuminate the extent of the problem", *Financial Times,* 17 December 2002

Jane Croft, "RBS fined over anti-laundering controls—No evidence of illegal transactions: £750,000 penalty on UK's second-largest bank seen as warning to sector", *Financial Times,* 18 December 2002

Edward Alden, "Ukraine and Nauru face money-laundering action", *Financial Times,* London, 20 December 2002 (U.S. Edition)

Richard McGregor, "China brings in new rules to stem capital flight", *Financial Times,* 14 January 2003

Edward Alden, "Bank fined over failure to report laundering", *Financial Times,* London, 17 January 2003 (U.S. Edition)

Nick Kochan, "Money laundering clampdown tightens regulatory oversight" *The Asian Wall Street Journal,* 25 May 2004

Reports

Annual Report 1999, 2000 and 2001 from the Criminal Assets Bureau, Government Publications, Dublin

Papers

European Commission Working Paper: Preliminary Draft Articles for a Directive of the European Parliament and of the Council on prevention of the use of the financial system for the purpose of money laundering and terrorist financing and repealing, Directive 91/308/EEC, as amended by Directive 2001/97/EC., Brussels, 22 March 2004.

Author Interviews

Felix McKenna, chief bureau officer, Criminal Assets Bureau, Dublin, 2003

Rowan Bosworth-Davis (see other references)

Financial Action Task Force

Larry Gurwin, security consultant and investigator

Louis de Koker, professor, Rand Afrikaans University, Faculty of Law, director for the study of economic crime, 2002

Martyn Bridges, Bridges and Partners

Emma Codd and Mark Tantam, partners, Deloitte & Touche, 12 October 2001

Helen Parry, lecturer in financial law at London Guildhall University

CHAPTER 14: London: Offshore, Onshore

Books

Nick Kochan and Bob Whittington, *Bankrupt: The BCCI Fraud* (UK, Gollancz, 1991)

Truell, Peter and Larry Gurwin, *False Profits: The Inside Story of BCCI, the World's most corrupt financial empire* (Boston: Houghton Mifflin Company, 1992)

J. Beaty, and S. C. Gwynne, *The Outlaw Bank: A wide ride into the secret heart of BCCI* (Random House, 1993)

Jonathan Reuvid, consultant editor, *The Regulation and Prevention of Economic Crime Internationally,* The British Foreign & Commonwealth Office Know-How Fund, Titmuss Sainer Dechert & Touche Ross, Kogan Page Ltd., UK, 1995

Bulletins

National Crime Squad, *Bulletin,* no. 3, July 2002 (UK)

"Attuning regulation to risk: FSA measures its own progress to date", *Compliance Monitor,* vol. 13, no. 6, Informa Publishing, February 2001

"Working to Rules", *Regulatory Bulletin,* no. 24, KPMG, May 2002

Legal Documents

Bank of Credit and Commerce International vs The Governor and Company of the Bank of England, folio 1309, 1993

Guidance Notes

BBA Enterprises Ltd., "Prevention of Money Laundering", Joint Money Laundering Strategy Group, UK, December 2001

Policy Statement

Financial Services Authority, "Money Laundering - The FSA's new role: Policy statement on consultation and decisions on Rules", January 2001

Reports

Annual Report 2000-2001, National Criminal Intelligence Service, UK, 2001

"Recovering the Proceeds of Crime, A Performance and Innovation Unit Report", UK Cabinet Office, June 2000

National Crime Squad, Corporate Plan, 2002 to 2005 (UK)

"Seizing Criminals' Wealth: The Proceeds of Crime Act", Home Office Communication Directorate, 2002

Serious Fraud Office, Annual Report, 2001/2002, 19 July 2002

The Fraud Advisory Panel, Fourth Annual Report, 2001/2002

Author Interviews

Rowan Bosworth-Davies, UK consultant, 2002

Carol Sergeant, former director for risk, Financial Services Authority, 2001

Alistair Monro, former UK law enforcement official, Northern Ireland, 2003

Adam Bates, partner, KPMG, 2002

Officials of the Serious Fraud Office, Metropolitan Police and the City of London Police Force, the National Criminal Intelligence Service and the UK's National Crime Squad, 2002 to 2004

Michael Adlem, formerly consultant with Arthur Andersen, now managing director, UK consultancy, Protiviti, 2002

Helen Parry, lecturer in financial law, London Guildhall University, 2002

Timon Molloy, editor, *Money Laundering Bulletin*, London, 2003

Sara Dayman, partner, BDO Stoy Hayward, restraint and confiscation unit, 2002

CHAPTER 15: Cyber Launderers, Cyber Detectives

This chapter has drawn extensively on the practical experience and theoretical insights of David Porter, director for risk at the consultancy, Detica.

Journals

Gordon Hutchins, "The Electronic Dimension to Money Laundering—The Investigator's Perspective", *Journal of Money Laundering Control,* vol. 3, no. 3, Winter 2000

Books

Peter Lilley, "Dirty dealing: The untold truth about global money laundering". Kogan Page, 2000

Author Interviews

David Chaikin, Frederick Jordan Chambers, Sydney, Australia, 2002

Neil Jeans, executive, ABN AMRO

David Porter, Detica, 2003

David Hughes, Partner, UK law firm DLA

Chizu Nakajima, director for Financial Regulation, City University Business School, London

Daniel J. Mitchell, The Heritage Foundation, Washington DC. The Heritage Foundation lobbies for reduction in taxation and a diminution in government influence in the economy

Bibliography

Adams, James. *The Financing of Terror.* Simon and Schuster, 1986.

Block, Alan A. and Constance Weaver. *All Is Clouded by Desire: Global Banking, Money Laundering and International Organized Crime.* Praeger 2004

Clark, Andrew, and Peter Burrell, consultant ed. *A Practitioners Guide to International Money Laundering Law and Regulation.* City and Financial Publishing, 2003.

Clarke, Thurston, and John J. Tigue Jr. *Dirty Money, Swiss Banks, the Mafia and Money Laundering, and White Collar Crime.* London: Millington, 1976.

Cohen, Rich, *Tough Jews—Fathers, Sons and Gangster Dreams.* Vintage, 1999.

Doggart, Caroline. *Tax Havens and Their Uses.* The Economist Intelligence Unit, 2002.

Friedman, Robert I. *Red Mafiya: How the Russian Mob Invaded America.* Little Brown and Co., 2000.

Gillard, Michael. *A Little Pot of Money—The Story of Reginald Maudling and the Real Estate Fund of America.* Private Eye, 1974.

Gunaratna, Rohan. *Inside Al Qaeda Global Terror Network.* Hurst, 2002.

Hart, Matthew. *Diamond: The History of a Cold-Blooded Love Affair.* Fourth Estate, 2002.

Lilley, Peter. *Dirty Dealing: The Untold Truth about Global Money Laundering.* Kogan Page, 2000.

Napoleoni, Loretta. *Modern Jihad: Tracing the Dollars Behind the Terror Networks.* Pluto Press, 2003.

Naylor, R. T. *Hot Money and the Politics of Debt.* Black Rose Books, 1994.

———. *The Wages of Crime, Black Markets, Illegal Finance, and the Underworld Economy.* Cornell University Press, 2002.

Possamai, Mario. *Money on the run, Canada and How the World's Dirty Profits are Laundered.* London: Viking, 1992.

Pulleyblank, Edwin G. *Essays on Tang and Pre-Tang China.* Variorum Collected Studies Series, Ashgate Publishing Limited, 1992, 19–20.

Raw, Charles. *Slater Walker.* Coronet, 1977.

Reuvid, Jonathan, ed. *The Regulation and Prevention of Economic Crime Internationally.* Kogan Page, 1995

Robinson, Jeffrey. *The Laundrymen: Inside the World's Third Largest Business.* Simon and Schuster, 1994.

———. *The Sink: Terror, Crime and Dirty Money in the Offshore World.* Constable, 2002.

Sampson, Anthony. *The Money Lenders: Bankers in a Dangerous World.* Hodder and Stoughton, 1981.

Sterling, Claire. *Crime Without Frontiers: The Worldwide Expansion of Organised Crime and the Pax Mafiosa.* Little, Brown 1994.

Varese, Frederico. *The Russian Mafia: Private Protection in a New Market Economy.* Oxford University Press, 2001.

Vukson, William B. Z., ed. *Organised Crime and Money Laundering.* G7 Report Inc. Toronto: Orca Book Services, 2001.

Yang, Lien-Shang. *Money and Credit in China, A Short History.* Harvard-Yenching Institute Monograph series, Volume XII, Harvard University Press, 51-52.

Index

C

H

I

J

K

L

Q–R